From Warfare to Party Politics

Syracuse Studies on Peace and Conflict Resolution

Harriet Hyman Alonso, Charles Chatfield, and Louis Kriesberg
Series Editors

Ralph M. Goldman

From Warfare to Party Politics

The Critical Transition
to Civilian Control

Syracuse University Press

First Edition 1990
90 91 92 93 94 95 96 97 98 99   6 5 4 3 2 1

The paper used in this publication meets the minimum requirements of
American National Standard for Information Sciences—Permanence of
Paper for Printed Library Materials, ANSI Z39.48-1984. ∞™

Library of Congress Cataloging-in-Publication Data

Goldman, Ralph Morris, 1920–
    From warfare to party politics : the critical transition to civilian
control / Ralph M. Goldman. — 1st ed.
        p.   cm. — (Syracuse studies on peace and conflict resolution)
    Contents: Includes bibliographical references.
    ISBN 0-8156-2500-6
    1. Political parties.   2. International cooperation.   I. Title.
II. Series.
JF2011.G65   1990
322'.5—dc20   90-34053
                        CIP

Manufactured in the United States of America

For Meg, Gary, and the next generation

Contents

Syracuse Studies on Peace and Conflict Resolution

Offering readable books on the history of peace movements, the lives of pacifists, and the search for ways to mitigate conflict, both domestic and international. Under the general editorship of Harriet Hyman Alonso, Charles Chatfield, and Louis Kriesberg, the series seeks to stimulate a wider awareness and appreciation of the search for peaceful resolution to strife in all its forms as well as to promote linkages among theorists, practitioners, social scientists, and humanists engaged in this work throughout the world.

Other titles in the series are:

Preface

War evokes emotion. We hate it. We fear it. We glory in it. And so on. War elicits panaceas. Throw all the guns into the ocean. Ban the bomb. Try brotherhood. World federation. And so on. How coldly analytical, then, to suggest that warfare is a primitive, inefficient, and costly tactic for handling a disagreement. How lost in theory is the question: "Can empirical inquiry reveal a tested means for making warfare obsolete?" How bizarre to hypothesize that party systems may provide that tested means.

That is what this book is about. And some of the reactions are predictable. Peace-movement activists are likely to find it laughable that political parties could have anything to do with making war obsolete. The military will insist that peace is an ordnance problem. Policy makers will see the extrapolations as one-worldish and visionary. Party leaders will perceive no connection between the "uniqueness" of U.S. political parties and emerging transnational parties. Historians may discount the institutional histories as typical of the research problems political scientists run into when they get outside their element. And so on.

This inquiry has an intellectual history three decades old. Initially, I shared all those views expressed above. I offer these results as a modest contribution to humanity's long effort to transform political conflict from violent and destructive forms to positive and integrative processes. Happily, as this book goes to press, political developments in Europe and elsewhere are apparently bringing its forecasts to reality.

For their help in bringing forth this volume, I thank Professor Randolph Siverson of the University of California at Davis for his contribution to the Mexican case and acquisitions editor Cynthia Maude-Gembler of Syracuse University Press for her unflagging support over publishing hurdles too numerous to recount.

Washington, D.C.   RALPH M. GOLDMAN
August 1990

Ralph M. Goldman is professor emeritus of political science at San Francisco State University, where he has been dean of faculty research, chairman of the political science department, and director of the Institute for Research on International Behavior. He has been a research associate at The Brookings Institution in Washington, taught at Michigan State University, and served as political commentator on the Voice of America and RKO-General Radio.

He is author of *The Party National Committees and Their Chairmen: Factionalism at the Top*, *An Introduction to Democratization: Behavior and Institutions*, *Dilemma and Destiny: The Democratic Party in America*, *Arms Control and Peacekeeping: Feeling Safe in This World*, and *Contemporary Perspectives on Politics*. He is coauthor, with Paul T. David and Richard C. Bain, of *The Politics of National Party Conventions*.

Ralph M. Goldman has edited *Transnational Parties: Organizing the World's Precincts*. He has coedited, with William A. Douglas, *Promoting Democracy: Opportunities and Issues* and, with Paul T. David and Malcolm Moos, *Presidential Nominating Politics in 1952*.

From Warfare to Party Politics

Chapter 1

Introduction: Critical Transitions from Warfare to Politics

Laws and institutions must go hand in hand with the progress of the human mind. . . . As new discoveries are made, new truths disclosed, and manners and opinions change with the change of circumstances, institutions must advance also, and keep pace with the times. We might as well require a man to wear still the coat which fitted him when a boy, as civilized society to remain ever under the regimen of their barbarous ancestors.
 —Thomas Jefferson (letter to S. Kercheval, 1816)

Men are great not for their goals but for their transitions.
 —Ralph Waldo Emerson

The inference to be drawn from this book is that a stable political party system is the most effective institutional alternative to warfare. Examples may be found in certain nations, some of which will be described here. Regional trends appear to be imitating the national experience. The components for a similar global political structure are coming into being. Specifically, the recent emergence of transnational parties is likely to have unforeseen potential for displacing international warfare as a means of elite conflict among nations. The possibility, a jarring one for Americans living in an antiparty ethic, requires a closer look at history.

Certain nations achieve an end to internal wars after experiencing turbulent centuries of domestic elite conflict. What elements are involved in this transition? By what process does this change occur? According to the assumptions of this study, the process consists of the developmental relationship among three types of political institutions: the military, the representative, and the partisan. At a particular phase of the developmental process, there occurs a successful passage of these institutions through a "critical transition" in their relationship to each other. As a consequence, there is a reordering of the influence of the three institutions. From superordinate, the military establishment becomes subordinate. From subordinate, the party system becomes superordinate. Thus is achieved civilian supremacy over the military. This study draws comparisons between these intranation histories and contemporary developments at the regional and world levels of political institutionalization.

This inquiry, to be hoped only the first of those to come, employed the soft methodologies of case study and analogy in describing and analyzing the relevant institutional histories of three nations: England, the United States, and Mexico. I found the pattern of institutional convergence and change similar in all three countries, as well as among the supranational institutions of the European region as a whole. Similar patterns are emergent among world institutions.

The basic pattern of institutional convergence is a developmental process that includes the centralization of the military establishment, the construction of a system of representation that is inclusive and comprehensive, and the rise of a stable political party system that is open, competitive, and adaptive. The period during which the three institutions converge and acquire new rankings of political influence is the critical transition, a process that is an antecedent condition for achieving civilian supremacy over the military and an end to internal wars as the dominant system of elite competition.

In periods leading up to and during the critical transition, transactions in various "political currencies" among competing elites result in fundamental alteration in authority relationships among the three institutions. Before the final transactions of the critical transition, the military leaders are senior, and leaders in the representative body are secondary; no party system exists, or, if one does, it is undeveloped and unstable. After the critical transition, political party leaders make up the most influential elite, representatives are secondary, and the military are in a subordinate role. Political transactions leading to this inversion of institutions are one of the most significant features of the developmental process, particularly during the critical transition.

This study concludes with speculation about public policy implications of the findings.

A Methodological Note

Human institutions evolve slowly, often requiring millennia to channel human behavior regularly in some premeditated direction. This glacial pace makes it difficult to trace the countless small events and transactions that make up the developmental history of such institutions. Students of religious, economic, social, and political institutions will readily recognize the nature of this difficulty. They will also appreciate the difficulty of tracing the development of relationships among two or more such entities.

In this investigation, for example, I have undertaken to identify and track relationships among military, representative, and political party establishments as they evolve into political systems in which the civilian representatives of the nation control the conduct of its military, and nonviolent competition between political parties replaces recurrent civil and other forms of internal warfare. This is no small research task.

The methodological hazards and shortcomings of this inquiry will be apparent to anyone with even modest training in the requirements of science. All the pitfalls of ex post facto historiography are present. The case studies are few and not randomly selected. Analogy, a valuable application of established knowledge to new settings, could turn out to be little more than a comparison of resemblances. Operational definitions of some of the principal variables are modest. Yet, new perceptions of reality and discoveries of unnoticed relationships must be somehow initiated. History, case analysis, and analogy are time-honored beginnings for more comprehensive and demanding investigations. Despite the fact that these approaches promise only limited confirmation of hypotheses, they may claim large successes with stimulating new insights into reality and building them into new theories.

If nothing else, historiography may focus the observer's attention upon the *process* aspect of institutional growth and development. In this book, the critical transition is a process. Much historical writing consists of "biographies" of such institutions as nations, political parties, governments, military establishments, churches, corporations, and so forth. For the most part, such writings are guided by the subjective perceptions and inclinations of their authors. Unfortunately, these historical accounts and ex post facto researches, although meritorious on other grounds, do not meet the usual standards of scientific tests.

Ex post facto research has been defined as "that research in which the independent variable or variables have already occurred and in which the researcher starts with the observation of a dependent variable or variables. He then studies the independent variables in retrospect for their possible relations to, and effects on, the dependent variable or variables" (Kerlinger 1966, 360). This procedure differs from the usual experiment in which the investigator hypothesizes: "If x, then y," using one or another method to control the manipulation and measurement of x, and at the same time watching for concomitant variation in y. If the hypothesis is confirmed, the investigator is able to predict y from the controlled variations in x. Experimental control is achieved by systematic manipulation of x and by applying the principle of randomization to the selection of the subject population.

In ex post facto research, however, variable y is the first to be observed. Then a retrospective search for x ensues, sometimes—rarely—guided by an explicit hypothesis. The problem in ex post facto research is an inability to control the independent variable x either by manipulating it (because it has already occurred) or by randomly selecting the events or subjects to be observed (because the entire universe of cases may either have already occurred or may have been incompletely reported by historians).

These are great obstacles to the production of well-confirmed historical or ex post facto knowledge. Nonetheless, historiography, particularly in the general form of case studies, continues to be one of the most economical and popular means of recording human experience, ranging from the case reports of the social worker to the expansive chronicles of the historian. (See also, Russett 1970, 425–43, and Yin 1984).

The case study is a common approach to exploratory inquiry. It is usually a detailed and intensive description of a single phenomenon: organism, person, group, institution, event, and so forth. In the social and behavioral sciences, the method may involve several cases at once in order to reveal the range of variation and comparability of a particular type of phenomenon. In this study, therefore, the English, American, Mexican, and European Community cases serve the comparative purpose.

The four cases were by no means a systematic sample. However, there were reasons for their selection. England, indisputably the cradle of political pluralism and the first modern competitive party system, was chosen as the classic case. With its long history of internal wars, Lockeian notions of social and political contracts, and political transactions that resulted in basic institutional changes, England seemed a prototype of the critical transition model.

At first glance, the United States, as the progeny of English experience and traditions, would be expected to be a mere continuation of the English case. In some ways this was true. However, constitutionalism, republicanism, and federalism brought to bear principles and problems that gave the United States case a distinctive character within the framework of the critical transition model. Despite the combination of English political culture and the rationalism of the founding fathers, the United States also had a critical transition, albeit its own version.

The Mexican case was a choice intended to represent a distinct political culture: Latin rather than Anglo-Saxon; authoritarian rather than pluralist; rigidly stratified rather than socially mobile; Catholic rather than Protestant. Institutionally, however, Mexico seemed much like the English and United States case; that is, experiencing recurrent internal wars, seeking a system of representative government, and aware of the need for political parties. The Mexican case had the potential for disconfirming the critical transition model.

Finally, the European case was chosen as the only regional case in which supranational military, representative, and party institutions were well along in their development. The European Community was a body with enough history to provide a possible example of the applicability of the critical transition model to supranational circumstances, particularly in other regions.

Case studies are often preliminary to additional, larger, or more systematic studies. In such situations cases may facilitate isolation of important variables, suggest plausible hypotheses, serve as illustrative or heuristic aids to speculation or model-building, and, if there are several cases, even provide initial quantitative data for testing hypotheses. Thus, country findings in this study of England, the United States, Mexico, and the European Community regional case may stimulate studies of critical transitions in other nations and regions.

Even when guided by a well-designed outline or questionnaire, the case study suffers all the methodological debilities of excessive observer subjectivity, inadequate operationalization of variables, insufficient quantitative data, and, as in all ex post facto research, inability to control the independent variable. In search of the most probable cause of a past event, the case method goes back in time, often to discover that there are many possible causes. This discovery is complicated by the frequent difficulty in obtaining reliable information about the past event and its causes. Although much of the theoretical fertility of the case approach depends upon the common sense and imagination of the researcher, this very subjectivity may also be a source of substantial error.

When these debilities are understood and taken into account, the case method remains an eminently practical way of investigating some general phenomena, discovering relationships previously unnoticed, providing factual illustration for theoretical speculations, and embarking upon the search for reliable, albeit after-the-fact, information.

The case method is generally thought to be strong on insight but weak on confirmability. The historical case studies of my investigation are intended to provide insight, hypotheses, and a sufficient degree of confirmation by analogy to stimulate further inquiry and, given the pervasiveness of warfare in this century, speculation about practical political strategies.

Analogy in itself is a risky method of analysis. If the institutional developments identified in the national case histories are indeed comparable, is it defensible to draw analogies between them and the regional and global patterns? Analogy is an assertion that enough similarity exists between the attributes of two otherwise different phenomena to make comparison both possible and useful. New phenomena are presumably better understood when analogies are drawn to familiar phenomena. In this study of institutional development, I show how the integrative patterns of newly emergent supranational institutions may be more readily recognized by comparison to well-known patterns at the national level.

The risks of error in the use of analogy are substantial. Are the essential attributes well-enough defined to be comparable? Is the fit between analogous elements good? Are the history and context of these attributes sufficiently similar to warrant the comparison? At minimum, strong analogies can provide useful insights and a sound basis for further investigation. At best, analogy can provide a beginning for more rigorous comparative studies. In the words of Morris R. Cohen and Ernest Nagel, "[I]f previously established knowledge can be used in new settings, analogies must be noted and exploited. . . . We generally begin with an unanalyzed feeling of vague resemblance. . . . And when we succeed in formulating a hypothesis analogous to others, this is an *achievement*, and the starting point of further inquiry" (1934, 222, 286–88, and 369).

Ex post facto case studies and analogies displaying the critical transition in relationships among military, representative, and political party institutions in England, the United States, Mexico, and the European Community are offered here with these methodological disclaimers. The ultimate research objective remains the same: the discovery of new and confirmable insights into possible institutional alternatives to warfare.

The Critical Transition Model

To facilitate the reader's interpretations of the flow of case-study events, I will describe the critical transition as a model of developmental process.

The status of an organization or institution within a community may be inferred from several formal and informal indicators: the salaries and other material rewards of its principal leaders; the money, property, and other resources at the disposal of the organization's executives; the degree of deference or obedience rendered its officers by leaders of other organizations; the scope of the decision-making power conferred upon the organization's executives by statutes, rules, and customs; and numerous other kinds of evidence.

For example, despite the many limitations and ambiguities regarding its constitutional functions, the office of president of the United States today (as compared to 1789) holds its greatest influence in the nation on the basis of both formal and informal factors. The president is the only public official elected by the entire citizenry of the nation. He holds a legislative veto power that makes him the principal legislator. He is the nation's chief diplomat and generally considered the first among peers who are heads of nations. He is the commander in chief of the largest and best-equipped armed force in the world, with power to launch nuclear weapons. He is the subject of daily attention in the mass media. Other factors could be named. The high status of the presidency is confirmed in law and may be inferred from observable behavior. A president is influential when he chooses to be and often when he does not.

Status is observably attributable to institutions in part through the deference accorded their leaders. In the U.S. president's cabinet, for example, the secretary of state is "senior" to the secretary of agriculture and others. Among churches, there are ministers in "high" and "low" denominations. Other examples abound. There is often contro-

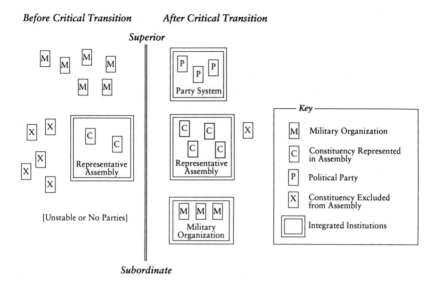

Fig. 1. The critical transition model.

versy about the seniority of leaders within particular institutions. Members of the U.S. House of Representatives frequently dispute assertions that they are "junior" to U.S. senators. Also, for example, will the newly created position of president of the Soviet Union be more influential than that of the general secretary of the Communist party? At the time of this writing, the debate has apparently been resolved by a constitutional amendment that significantly increases the powers of the Soviet presidency. There is no doubt, however, that Soviet civilian offices and institutions are senior to the leadership of that nation's military defense forces.

The critical transition model defines the status of specific political institutions according to their general authority or influence within the nations described in this study. The military organization, the representative assembly, and the political parties are viewed as having ranks: superior, intermediate, and subordinate. An institution's rank will depend upon the consequences of its activities, the resources possessed by its organizations, and the deference accorded its principal leaders, as inferred from general historical evidence.

As illustrated in the figure, the institutional hierarchy *before* a period of critical transition is as follows:

SUPERIOR: military organizations (plural)
INTERMEDIATE: representative assembly
SUBORDINATE: political parties (if any exist)

As a consequence of political transactions consummated by adversary political leaders, particularly during the critical transition and the emergence of competing political parties (or competing factions within a single-party system), the rank order of the institutions *after* the critical transition is reversed, as follows:

SUPERIOR: political parties
INTERMEDIATE: representative assembly
SUBORDINATE: military organization (centralized)

During the transition, numerous military organizations (usually independent armies) are integrated into a single force, the representative body expands to include major constituencies previously unrepresented, and the political party system comes into being where there was none before. *Instead of competing through armies, as before the critical transition, adversary elites now compete through political parties.* The military is no longer the principal instrument of conflict within the community. Instead, the military becomes agents of internal order under the control of the civilian representative body. In other words, civilian supremacy over the military is established.

The post-transition relationship among the three institutions allows serious competition among adversary leaders, progressively reduces or eliminates the prospect of violence among them, promotes political trust, and facilitates the integration of the political community. As trust-promoting transactions become the customary and successful procedures of governance, it is progressively easier for political adversaries to trust each other. Civil war is no longer a reasonable or profitable activity.

When the period of critical transition is not successfully traversed, there is regression to warfare as the principal method of elite conflict.

Chapter 2

A Conceptual Context for Observing
Critical Transitions

Conflict among groups and nations, led by their respective elites, is an inevitable, continuing, and often constructive aspect of human affairs. Conflict, however, tends to induce distrust among elites, who often find themselves drawn by mutual fear and distrust into such tactics of violence as arms races and warfare.

Distrust and violence, through sheer recurrence, may become institutionalized; witness the frequent reference to war as an institution. Wars occur when political institutions insufficiently constrain conflict behavior or fail to provide alternative conflict-managing, trust-promoting avenues of choice. The critical transition model of institutional development suggests that it is important for political communities to develop institutional capacity, or sufficiency, in order to reduce or eliminate violence as a tactic in collective decision making.

The Problem: Conflict and Distrust among Elites

Plato initiated a centuries-long debate about political leadership when he called attention to the fact that every community needs a special "higher" class of individuals, the guardians, whose principal functions would be to protect the community against foreign enemies and to maintain peace among citizens at home. In modern terminology, these are the functions of national security and domestic order.

By the nineteenth century, European social theorists were describing guardians as "ruling classes" and "elites." A connection between elites and physical force became firmly implanted in political theory. Vilfredo Pareto, for example, wrote of elites as aggregations of powerful or governing individuals who remain in power only so long as they are willing to use physical force. If one elite loses its ability or willingness to use force, it is eventually overthrown by another.

Elites are common to most societies. In primitive societies, elders, priests, or warrior-kings comprised the elites. Later societies had various types of elite whose character often reflected the principal skills or preoccupations of the society. For example, a religious community's ruling elite would often be a priestly caste. Other distinguishing characteristics included kinship, language, residence, wealth, occupation, or social prestige. Aristocrats in key leadership positions usually were elevated on the basis of family ties, landed property, wealth, or distinctive life-styles.

In more recent times, advancement to elite status in developed nations has been influenced by skills and merit, reflecting the highly organized and specialized character of modern industrial societies. These modern elites have been known for their political, economic, military, diplomatic, scientific, moral (priests, philosophers, educators), and even emotional (celebrated artists, film stars, athletes) talents and achievements.

Members of elites, like other human beings, have disagreements and engage in conflicts. The sources of conflict are many: differing perceptions of reality; different value priorities; fear and anxiety; ego-defense; irrational personal dislikes; scarcity of resources; intergroup competition; and so forth. The literature of social and political science is rich with speculation and experimentation about the causes, consequences, and management of social conflict (*International Encyclopedia of the Social Sciences* 1968, vol. 3; Porter 1982; Coser 1967; Deutsch 1973). Politics itself has been described as a conflict process in which elites are the conflict managers. "Political strategy deals . . . with the exploitation, use, and suppression of conflict. Conflict is so powerful an instrument of government that all regimes are of necessity concerned with its management." As a consequence, public policy about how to conduct conflict is "the policy of policies, the sovereign policy" (Schattschneider 1957, 51: 933–42).

The politics of elite conflict raises the subject that adversary elites tend to distrust each other. Although much is said and written using the terms trust and distrust, few have investigated the behavioral dynamics of these attitudes, least of all in connection with analyses of elite competition and warfare. However, it has been demonstrated that trust and distrust are definable, observable, measurable, and containable (Deutsch 1973, chaps. 7 and 8). Indeed, containment of political distrust is a principal purpose of certain of the political institutions with which this inquiry deals. Creating institutions that reinforce trust also tends to ameliorate the negative consequences that flow from elite conflict.

Tactical Tools of Elite Conflict: Weapons, Words, and Numbers

Elites try to influence the decisions and actions of their adversaries through the use of one or more of certain types of means; namely, weapons, words, and numbers.

Use of *weapons* of violence or the threat of violence are ancient tactics for either bringing another party over to one's own point of view or eliminating the other party entirely from the decision process. *Words*—commonly in the form of laws, rules, reasoned arguments, propaganda, or scientific theories—have less antiquity, coming into their own during the Classical Era of Greek philosophy. Free discussion, reason, and rhetoric (that is, the thoughtful, nonviolent, and skillful use of words) have, in modern times, been considered fundamental requirements of constitutional democracy. The use of *numbers,* that is, numerical tactics, is of most recent vintage. Although occasionally employed in ancient Greece and Rome, numerical tactics—most commonly numbers of votes—were rationalized for decision making in the medieval church.

Decision making is essentially an individual act. When two or more persons decide in concert, decision making becomes collective, requiring some procedure for summarizing individual decisions into a form reflecting the collective preference as the basis for action. Collective decision making must have a collective "decision rule" that is overt, specific, and legitimized if it is to result in collective action (Buchanan and Tulloch 1962, 5–6; Goldman 1976, chap. 6). For example, in some nations, decision making on specific subjects (national emergencies) is explicitly delegated by law (legitimization) to a leader (a monarch, a dictator, a president) whose choices then become the decisions of the entire nation. In another example, the collective decision rule may call for a popular voting system wherein the publicly recorded preferences of a simple majority of participating citizens may produce the collective decision. There are innumerable other procedures by which individual decisions may be systematically translated into collective choice. At the outset, for a group to function at all as a group, the very first collective decision it must make is to adopt a procedure by which it will make its collective decisions; that is, it must choose its basic collective decision rule.

It is during the implementation of collective decision rules that the members and factions of groups and nations employ the aforementioned means—weapons, words, and numbers—to influence the outcome. Violent, verbal, and numerical means are essentially tactical in character. As we shall argue below, different political institutions tend to "specialize" in the use of one or another of these tactics during the political conflicts that precede collective decisions.

The choice of tactics is also affected by different degrees of trust among members of the collectivity. Extreme distrust tends to elicit tactics of violence. Great mutual trust maximizes the use of verbal and numerical tactics. Violent tactics tend to escalate to all-or-none (zero-sum, in the language of game theory) outcomes; numerical tactics, on the other hand, tend to produce compromises or non-zero-sum outcomes.

The tactics of violence usually depend on the availability of weapons and other physical means—fists, rocks, spears, bullets, atom bombs—and the member's or group's willingness to use them to influence or eliminate other participants in a collective decision process. The physical means are designed to produce discomfort, pain, deprivation, death, or reduced resources. These means either produce in adversaries a state of psychological readiness to submit or remove them entirely from participation by destroying them or preventing them from following the procedures of participation. For countless millennia violence has been viewed as the decisive sovereign procedure, particularly among nations. Within nations, revolutions, civil wars, genocide, purges, and assassinations are familiar violent tactics.

To be influential, however, the possession of weapons may not be enough. There usually must be a demonstrated willingness to use the weapons. Once this will is demonstrated, possession of stockpiles of weapons may suffice to influence or deter other adversaries. A skillful practitioner of violent tactics will not only possess weapons but know how to brandish them influentially without actually expending them. Threat may be enough. A bullet fired, after all, is a resource expended and no longer available.

Verbal tactics employ spoken or written language, signs, and symbols as the means for influencing a collective choice. In the United States Senate, for example, the filibuster is a verbal tactic intended to demonstrate the intensity of a minority's resistance to an impending collective decision. It may be enough to prevent the decision. Debate over the definition of key words in the writing of statutes or party platforms is a verbal tactic, with collective decisions usually depending on whether a particular word or definition can be made acceptable to most disputants (Rapoport 1960, pt. 3). Conversely, a Quaker meeting is said to have reached a collective choice when verbal activity—discussion and debate—ends, at which point, the "sense (consensus) of the meeting" is announced.

Numerical tactics take advantage of explicit and precise quantification to determine the ratio between consent and dissent in the making of a collective decision. The vote is its most common unit of measurement. Numerical tactics are of relatively recent development, lent early significance by the papal elections of the medieval Catholic church.

Votes enable a group to determine with some exactness the ratio between agreement and disagreement evoked by the alternatives in a particular collective decision. Numerical procedures offer great flexibility in that they allow for changes in voter preference, in the composition of coalitions, and in the sequencing of issues for decision. Because their dimensions can be systematically varied, numbers lend themselves to various kinds of modification. For example, votes can be fractional or multiple. Or the total number of voters may vary. The latter is illustrated in the history of suffrage, wherein the total vote is shared among an increased number of participants, thereby reducing the weight of each previous voting unit.

Apportionment is another way of changing shares of power among participants; witness the change from "one class, one vote" in the earliest parliaments to the "one person, one vote" principle today. The timing of votes, the proportion of votes (majority, two-thirds, unanimity, etc.) needed for a decision, the issues submitted for a vote (leadership selection, referenda on statutes, etc.), and other aspects of numerical procedure afford many opportunities for modifying a group's collective decision rules. Numerical tactics, by offering such flexibility, are a contrast to the apparent finality of violent tactics and the frequent rigidity of verbal tactics.

In actual practice, adversaries participating in a collective decision process often employ a mix of tactics, with greater or less emphasis upon one or another. In the international community, for example, although much attention is given to propaganda (verbal tactic) and votes (numerical tactic) in such organizations as the United Nations, the underlying assumption is that disputes between nations may ultimately be resolved by force; that is, the tactics of violence. In contrast, the use of violent tactics in the domestic conflicts of an integrated democratic nation is usually limited to civil demonstrations and certain police activities; the greater emphasis is on verbal tactics in courts and legislatures and numerical tactics in the election of the nation's representatives.

A Related Problem: Institutional Insufficiency

Institutions grow through the repetition of particular patterns of activity carried on within certain social organizations or sets of related organizations. What, then, is an institution? Institutions, according to one scholar, "are patterns of recurring acts structured in a manner conditioning the behavior of members within the institutions, shaping a particular value or set of values, and projecting value(s) in the social system in terms of attitudes or acts" (Robins 1976, 7; Blase 1973). The rubrics "organization" and "institution" are often used interchangeably (for example, Huntington 1968).

Another authority offers the following definition. "An institution is an orderly and more or less formal collection of human habits and *roles*—that is, of interlocking expectations of behavior—that results in a stable organization or practice whose performance can be predicted with some reliability." Examples include governments, corporations, legislatures, courts, churches, and the family. Institutional practices are activities such as buying in marketplaces, voting in elections, getting married, or holding property. To *institutionalize* a practice, process, or service "is to transform it from a poorly organized and informal activity into a highly organized and formal one" (Deutsch 1980, 175).

As in the case of other concepts, the meaning and implications of the term *institution* have also undergone change. More recent usage tends to emphasize the relative autonomy of political institutions. Policies and programs adopted as political compromises between adversary parties, for example, may become endowed with separate meaning and force by having a public agency or other organization established to deal with them (March and Olson 1984, 78: 734–49). Something as simple as a majority-rule principle in an electoral college, as in the selection of a United States president, may lead to the unanticipated development of a two-party system. This development was not foreseen by the Founding Fathers, for whom the majority-rule principle was part of a negotiated compromise.

In general, institutions offer the advantage of keeping human behavior relatively predictable and bringing to human interactions some of the economies of fixed expectations and habits. Nations reinforce institutional behavior through custom, tradition, law, and similar consensual and regulatory means. Leaders of political organizations that are part of institutions implicitly bear responsibility for teaching, perpetuating, and protecting the relevant institutionalized behaviors. When institutions are effective, they may guide human conduct along desirable and predictable lines. The accretion of institutional arrangements and behavior patterns is the stuff of institutional development and history.

Different institutions often employ distinct influence tactics to guide or control behavior. A religious institution, for example, ordinarily employs verbal methods (holy crusades aside)—for example, theology, prayer, and sermons—in its daily practice. The religious institution may also consist of several organized churches interacting with each other in a systematic way over long periods of time. Similarly, a political party institution may be made up of enduring patterns of electoral and related activity and numerous organizations with stable patterns of relationship among themselves. The United States party system, for example, emphasizes the use of verbal (campaign propaganda) and numerical (elections) methods and consists of the Democratic party, the Republican party, and a number of minor parties in relatively systematic relationships with each other, the electorate, and the citizenry at large.

The political institutions that seem most intimately involved in elite conflict, distrust, and warfare appear to be those that have to do with the management of weapons and other military resources, representative assemblies as arenas of conflict over laws and governmental policies, and political parties as competitors for control of public offices through electoral processes. Each of these institutions tends to "specialize" in the exercise of a particular tactic of influence: weapons by the military, words by the representatives, and numbers by the political parties.

In any political system, whether democratic or totalitarian, the creation and maintenance of an enduring institution is a difficult assignment for any set of leaders, particularly elites distracted by their animosity toward each other or untalented in the building of political institutions. Thus, human inability and lack of foresight may, and all too often do, lead to the pathology we may refer to as "institutional insufficiency." Weak institutions, such as those reported in the case histories of this study, have deterred nations from harnessing their elite conflicts to positive outcomes.

Examples of institutional insufficiency may be drawn from the histories of undeveloped or unstable nations throughout the world. A familiar example from American history would be the U.S. Civil War. When, in 1860, the Congress of the United States could no longer effectively represent the interests of both North and South on the issue of slavery, when the political parties were unable to select presidential nominees to whom all sections of the country could have political access, and when the federal army was a meager force in Washington at a time of military threat to the nation's capital, these representative, partisan, and military institutions were suffering institutional insufficiency. They could not adequately perform their assigned functions. The institution of representation (Congress), party competition (particularly the Democrats), and military power (federal army) were incapable, together or separately, of containing the stress and disequilibrium that soon led to civil war.

Other examples at the level of world affairs are World War I and World War II. World War I occurred soon after the collapse of the system of international conflict management that had been developed at the Congress of Vienna. World War II followed the institutional failure of the League of Nations. In contrast, the current feeble, but nonetheless enduring and modestly effective, institutional capacities of the United Nations and related supranational agencies have thus far limited the scope and devastation of international conflicts. Of the more than four hundred international conflicts since 1945, the United Nations has played a constraining and peacemaking role in more than one hundred. At this writing, the UN's role appears to be expanding with substantial success.

According to the critical transition model, it is institutional insufficiency, particularly of the party system, that most often triggers regression into domestic warfare as competing elites fail to grasp an opportunity for successfully negotiating the transition: in this book, notably the seventeenth-century civil wars in England, the Civil War in the United States, and the Mexican Revolution.

The Evolution of Core Political Institutions

As implied thus far, the institutions most directly concerned with large-scale elite conflict are the military, the representative, and the partisan, particularly as these relate to one another. The military are mobilizers and managers of weapons and armed forces that, in pre-critical-transition periods, elites use to exercise power over each other. Representative assemblies, if they conduct their activities in an open and free fashion, provide another arena for elite competition, particularly regarding laws, public policies, and the allocation of community resources. Political parties are the vehicles of elite competition for the offices of government through electoral processes.

The *military,* in many cases the most organized institution in a nation, has been characterized as destructive and authoritarian. Although this is functionally true, no other institution has evolved to perform the military's principal constitutional (where there is a constitution) contribution to the community; namely, providing safety from external attack and maintaining internal order. Yet, defense and order are both necessary antecedent conditions for the pursuit of nonviolent domestic policies and, in democracies, for the preservation of freedom.

As the history of every nation will confirm, it is no simple matter to establish a nation's collective-decision rules. The initial decision rules are usually put in place under conditions of war, revolution, or rebellion, during which elites are extremely divided and suspicious of each other's intentions. These divisive conditions tend to cause recurrent regression to warfare and other violent tactics. Witness the number of revolutions that have "consumed their children." Witness the number of empires dissolved because of leaders' failure to modernize in a timely fashion the collective-decision rules that could incorporate the aspirations of new generations or newly conquered peoples.

Violence tends to breed violence. Only strong and effective political institutions seem able to harness such conflicts to transactions leading to trust, nonviolence, and political integration. Some political institutions have greater potential than others for placing constraints upon violent elite conflict and for reducing the uncertainties, risks, and costs of the conflicts that do occur. Which institutions, and how do they achieve these constraints?

Representative assemblies have been the principal institution for dispersing units of collective-decision prerogative among participating constituencies and for reducing distrust among competing elites. When effective, these assemblies have often become "gentlemen's clubs." Representative assemblies, ordinarily organized as legislatures or cabinets, have been the agencies within which competing elites may share the nation's sovereignty (collective prerogative) and resort to verbal tactics in their collective decision making, that is, conduct debates, enact laws, and declare public policy. Properly institutionalized, these assemblies include political claimants with demonstrated capacity— usually constituency voting support—for insisting that their interests be taken into account. Representative assemblies have also been a convenient place for competing elites to form political-party coalitions.

Political parties are usually extragovernmental organizations. They mobilize representatives in legislatures and constituencies in the electorate in order to capture the offices and programmatic initiatives of government on behalf of their leaders and constituents. The more mature and inclusive parties usually have some system of internal representation—committees, conventions, and so forth—that reflects the relative influence of their various constituencies. A party system usually has achieved stability when it peaceably conducts succession contests among its parties or factions.

The three types of institution—military, representative, and partisan—have had distinct developmental histories in different nations. Overall, however, military institutions are among the world's oldest. Representative institutions have great antiquity, although they came into their own only some five or six hundred years ago. Political party systems are the most recent, having been distinct institutions for only two to three hundred years. The evolution of the three types of institution, regardless of country, has influenced their specific development in particular nations during different historical periods. For example, the military in twentieth-century Mexico's civil war differed from the military in the civil war of seventeenth-century England. Therefore, the following brief survey of military, representative, and party institutions in general may serve as useful background for the particular institutional histories in England, the United States, and Mexico.

The Military and the Management of Violence

Military institutions are among the oldest created by humanity. Primitive societies that engaged in warfare were small, territorially ill defined, and nomadic. Revenge for wife stealing, adultery, or divorce was a principal motive for engaging in battle. Other motives related to religious duty, sport, or personal prestige. As societies became more organized, a major motivation for engaging in military activity was to achieve senior status in the tribe or community. Territorial and economic motives came much later.

Warfare in primitive societies was the norm rather than the exception. Fully 30 percent of the deaths in the adult male population were attributable to the state of perpetual warfare. Military activity, therefore, was a major function of society from the outset and soon led to specialized skills, distinct social roles, organized military groups, and experimentation with military technology. All men in a tribe were usually expected to prepare for a warrior role by learning war rituals and weapons skills such as rock hurling, spear throwing, arrow shooting, and dueling with knives and swords.

Military encounters took the form of feuds, raids, and pitched battles in predesignated areas. Warrior bands grew in size and complexity, which led to specialized types of military leadership and modes of organization. Alliances and treachery demanded particularly careful coordination and leadership. Military administration was therefore an early and significant form of community leadership.

As societies changed from nomadic hunters to settled agricultural communities, military leaders acquired even greater responsibility and status as protectors of the community's stores of produce, its herds, and its commerce. Weapons and military tactics became more complex and efficient. Warrior units became better organized and better prepared through systematic training. Military equipment such as chariots, heavy archery, and guns required sophisticated engineering and manufacture. Armies fortified and patrolled entire cities. In the field, armies had to be moved and maintained by elaborate logistical systems and large contingents of ships, horses, and camels. By the eighth century B.C., imperial armies consisting of 50,000 to 150,000 men were not uncommon. In the fourth century B.C., Alexander the Great built his empire with a force of some 30,000–50,000 men operating in highly disciplined phalanx infantry formations and using powerful siege engines.

Beginning in the third century B.C., the Romans carried military organization, tactics, and administration of captured territories to new levels of sophistication and professionalism. At its height, the Roman Empire governed some 150 million people and maintained a military force of at least three hundred thousand men.

In subsequent centuries there were numerous similar but usually smaller military enterprises. Attila's army of two hundred thousand Huns and Germans prevailed until their decisive defeat in A.D. 451. The horsemen of Muhammed and his successors extended Islam across North Africa and southern Europe between A.D. 622 and 732. Charlemagne's army of feudal knights brought together an eighth-century empire that included most of France, Germany, and Italy. From the ninth to the eleventh centuries Vikings raided and settled communities in Normandy, England, and Iceland. The eleventh to the thirteenth centuries were dominated by the Christian Crusades against Islam. In the Hundred Years' War, from 1337 to 1453, the English undertook the ambitious venture of trying to conquer France. These continent-wide military enterprises began to have significant consequences for the development of domestic institutions in emerging nations, as will be evident in the case studies of this inquiry.

From the eighth to the thirteenth centuries Europe's feudal system brought economic and military organizations into one structure. At the heart of the feudal economic arrangement was the tenant farmer who paid fixed dues, rents, or taxes to the local lord who held title to his tenants' lands. Over the centuries a hierarchy of tenancy developed. Local and regional lords came under obligation to higher nobles, kings, or the Church. Title to lands became a function of alliances, conquest, and fealty to a sovereign.

This landholding and agricultural system carried with it a system of vassalage, which included military service. Each local lord owed military service to a senior noble, and this formed the base of a hierarchy that pyramided up to the king. The noble at each feudal level maintained a band of armed retainers attached to his household to protect landholdings, maintain local order, and render military service when called upon by his superior. Military leadership depended less on competency than upon landholding and noble status. As a consequence, the bands of armed retainers were rarely trained in earnest for real battles.

The royal need for skilled soldiers on short notice gave rise to mercenaries; that is, hired soldiers of fortune. When salaries and maintenance of mercenaries became important, primitive tax systems were strained to the extreme to support them. In major campaigns, therefore, mercenaries were promised conquered land in lieu of money, a motivation that in 1066, for example, spurred many of William the Conqueror's army of fifty thousand men. By the end of the twelfth century, Philip II of France and Henry II of England were able to design tax structures that permitted them to hire large numbers of mercenaries on a permanent basis. In Philip's case this meant about twenty-eight hundred men with skills as infantry, mounted crossbowmen, sappers, and so forth. In this way, kings began to escape their dependence upon the unreliable financial and manpower contributions of their nobility.

New technologies changed the management of warfare in the thirteenth and fourteenth centuries. Cavalry, too heavily armored, declined in importance. The longbow gave the infantry archer a major role. Edward III brought the age of castle fortification to an end when he introduced cannon and gunpowder during the Battle of Crécy in 1346. Edward also inaugurated a contract system of recruitment. He paid fees from the royal treasury to contractors who would raise the armies with the skills he needed. Technology, specialization, nonfeudal sources of military personnel, and new methods of taxation evolved together to hasten the process of military centralization in several countries.

Over the next two centuries military technology and organization adopted modern patterns of operation. Artillery units grew as cannons were refined, placed on wheels, and drawn by horses. Light horse cavalry—lightly armed, highly mobile, and open in formation—was adopted from the Turkish model. Archers, crossbowmen, swordsmen, and javelin throwers continued to be prominent, although their skills became obsolete as hand firearms made their appearance.

Mercenaries in growing numbers were hired for specific campaigns; there was no permanent military force. Systems of officership, previously based on noble status and specialized military skills, began to emerge for different kinds of units. By the seventeenth century, occasional efforts were made—without lasting success—to establish officer training schools. During the seventeenth century, too, the musket became the principal infantry weapon, infantry became disciplined and mobile, and navies emerged as a major military force. In the eighteenth century the flintlock musket replaced the matchlock, the bayonet was used in place of the pike, nation-states were gathering larger armies, and military organization was increasingly hierarchical, complicated, and professional. The nationalization of military institutions proceeded rapidly as nations struggled to capture, extend, or protect colonial empires.

The American Revolution was an event of substantial significance in military history. What was later known as guerrilla warfare was for the first time demonstrated to be tactically effective. These were tactical light troops; that is, mobile regulars to whom local partisans attached themselves for specific local actions. Particularly important (and threatening to Europe's monarchs) were the new republic's constitutional provisions for civilian control of the military, its decentralization of military forces into state rather than national militia, and its preference for short-enlistment armies whose citizens' right to bear arms it guaranteed.

In the nineteenth century, large-scale wars in which mass armies moved in and out of densely populated civilian areas arrived. Mass production of weaponry created flourishing arms industries in many countries. Liberty, equality, fraternity, slavery, and other ideological rationales energized the rank-and-file of large armies and justified invasions and counterinvasions. The American Civil War turned out to be the bloodiest on record to that time. Also in the nineteenth century the profession of military officership was firmly established, with the Prussian military academies leading the way.

Armies became even more massive in the twentieth century. World War I caused nine million military and thirty million civilian deaths. The figures for World War II stood at seventeen million military and thirty-four million civilian deaths. Airplanes, rockets, intercontinental missiles, and satellites added space to the battlefields and oceans already filled with armies and navies. Vast and highly centralized military bureaucracies conducted wars and maintained preparedness for national defense. Military-industrial complexes; that is, interlocking economic, military, and political interests, became pervasive new influences in the lives of nations. Nuclear weapons and their uncontrolled proliferation made it technically possible for humanity to destroy itself within a matter of hours. Most major nations had highly centralized military institutions. Two hostile alliance systems—the North Atlantic Treaty Organization (NATO) and the Warsaw Treaty Organization (Warsaw Pact)—consumed two-thirds of the world's military budget.

There are those who argue that the arrival of the nuclear age and the ultimate doomsday weapon have made major wars obsolete. This assessment may be true, but it misses the point. Weapons continue to be built and massive armies trained because the tactics of violence require them to be, whether for attack, defense, or deterrence. Military institutions will continue to be tactical resources for political elites trying to influence each other's decision making, which, in this era, encompasses decisions about global as well as national issues.

Representative Assemblies and Verbal Tactics

The concept of representation is at once comprehensive and precise. In the broadest sense, anything that functions in the place of something else is representative: a flag as the symbolic representation of a nation, a check in place of cash, a lawyer on behalf of a client, a delegate to the United Nations authorized to speak for the entire nation. In the statistical sense, to be a representative sample of a larger population, every member of the larger population must have an equal chance of being included in the sample (Gosnell 1948; deGrazia 1951 and 1963; Pitkin 1967 and 1969; Pennock and Chapman 1968).

The idea of human beings representing or standing in place of other human beings, however, is a relatively recent one. Institutions designed to accomplish political representation are even more recent in development. "Such uses [of the concept of representation] began to emerge in Latin in the thirteenth and fourteenth centuries, in English even later, as persons sent to participate in church councils or in the English Parliament came gradually to be thought of as representatives" (Pitkin 1967, 3).

The first thorough theoretical analysis of representation as a political relationship between leaders (representatives) and followers (congregants, citizens, constituents, etc.) was made by Thomas Hobbes in chapter 16 of *Leviathan,* published in 1651. Another two hundred years passed before John Stuart Mill, in 1861, devoted an entire book to *Considerations on Representative Government.*

Meanwhile, in the Catholic church and in England, the United States, France, and other countries, the development of political representation went forward in constitutional arrangements, particularly in the United States in 1787 and France in 1791; in debates among leaders; for example, Edmund Burke's speeches and writings in the 1780s and 1790s and James Madison's papers in *The Federalist;* and in political practice; for instance, the evolution from class to district representation in the English Parliament and political party control of slates of presidential electors in the United States.

At times, political representativeness is attributed to particular officers or agencies of government. Kings, dictators, and presidents have been referred to as representatives of their diverse constituencies. Small oligarchic committees in the form of councils, cabinets, politburos, and the like have also been considered representative of major interests in a political community. It is in the representative assembly of several score or several hundred members, however, that any comprehensive representation of interests has the best, but not necessarily assured, opportunity for representation.

Representative institutions have not always been instruments of popular democracy. They were initially a political convenience of kings. In the beginning, representation was a royal technique for communicating with and controlling different elements of the kingdom; for example, the church, nobles, merchants, and so on. Later, systems of representation gave various groups the opportunity to constrain royal power. Much later, political parties made possible the popular control of representative institutions and government.

Scholars disagree about the earliest origins of representative institutions. Some believe that Indian tribal federations, Teutonic tribal communities, and some of the Greek city-states nurtured the seeds of modern representative government. Others, notably Harold F. Gosnell, have taken the position that "the ancient world was basically non-representative in form . . . a representative assembly by election was utterly lacking." The earliest more or less systematic writings on the concept of representation came in the Middle Ages in connection with the emergence of the corporate concept of the church (Gosnell 1948, 154–157).

There is little disagreement, however, about the modern origins of representative government some 500 years ago. The struggle between the English Crown and Parliament gave the development of representation its strongest impetus. Representative government in England was not a spontaneous invention of Teutonic political genius. Rather, as mentioned above, it began as an instrument of royal power. As monarchs, particularly the English, established their influence over remote geographical areas and communities, they found themselves dealing with a large number of political and social organizations and classes such as the church, feudal estates, noble families, guilds, cities, and other local communities. In order to preserve the peace and maintain efficient arrangements for the flow of resources to the royal household's treasury, kings needed to communicate with and eventually to consider, at least to some degree, the many local and other interests of their subjects. As a consequence, parliaments were convened to represent "estates of the realm"; that is, clergy, nobility, landed gentry, and local communities.

Parliament as a representative assembly became a lawmaking institution in gradual steps. The members of Parliament were at first agents of the various estates, serving these interests vis-à-vis the king. In time, the members of Parliament began to participate in the negotiation of royal taxes. Parliament soon learned how to use the tax levy as a trade-off for political concessions from the king. The procedure took the form of petitions expressing public grievances. These were submitted to the king, often in conjunction with the tax levy. If the king approved the petition, it became law. In time, various interests within Parliament formed coalitions—later to become political parties—in order to lend their aggregate weight to the petitions, later known as bills, as well as to arrive at a parliamentary consensus regarding the amount of money that should be raised at any particular time for the royal household and its administration of governmental functions.

It was during the revolutionary seventeenth century that Parliament diminished the king's lawmaking and taxing powers to the point that his role in the process was perfunctory. By this time, coalitions of representatives in Parliament were sufficiently stable in composition to be prototypes of modern political parties. The nineteenth-century extensions of popular suffrage and party competition for popular electoral majorities brought into its modern phase the evolution of representative institutions in England and other parliamentary systems. What began as a royal and elite agency was now popular and partisan.

The American and French revolutions hastened the transformation of representative institutions into instruments of popular sovereignty. The American Founding Fathers, however, hesitated to give popular representation too large a role. Popular influence in the selection of the president was kept indirect through the establishment of a unique, albeit representative, electoral college. Senators were to be elected to Congress by their state legislatures; that is, state representative bodies. Only the membership of the House of Representatives was to be subject to the direct and frequent choice of the people.

In the contemporary world, various stages of institutional evolution appear to be taking place at different places and paces. Numerous totalitarian regimes have employed representative assemblies, with the aid of authoritarian party organizations, for the purpose of exercising tight political control over all sectors of society. In other nations, it is the military establishment rather than a political party, or some combination of both, that maintains political control through ostensibly representative arrangements. In some one-party states such as the Soviet Union, Mexico, and China, competition among factions within the single authorized party has been manifest through some form of intraparty representation.

At the regional level, the European Parliament continues to experience an important and precedent-setting transition in its evolution as a supranational representative assembly. In 1979, the representatives to this Parliament were, for the first time, directly elected by the voters of each of the nine (now twelve) member nations; subsequent elections took place in 1984 and 1989. In the United Nations, previously dominated by the permanent members of the Security Council, increasingly important political activities take place in the General Assembly where delegate coalitions are emerging in somewhat the same way as in the early English parliaments; that is, as competing coalitions.

In general, representative institutions have become a familiar feature of political structures in the modern world. The specific arrangements for representation vary widely between democratic and totalitarian settings, particularly with respect to the political interests that are included, the manner in which community power is distributed, and the degree of their accuracy as gauges of consensus and dissent. The principal products of representative assemblies tend to be verbal: debate, laws, policies, public programs, and other verbal guides for civic conduct. Where representative institutions are vital, comprehensive, and efficient, they also serve as essential mechanisms for the political integration of the nation.

Political Parties and Numerical Mobilizations

Political parties are a more recent form of social organization than the military and the representative assembly (Sartori 1976; *International Encyclopedia of the Social Sciences*, vol. 11). There were party-like groupings of parliamentary factions and party-like clubs and cliques among influential leaders during the late seventeenth and most of the eighteenth centuries, particularly in England and the American colonies, but political parties as distinctive human organizations, with both legislative and electioneering functions, assumed their modern form at the end of the eighteenth century. Their institutional development went forward rapidly in the nineteenth century, stimulated by the implementation of the principles of popular sovereignty and the emergence of mass electorates. In the twentieth century, nearly every one of the more than 160 nations in the world has at least one political party organization that is institutionally central to the governing system. In addition, transnational parties have arisen, particularly since World War II, to pursue global objectives (Goldman 1983).

In a numerous body such as the English Parliament of the seventeenth century it was relatively easy for small cliques of members representing common interests to cluster around particular spokesmen. Not quite a modern legislative body, the seventeenth-century Parliament was busy defending its integrity against royal dictatorship, reflecting England's tumultuous religious constituencies, and enacting tax measures for military and other governmental functions. Cliques and coalitions of members of Parliament learned to act en bloc to achieve their objectives. The development of the cabinet as the central institution of English politics during the eighteenth century tightened party lines, as Tories and Whigs competed for voter support and government control. Because votes were the essential decision-making technique and source of legitimacy, the basic partisan tactic was numerical, first in Parliament and later extending to the electorate.

These developments were imitated in the American colonies where, in several colonial legislatures, partisans of royal governors came to be known as Court parties and those opposed became Country parties.

Urban "machines" such as the Boston Caucus and other electioneering clubs and societies gave the colonial parties a popular base long before this occurred in England. Thus, the world's first modern party systems were the English and the American. The French and others followed suit by the end of the eighteenth century.

After strong beginnings in the late 1790s, the Federalist party of Alexander Hamilton and John Adams disappeared during the first two decades of the nineteenth century. The Whig party was its principal successor for a brief period. The Democratic-Republican party of Thomas Jefferson and James Madison was given strong national organization by the Jacksonians in the 1830s. A well-matched two-party contest between Republicans and Democrats appeared, stabilized, and was still mass-based by the end of the Reconstruction era following the Civil War.

In England, the Reform Act of 1832 gave rise to the local registration societies of the Liberal party. A two-party competition between Liberals and Conservatives lasted throughout the following century. The European revolutions of 1848 brought mass party organization to France and other nations on the continent. In Asia, the Japanese began to establish party institutions in the period between the Meiji restoration (1867) and World War I. After the first World War, the organization of political parties became popular in other parts of Asia, Latin America, and Africa. In most cases these remained oligarchic groupings with fragile institutional structures. Transnational collaborations among Marxist parties were adding another dimension to party development at this time.

There have been one-, two-, and multi-party systems. They have been competitive or monopolistic, depending on their number, the nature of their internal factionalism, and their relationship to the governing elites. Parties have been revolutionary, quasi-military, or conservatizing, depending upon the stage of their institutional evolution. Political parties have built coalitions in legislative bodies, among organized interests, and in electorates. They have operated in control of governments or in opposition. Invariably, however, modern political parties have been the organization vehicles through which political leaders have employed predominantly numerical tactics to capture or retain control of governmental offices and public policy-making initiatives.

In political systems where collective decision power has been widely dispersed, political parties have been the principal developers, defenders, and mobilizers of numerical tactics and voting systems. In contrast, where participation in governmental powers has been narrowly held, parties have tended to be instruments of authoritarian control over the populace and, in collaboration with the military, heavily committed to the tactics of violence.

These brief general histories of military, representative, and party institutions suggest that changes in these institutions have been in part the consequence of elite responses to technological developments, shifting group interests, and changing attitudes toward each other. Perhaps the most important attitudinal change, when it occurs, is the elites' diminished distrust of each other. Elites are constantly testing each other's trustworthiness, and, as the centuries have shown, the least costly of these tests have been conducted within the framework of open and competitive party systems.

One other aspect of institutional development worth noting pertains to the character of the elites nurtured by the different institutions. Military institutions, for example, tend to produce elites who are skilled in the management of hierarchic and authoritarian forms of organization. Hence, societies in which the military provides the principal political leadership tend to have feeble representative institutions and authoritarian one-party systems.

Elites raised in communities with comprehensive representative institutions tend to be skilled in advocacy, legal process, and political brokerage. In some places, for example, the United States, this political elite is made up largely of lawyers. Such systems of representation tend to develop coalitional parties that capture shifting group interests in order to achieve a majority consensus. Societies with strong representative assemblies also tend to separate internal police agencies from external military defense organizations, and this helps serve the objective of civilian supremacy over the military.

Finally, strong political party institutions tend to promote open elites made up of highly competitive leaders skilled in symbolic and electoral management. These societies tend to have strong civilian control of the representative institutions. Thus, in a strong and stable party system, elite competition is likely to be carried on vigorously and safely. In the words of Quincy Wright, "Peace requires an organization of conditions favorable to the rise of a just and reasonable elite throughout the area of contact" (Wright 1942, II, 1385, app. 28).

Transactions as Increments of Institutionalization

A principal discovery of this investigation is that cessation in the use of military violence as a tactic of political decision making, civilian supremacy (a form of arms control), and political integration is the outcome of a developmental process that includes a special convergence in the development of three institutions: the military, the representative, and the partisan. When the rank order of influence among these institutions reverses during a critical transition, conditions emerge that promote institutionalized trust and nonmilitary modes of conflict among adversary elites.

Nations that have experienced this process are England, the United States, and Mexico. Study of these cases reveals the following patterns of development.

1. Each nation's armed forces became, organizationally speaking, centralized and nationalized. This may have occurred through conquest or negotiation among competing armies. A nation is considered integrated when its government possesses an accepted and legitimate monopoly of the principal instruments of violence; that is, full control of the major armed forces and weapons systems. Under constitutional arrangements, this monopoly is to be exercised in the defense of the nation against external attack or internal rebellion and in the general maintenance of internal order. When the nation's representative and political party institutions are undeveloped or incapable (institutionally "insufficient") of exercising control over the military, military forces tend to be used for aggression against other nations or for the oppression of the nation's own citizenry.

2. The essential function of systems of political representation is to disperse, realistically and comprehensively, shares of collective decision making prerogative among the significant elites and constituencies of the political community. The sharing of prerogative (sovereignty) has usually taken place within cabinets, high councils, legislative assemblies, and political parties. Institutions of representation provide an arena wherein civilian authorities may exercise ascendancy over the military.

3. Political elites within any community—city, nation, or world—compete with each other for control of governmental offices, public policies, community resources, shares of public decision power, and so forth. In such contests, elites may find themselves engaged in very serious conflicts with very high stakes; hence, they often are willing to employ any tactic to succeed against their adversaries. Military tactics have often been the most concrete, most dramatic, and most immediately available, although not convincingly the most efficient or enduring.

The emergence of political party systems over the past three centuries has introduced an alternative instrument of contest. In nations that have developed effective political-party institutions, military methods of conducting domestic rivalries have diminished or disappeared. Ballots have literally replaced bullets as the predominant instrument with which elites pursue their conflicts against each other.

The Relevance of Transaction Theory

How were the incremental changes in institutional arrangements and behavior accomplished? As the case studies will demonstrate, institutional change was usually the consequence of a political transaction between adversary elites. Transactions, accompanied by violent, verbal, or numerical modes of influence, established new patterns of institutionalized behavior or modified previous ones. The transactions involved exchanges of various types of political "currency." An important by-product of elite transactions, particularly those transactions reducing the importance of violence and providing good "profit" to each side, has been the development of attitudes of trust among the adversary leaders.

Exchange, or transactional explanations of political behavior and events, has great antiquity. Plato, discussing the essential activities of the inhabitants of a state, observed that "they exchange with one another, and one gives and another receives, each under the idea that the exchange will be for his own good." Aristotle's conception of distributive justice viewed the distribution of the offices and rights of a community as a transaction in which each citizen receives these goods in proportion to his contribution to the goals of the state (Barker 1946, 116–37).

In traditional economic usage, a transaction involves the giving up of goods by one party under circumstances contingent upon receipt of goods from a second party. A transaction is an exchange, along with the attendant bargaining or negotiation. Homans defines all social behavior as a form of exchange, that is, more or less rewarding or costly to each individual. Each person's "activity" includes, according to Homans's usage, not only the transfer of objects and materials, but also the emission of "sentiments" by one party toward the other; for example, deference or affection in exchange for advice. Each party nets a social profit if his or her perceived reward from the interaction exceeds the perceived personal cost (Homans 1961).

Homans's conception of "activity" may be translated or refined to describe certain types of social and political currencies (Goldman 1969, 62: 719–33). A currency may be defined as any empirically observable object, action, or condition valued by a set of transacting persons and capable of being transferred by one to the other. Social currencies may be considered a more generic version of political currencies.

Social currencies may be classified as positional, decisional, or material. Positional currencies include such familiar phenomena as jobs, positions, offices, and certain of their attributes, such as titles and duties. For example, when an employee agrees to take on additional job duties in exchange for a better title and higher wage offered by the employer, the employee is trading positional (duties, title) for material (wage) currency.

Decisional currencies are shares of power based on participation in the decision making prerogatives of a collectivity. For example, each stockholder in a corporation holds voting power in corporate decisions according to the number of shares of stock he or she possesses. Similarly, each member of Congress can exercise one vote as a share of collective prerogative in legislative decisions.

Material currencies are perhaps more familiar than the other two. Material currencies refer to the goods and services (or their surrogate, money) that are commonly exchanged, usually in commercial transactions. For his medical advice (a service), the family physician is paid in money (a surrogate for goods and services); together, the exchange consists entirely of material currencies.

Political currencies may be classified as incumbencies, shares, and commodities. These may be considered subtypes of the more generic social currencies. The two typologies are parallel. Thus, incumbencies are a type of positional currency, shares parallel the decisional currency; and commodities may be classified as a kind of material currency. For analytical purposes, we may consider specific manifestations of a political currency as a denomination; for example, job patronage is a denomination of incumbencies, which in turn is a subtype of (social) positional currency.

An appointive governmental job as payoff for services rendered in a political campaign is a familiar political transaction; an incumbency (the job) is given in exchange for a commodity (campaign services). Another familiar transaction occurs as a result of the apportionment of seats in a legislature in which a community's collective decision power is distributed in shares to particular districts. When a governmental agency is performing a service, such as regulation of pollution or maintenance of a park system, the exchange may be viewed as a transaction between the agency and the taxpayers; that is, an exchange of commodities (agency service in exchange for citizens' taxes).

The principal utility of the political currency classification scheme is analytical. The observer is aided in assigning a name to components of a transaction that might otherwise be overlooked or dealt with unsystematically in a transactional analysis.

Social and political exchanges are carried on in a number of marketplaces and time-frames. Commercial marketplaces include such familiar settings as stores at a shopping center, stock markets, or a real estate market (the latter usually at realtor's offices and in classified advertisements). Less familiar, but nonetheless places for making political "deals," are legislatures, political party conventions, courts, diplomatic conferences, and similar political settings.

The time frames of transactions vary. The simplest transactions are those in which two parties transfer goods between themselves simultaneously: for instance, two hundred dollars given in payment for a bicycle that is delivered at the time of payment. There are transactions in which a period of time, either specified or unspecified, passes before the exchange is completed, if ever; for example, an automobile purchased on an installment plan. The latter delayed-exchange time frame may be of consequence for an additional factor: trust.

Social and political exchanges, according to Blau, are usually somewhat different from the simultaneous and precisely quantifiable transactions that take place in commerce (Blau 1964). Commercial transactors can bargain over price, for example, but two friends can hardly bargain about the expectation that an invitation to dinner will be reciprocated at some future time. Nor are the units of currency in social and political exchanges readily quantifiable; they are, in fact, often quite ambiguous. (How many "units" of advice are worth how many "units" of deference?) Furthermore, many social and political transactions take place within a delayed-exchange time frame, wherein something is given now in the expectation that something will be received in the future.

As a consequence, social and political exchanges tend to create diffuse rather than precisely specified future obligations. The timing and amount of return for something given is often left to the discretion of the party obligated to complete the exchange. This delay in the completion of the exchange makes time an important feature of the transaction and *significantly affects the attitudes of trust or distrust that the transactors may develop toward each other* (Pilisuk et al. 1967, 11: 116). To illustrate, the local merchant will extend interest-free credit until payday to a longstanding customer because, on the basis of previous experience, he knows that the customer is honest and pays his bills on payday, and the merchant's well-founded trust is profitable in that it keeps the customer buying at his store.

A more complicated delayed-exchange transaction occurs when a home purchaser applies for a mortgage at a bank where he or she may be a total stranger. In this case, the bank's officers must decide whether or not to trust the prospective borrower. The loan officer must assess evidence about two factors pertinent to the granting of trust and credit: the applicant's past behavior as a borrower in the bank or elsewhere and the desire of the bank to make profitable use of its funds.

To determine the predictability of the applicant's repayment behavior, the bank investigates the applicant's past credit rating, determines if he or she has regular employment, and, upon making the loan, retains legal title to the dwelling until the mortgage is fully paid. If the borrower fails to make payments on schedule, he or she may lose all accumulated equity in the property. Because trust arrangements such as this are so well institutionalized, this borrower, if granted a mortgage, can have a home immediately; the bank, for its part, can begin to earn interest on the loan. This is a mutually profitable transaction involving a prolonged period of trust as well as penalties for unkept promises. An appropriate name for this type of delayed-exchange system could be "institutionalized trust."

Deals between politicians tend to be less overt than those for mortgage loans, but reputedly are equally binding. In the field of diplomacy, treaties are published records of delayed-exchange expectations associated with particular international transactions; hence, treaties are important for establishing and testing trustworthiness.

Foreclosure or loss of one's credit standing is a significant penalty in a consumer society; it leads to a loss of opportunities to possess goods in advance of having the cash to pay for them. In political exchanges, unkept promises and unreturned obligations may also lead to the loss of reputation, friendship, honor, peace, credibility, access, affiliation, and the like. When transactors become less trusting of each other, grounds for cooperation or coalition become less tenable. If enough distrust is generated by unmet obligations, the aggrieved first (or giving) party may try to recapture the political currency previously given. As hostility increases, conflict escalates and political relationships regress, often into violent tactics. It is this kind of regression into warfare that occurs when critical transitions fail.

Trust is one of the most significant consequences of social and political exchanges, according to Homans, Blau, and others (Homans 1961; Blau 1964; Foa 1971, 171: 345–51; Foa and Foa 1976). Because trust is a significant outcome of successful political transactions and a facilitator of institutional development, a more precise definition of the concept may be helpful.

Trust and distrust describe polar extremes of a particular attitude. The attitude is anticipatory; that is, an expectation about the consequences for oneself of another's probable behavior. Two questions arise from this expectation: Will the consequences for oneself be positive or negative? Will the other person or group behave as predicted? If a person, A, anticipates that the other, B, will reliably act as expected, with positive consequences for oneself, A's attitude toward B will tend to become a trusting one. If there is substantial doubt about the predictability of B's behavior or if the consequences for A are likely to be negative, or if both these conditions prevail, A is likely to distrust B.

From the perspective of institution-building, transactions negotiated by adversary elites are likely to be of the delayed-exchange type, with obligatory future behavior based upon present compromises. Obligations fulfilled are likely to provide grounds for further behavioral exchanges; as a consequence, there may be increased trust and further institutionalization of the activities jointly undertaken. Joint efforts at institutionalization will cease if obligations are unmet, exchanges will terminate, and distrust will be revived.

Examples from the Critical Transition Cases

What is the relevance of political transactions to the critical transition among the three institutions under study? As the English, American, and Mexican cases will demonstrate, the development of the institutions, both internally and relative to each other, was in large measure the cumulative consequence of long series of exchanges of political currencies between series of adversary leaders. These competing elites, at the head of their institutions or organizations, struggled for ascendancy; that is, senior political status. In victory, defeat, or at a stalemate, they eventually negotiated exchanges of political currencies (incumbencies, shares, or commodities or all three). Upon fulfilling or betraying their contracted obligations, the competitors moved on to the next conflict cycle. Fulfilled obligations were likely to diminish the scope of their disagreements. Unfulfilled obligations aggravated their conflicts and increased their distrust of each other.

These transactions, which often went on for decades or generations, strengthened or weakened particular institutions. In this way, one institution grew to higher status (read: leadership influence, available resources, etc.) while another institution declined. For example, political party leaders became more influential while military leaders became less so. One of the purposes of this inquiry into English, American, and Mexican institutional history was to identify some of the long series of political transactions that eventually led these nations through their critical transitions. What follows are examples of the development processes involved.

In England, rival elites and their armies carried on internal wars for a thousand years. The Settlement of 1689 brought this strife to an end. Thereafter, English elites no longer depended on rival armies but turned to party institutions in their efforts to influence each other and national affairs. There has since been no full-scale civil war in England.

Similar conditions occurred in Mexico during the period from independence in 1820 until the regime of President Plutarco Calles in the late 1920s. Between 1820 and 1920, coalitions of caudillos battled each other with costly regularity; internal war was the normal state of

Mexican politics. By the 1930s, however, the nation's party and representative institutions were sufficiently influential to discourage further civil war. Mexico has since been free of internal war.

In the history of the United States, the most devastating war to that date began in 1861, ended in 1865, and almost reignited during the disputed Hayes-Tilden election of 1876. The Civil War was the first and, it is to be hoped, last internal war of the Republic.

Were the patterns of change similar in the three nations? This investigation revealed institutional patterns with similarities that appear to be more than coincidental. During the tumultuous seventeenth century in England, that nation's military institutions experienced substantial centralization, particularly under Oliver Cromwell's New Model Army. At the same time, Parliament asserted itself as the ascendant representative body for the entire nation. This claim to ascendancy was made by the leaders of the emergent parliamentary political parties. Changes in the power relationships among the three political institutions—military, representative, and partisan—culminated in civilian control of the military; that is, the political parties controlled Parliament, and Parliament controlled the military. There were no more internal wars. Civilian supremacy prevailed. The parties were accountable to the electorate. The Parliament was accountable to the parties. The military was accountable to the Parliament.

A similar critical transition among political institutions took place in Mexico during a briefer period: from 1919 to 1940. With varying degrees of success, each Mexican president during this period sought to build a centralized and professional national army while at the same time diminishing, through conquest or bribery, the influence of the armies of local caudillos. During this same period, Mexico's system of political representation evolved slowly and, for the most part, comprehensively.

At first, major interests were represented in the president's cabinet, later in the nation's principal political party in what became a one-party system. During 1928–29, a Partido Nacional Revolucionario (PNR) was inaugurated; its factional structure provided the arena for elite representation and accommodation. Here again, as in England, the military, the representative, and the party institutions converged in critical transition. The party co-opted and later controlled the military; representation in the presidential cabinet was succeeded by the more comprehensive representation afforded by the Mexican Congress; the Congress, controlled by the party, eventually achieved control of the military. There was civilian supremacy and an end to internal wars.

In the American case, a great deal of military centralization occurred during the Civil War, but diminished significantly thereafter. What appeared to be a stable political party system during the 1830s and 1840s disintegrated on the eve of the Civil War, a development that can be blamed for the events leading to that bloody conflict. Additionally, the Congress became ineffectual as an agency for representing and balancing powerful conflicting interests, especially between the North and the South. Not until the 1880s and 1890s did the nationalization of the military; that is, the firm establishment of federal military ascendancy over the state militia, take place. During these same decades the party system was rehabilitated and stabilized, and Congress once again came into its own as a powerful representative assembly. Political integration of the nation then went forward without further risk of civil war.

The components of each nation's institutional development followed a similar pattern: centralization of the nation's military institutions; emergence of a comprehensive system of political representation; and stabilization of a political party system that permitted serious but nonviolent elite competition. When the rank-order of influence among the three institutions found the party system in the superior position and the military establishment third in rank, it was reasonable to conclude that the nation had successfully passed through its critical transition.

The process that led up to and carried change through critical transitions usually consisted of series of specific transactions consummated by adversary elites. The Settlement that concluded the Glorious Revolution in England in 1689 is an important example of a contractual document that consummated just such a transaction (Randle 1973, 103–4).

The principal adversaries in the Glorious Revolution were a coalition of English nobles versus King James II. After a few minor military engagements, the king found that he could not rouse popular support for his cause. He fled the country, leaving the field to the coalition of nobles and their parliamentary allies. Parliament declared the throne vacant by abdication.

Acknowledging that it could not function constitutionally without a king, Parliament invited Mary, the daughter of James II, and her husband, William of Orange (The Netherlands), to assume the throne as joint sovereigns. The political currencies implicitly exchanged were an incumbency (kingship) for shares of prerogative (Parliament's expanded power in English lawmaking and control over the military).

The Settlement that followed consisted of more explicit exchanges of political currencies between Parliament and the new sovereigns.

1. Parliament and the coalition of nobles swore allegiance to William as de facto king (legitimizing his incumbency) in exchange for his promise that no Roman Catholic could wear the crown (an incumbency condition).

2. English laws could be promulgated or altered only if a statute were passed by both houses of Parliament (increased share of national prerogative) and received the perfunctory consent of the king (reduced share of collective prerogative).

3. To end the royal power of arbitrary removal of judges (reduced share of royal prerogative), exercised often by earlier kings, it was agreed that judges would have tenure during good behavior (an incumbency condition).

4. Royal prerogative was further limited by the requirement that the army would be financed (commodity, in the form of funds for the military) for only one year at a time and could not be subject to mobilization by the king unilaterally (reduced share of royal prerogative).

The Settlement was a contract that recorded a major political transaction among the leaders of several institutions: Parliament, the royal household, the Church of England, and the military. The contract had consequences for the development of each institution. All statutes would be required to have the approval of the House of Lords, the House of Commons, and the king. This would compel negotiation and transactions among them before the enactment of laws. Any attempt by the king or Parliament to enact laws in other ways could immediately be recognized as a breach of contract and trust, hence unconstitutional. There would be prompt and substantial punitive responses in such situations.

The political currencies traded in the Settlement, only in part summarized here, were shares of national decision-making power (for example, full statutory power was given to the two houses of Parliament), incumbencies in particular offices (such as the kingship, the judgeships), and public commodities (such as annual appropriations for the army). The Settlement was the culmination of a century-long series of political transactions.

Recording the type of political currencies involved in such political transactions enables the historian to gather and analyze two otherwise seemingly inaccessible kinds of data: the substantive content of negotiated political contracts and the sequence of such transactions that contributes to the growth of a particular institution. These transactions may take place not only within a particular institution but also between institutions.

In sum, wars are likely to occur when political institutions inadequately constrain elite conflict behavior or fail to provide alternative nonviolent conflict arenas and processes. The critical transition model describes an aspect of institutional development in which adversary elites incrementally exchange political currencies that result in elevating political party institutions to first rank in national influence while at the same time reducing the military to a subordinate political role. This critical transition, when completed, leads to the reduction or elimination of warfare as a tactic of influence.

Are the national processes and findings relevant for supranational development? Very much so. Studies of small communities have furnished insights into the patterns of political development of larger ones. Investigations of tribal politics and the Greek city-states, for example, have given scholars important understandings about the development of nations. The disappearance of internal wars within certain nations may offer lessons for the elimination of international war.

Chapter 3

England: The Millennial Case

One thousand years were required to end internal wars in England. Over this millennium, the nobility's private feudal armies gradually emerged from a sequence of shifting military alliances into a single national defense force. A series of representative bodies—the Witan, the Great Council, the House of Lords, and, finally, the House of Commons—provided the arena in which most of the shifting alliances were consummated. Eventually, the merchant class and others gained power. The Parliament was also the place in which the political parties were born and gained ascendancy.

The political parties emerged at first as clusters of parliamentary colleagues voting together. Then, with the rise of popular suffrage, these clusters became teams of political colleagues cooperating systematically to win popular electoral support. The nation's critical transition was completed as the English party system achieved stability. The main period of the critical transition occurred in the seventeenth century, chiefly between 1648 and the Glorious Revolution of 1688. It was the culmination of a process that had begun many centuries earlier.

The Armies and Councils of Early Kings

England was settled before the fifth and sixth centuries by Jutes, Saxons, and Angles, three Germanic tribes that migrated from the European continent. Each migrating group had its own king, many of whom claimed to have special authority because of descent from ancient Germanic gods. From about 55 B.C. to A.D. fifth century, in response to invasions from the Continent, contact with Roman armies, and shifting alliances among themselves, numerous tribal kings formed coalitions, giving nominal deference to a senior king heading the coalition.

The first of these senior kings was Humber, king of the South Saxons during the late fifth century. The marriage of one of the senior kings, Aethelberht of Kent, to the daughter of the king of Paris on the Continent, led to the introduction of Christianity among the heathen tribes of England at the close of the sixth century. In one, the Kingdom of Kent, the cathedral of Canterbury was built. Thus, at the outset, even within the confines of their small island, the English were a heterogeneous people whose leaders were competitive, accustomed to dispersed and limited power, and skilled in the formation of coalitions.

With the departure of the Romans, several tribes fell into warfare. Alliance systems changed with relative frequency. Between the sixth and ninth centuries, seven relatively independent kingdoms emerged: Kent, which had been settled mainly by Jutes; Essex, Sussex, and Wessex, ruled by Saxon kings; and East Anglia, Mercia, and Northumbria, predominantly made up of Angles. The prominence of Mercia at this time prompted the papacy to address Offa II of Mercia (757–96) as "king of the English," even though the other rulers of the heptarchy, that is, the seven kingdoms, rendered only minimal allegiance to him.

Intermittent warfare among these kings was usually carried on by unorganized armed bands. The tribal leaders of the fifth and sixth centuries had military units that were essentially personal bodyguards. Each unit member was known as a *gesith,* sworn in personal allegiance to the king in peace and war. The sworn allegiance gave a contractual character to the relationship. The aura of contract has since been a customary feature of military-political relationships in English affairs. In return for allegiance, tribal leaders divided among the gesiths much of the land of the district in which they settled. The kings also assumed responsibility for providing the gesiths with food, clothing, and arms.

As tribes grew to be kingdoms, defense of the kingdoms began to require greater numbers of men. The gesiths remained as personal retainers of kings, but were not adequate for the more general defense. Tribal traditions, when a defense emergency occurred, began to call for the mobilization of all able-bodied men. The English kings of the seventh, eighth, and ninth centuries rendered every able-bodied free-man liable for military service in the event of invasion. This obligation became firmly rooted in practice. The result was a primitive national militia known as the *fyrd*.

Free landowners between the ages of sixteen and sixty were subject to service in the fyrd for two months a year in time of war. These citizen-soldiers had little training, little specialized skill, and little discipline. They were capable of little more than massed tactical formations, although some of their formations reflected lessons learned from the Romans. In time, foot soldiers became somewhat specialized, depending upon which weapon they used. The boundaries of some kingdoms were fortified with trenches and mounds in strategic places (Fortescue 1899–1930, I: 5; Curtis 1943, 5).

During the ninth century, the Danes swept across many parts of the European continent seeking plunder and conquest. One of these armies, known as the Great Army, invaded eastern England in 865 and succeeded in converting the kingdoms of Mercia, East Anglia, and Northumbria into Danish colonies. The Great Army was a highly disciplined force. There were distinctions in rank. The men were skilled as both seamen and soldiers. Battlefield organization and tactics were sophisticated for that era. Most of England fell under Danish control.

Not until the reign (871–99) of King Alfred the Great of Wessex were the English able to turn the tide. Alfred's successes, the first occurring in 878, eventually enabled him to capture London, which by then had become the political center of England. Kings, nobles, and other Englishmen began to defer to Alfred as overlord of all those parts of England not under Danish control. Their deference was voluntary and their declarations of allegiance were total. The nobility's active participation in designating him as senior king reinforced existing precedents in English leadership selection and established new ones. Their actions also placed Alfred at the head of all English military forces, such as they were, in the common effort to drive out the Danes. Alfred used the occasion of this recognition to inaugurate the first great reforms aimed at centralizing England's civil and military administration.

Alfred constructed a three-part system of national defense. He built a navy with vessels larger and faster than those of the Danes. In addition to personal gesiths, Alfred recruited soldiers by requiring all owners of five *hides* of land (about 600 acres) or more to send, at his summons, one armed man provided with food and pay. These recruits and the king's gesiths were together known as *thanes* and constituted a separate royal standing army. The thanes were organized into units according to shire. This practice in English military organization recognized the importance of local pride and control.

In addition to navy and thanes, the national militia; that is, the fyrd, was made Alfred's third line of defense. The fyrd was reorganized so that only half of all able-bodied freemen were called to service at a time, while the other half remained to till the soil during an invasion. Alfred and his successors also fortified strategic locations with earthworks and stockades known as *burghs,* a term that was later appended to the names of many towns fortified in this manner.

Burdened by endless warfare with the Danes, many English landowners and farmers during the tenth century began to give up their land in exchange for the military protection provided by the king and other senior nobility. This type of exchange (the commodity of land for the service of protection) marked the beginning of the feudal manorial system. At the same time, the transactions spurred the centralization of the nation's military establishment.

Alfred's descendants, successfully turning back the Danish and Norwegian raids from the north, won the allegiance of additional nobles. They also began to develop foreign alliances as part of their defense strategy. It was all in vain. In the end, the Vikings conquered England.

Kind Edmund Ironside's death in 1016 left the English throne vacant, whereupon Canute, king of Denmark, launched a successful invasion. The Witan, or Witenagemot, the council of senior nobles, which had by this time established itself as the principal advisory body to English kings, legitimized Canute's incumbency by pledging their allegiance to him. Canute in turn agreed to send his army back to Denmark, with the exception of from three to six thousand *huscarls* (household troops). The huscarls, like the thanes before them, became the royal household's special army, to be supplemented by the fyrd during invasions. The huscarls' special weapons at this time were the two-handed axe and the five-foot shaft. As it turned out, this royal army's lack of archers and cavalry was later a major cause of King Harold's defeat at the hands of William the Conqueror of Normandy in 1066.

The Witan's presumptive prerogative was again exercised in 1066 in the election of Harold as king. The Witan subsequently selected Edgar when Harold was killed in battle against the Norman army of William the Conqueror. Soon after, the Witan obtained Edgar's resignation so that it could bestow the crown upon William, thereby ending the invasion. William's acceptance of the decision-making procedure as well as the crown (baronial shares in exchange for William's incumbency) brought the Norman kings to the English throne and firmly established baronial participation in matters of royal succession.

At the time of the Norman conquest, England was already a relatively well-organized state. Royal authority was widely recognized. A system of national taxation existed and was administered by the king's local agents. There was also a system of law administered by local courts in the king's name. The minting of currency was under the control of the central government. On the principle that all the land of England belonged to the king, William was able to divide four-fifths of the land among the military adventurers who had joined him for the invasion and among the English nobles who agreed to hold all their lands as feudal fiefdoms obligated to him.

English military service was intermittent and part-time, activated mainly by invasions and other security emergencies. Across the English Channel, however, Normandy was absorbed by its military needs arising from the incessant warfare among Continental nobility. To avoid similar chaos in England, William the Conqueror instituted a fundamental military reorganization based upon a new contractual relationship with the nobility. When the English nobility agreed to hold all their lands as feudal fiefdoms, in exchange for title to their land, they gave the king the right to demand either military and related services or *scutage*, a tax paid in lieu of military service (land as a commodity exchanged for another commodity, that is, military service or scutage). Thus, institutionalization of the nation's military force advanced another step. As vassals, the nobles owed fealty to the king, a breach of which was a felony, a crime of great seriousness.

Under the Norman kings, cavalry, with horsemen clad in ringed mail, became a high-priority military resource and were recruited according to feudal principle. One of the nobility's obligations was to provide a specified number of horsemen or knights as requested by the king. Small estates were expected to send small numbers of knights, perhaps the lord of the manor and one or two additional men; great estates were to send perhaps a hundred or more. To prevent the development of small and potentially rebellious armies, in 1086 William had all the landowners of England pledge allegiance to him as supreme head of the feudal levy. Part of the levy involved replacing the burghs with stone-walled castles, which, in time, became a strategic defense network throughout England.

William also strengthened his authority to call up the fyrd in times of invasion. The fyrd, however, now had several disadvantages as a military force. England had begun to be involved in wars on the Continent, but the fyrd could not be called out to fight abroad. Soldiers in the fyrd were usually ill-trained, ill-armed, and liable to service for only forty days a year. The king therefore began to allow landowners and freemen to substitute a money payment for their military obligation. Instead of furnishing a knight, or a shield (*scutum* in Latin) as knights were also known, the landowner could pay an annual fee instead, that is, the scutage referred to above. With these funds, the king could hire professional mercenaries, or soldiers (from *solidus*, Latin for wages), who would fight under whatever circumstances the king wished, including foreign wars.

The Great Transaction: Magna Carta

By the twelfth century most Continental kings had gathered large armies of paid mercenaries. By comparison, the mercenaries of the English kings were a relatively small force. National and royal security still rested primarily upon the whole body of English freemen. As a consequence, much attention was given to the organization and quality of the fyrd. When Henry II, Duke of Normandy and Aquitaine and Count of Anjou in France, came to the English throne in 1154, he found himself spending nearly half his time in France defending or extending his lands there. A strong leader and administrator, he also gave a great deal of attention to building an English army that he could use on the Continent.

In a famous edict, the Assize at Arms of 1181, Henry II reiterated the obligation of every man to serve the nation in time of military need and set forth the kinds of arms and equipment each should bring with him when called into service. Poorer men were to bring daggers, knives, and any weapons they could find; the rich were to come elaborately equipped with lances, coats of mail, and steel helmets. (During the following century, lances were replaced by longbows as the formidable weapon of the English infantry.) The individual citizen's obligation was made more direct than hitherto, when the noble vassals were the middlemen of the military service system. The direct obligation derived, according to Henry II, from every man's status as the king's subject.

Henry modified royal tax arrangements in order to promote centralization of the royal military establishment. Taxes on land were either dropped or subjected to negotiation between the king's agents and tenants. Scutage was encouraged among noble vassals. In 1166, the first tax on personal property and income was levied, evidence of growing mercantile and industrial wealth. Before long, Henry was able to hire a mercenary army with the revenues received from scutage and income taxes. He could then use the mercenaries on the Continent.

The Catholic church played a leading role in English politics up to the time that the Settlement of the Glorious Revolution in 1689 forbade the elevation of a Catholic to the throne of England. Henry's various alliances on the Continent and his quarrel with Thomas Becket reflected the political power of the medieval church. Thus, taken together, Henry's military reforms and the church's political influence paved the way for Richard the Lion-Hearted's great military exploits in the Crusades at the close of the twelfth century.

It was King John (1199–1216) who increased taxes and scutage arbitrarily and collected them abusively. This led to a historic baronial rebellion against John. The conflict was resolved by the political transaction recorded in the Magna Carta in 1215, one of the most significant political transactions in human as well as English history. It was a contract of some sixty-three clauses recording the outcome of a multilateral negotiation: first, among a number of England's leading clergy, earls, and barons; and then, between this coalition of rebellious nobles and King John. The negotiations as well as the details of the agreement are reported elsewhere (Henning 1949, 23–38).

Lunt summarizes this great English constitutional contract as follows:

Since the Norman conquest the king of England had been both a national king and a feudal overlord, but his position as suzerain, which had been emphasized in the actual practice of government, was the side of the royal power which affected the barons particularly and against which the Great Charter was directed. The King's position as feudal suzerain rested upon a contract, actual or implied, between him and his vassals. He gave lands and protection in return for certain specific services. Since the arrangement was contractual the king had duties as well as rights. What those duties were varied from time to time in accord with the content of a fluctuating body of unwritten feudal custom. But from the days of William the Conqueror the tenants-in-chief of the king had been attempting by rebellion or by other means to force the king to keep his side of what they considered the feudal contract to be. Henry II so limited the powers of the tenants-in-chief and so increased his own, that the contractual element nearly disappeared. Richard and John continued to break the contract in ever-increasing ways. In 1215 the barons rose in rebellion and refused to return to their allegiance, until the king should have promised no more to break his contract in those particulars which they specified. The Great Charter revived the nearly extinct theory of the feudal contract, and it was consequently an acknowledgement on the part of the king that the powers of the crown were limited (Lunt 1947, 147).

This historic document is best known for the constraints it placed upon royal power to take life, liberty (by imprisonment), or property without fair trial by the defendant's noble peers in the courts. This established the basic propositions and rights of due process of law.

The military provisions were also of profound significance. The king could no longer levy scutage and other aids (direct taxes or requests for special financial grants) without the consent of the Great Council of the Curia Regis, which had by this time become a quasi-representative assembly (Great Council shares exchanged for taxes as a commodity). Because support of the royal military forces was the major purpose of these revenues, the nobility could now influentially constrain the king's military capacity and actions.

The Magna Carta further provided for a permanent committee of twenty-five barons to review reports of royal breaches of the agreement, in which cases all were bound to unite in military action; that is, civil war, against the king. Disloyalty to the king, ordinarily a felony, was, with typical English constitutional ingenuity, transformed into an act of honor if implemented by due process.

A decline in scutage revenues, an increase in wages for mercenary knights, and a growing need for mercenaries arising out of England's expanding involvement in continental wars compelled John and subsequent kings to find another way of raising armies, namely, the fine *pro servicio*. This fine was imposed in place of, or sometimes in addition to, scutage. The fine was usually set at an arbitrary rate in excess of the scutage rate, and, in time, became an undisguised form of royal extortion (Hollister 1965, 214–15).

Subsequent to Magna Carta, the English military establishment in theory consisted of three components: the nobility, or principal tenants of the king, and their armed vassals; the minor tenants; and the freemen subject directly to the assize of arms of the king. The freemen received assize orders from the county sheriffs, who had by now become important agents of the king in matters of local order and justice as well as national defense. It was the sheriff who enforced the assize of arms and saw to it that a fixed contingent of properly outfitted men-at-arms could be furnished upon call of the king. The sheriff was, in effect, an agent of military centralization, putting the king in direct contact with citizen-soldiers and thereby further circumventing the feudal hierarchy.

One other aspect of military organization was the network of castles and castle service. Although the number of fortified castles dropped from about six hundred at the end of the eleventh century to fewer than four hundred at the end of the twelfth century, castle guard and related services were an important form of feudal military obligation. The arrangements for fulfilling the obligations of castle guard and castle labor varied from district to district: sometimes paid for by the lord, sometimes at the vassal's expense, sometimes for a few days to a few months at a time, sometimes for permanent duty on a paid basis, sometimes perceived by the local community as forced labor, sometimes as patriotic duty. Scutage and castle guard service were often assessed at different rates, and the regulation of these obligations became quite complex. By the end of the thirteenth century, castle guard service became relatively insignificant as the king's military needs began to transcend those of mere local defense (Hollister 1965, chap. 5).

Expanding Representation and Centralizing the Military

Following King John's reign, the House of Plantagenet continued to rule until 1399. Henry III was on the throne for fifty-six years (1216–72). Then came Edward I (1272–1307), Edward II (1307–27), Edward III (1327–77), and Richard II (1377–99).

Before the reign of Edward I, there were numerous experiments aimed at making the membership of the king's Grand Council, which was predominantly baronial and clerical, more comprehensive and representative. Simon de Montfort's effort in 1265 was the most noteworthy, adding two knights from every shire as representatives of the rural middle class and two burgesses from every city and borough to represent the new urban middle class. The trade-off was straightforward: more middle-class participation (shares) in national policy making in exchange for more middle class revenue and service (commodities) to the royal household. Edward I institutionalized these changes in the Model Parliament of 1295, which he thereafter called into session almost every year.

The functions of Parliament under Edward I were primarily judicial and revenue-raising, but a novel legislative device was also inaugurated at this time; namely, the petition. Although only the king could enact a law, his power subsequently came to be shared with Parliament through the latter's use of petitions. If representatives united to present a petition and if the king granted the request, then the king and Grand Council would convert the language of the petition into a royal statute. Edward's concern for public opinion and revenues (commodities) from the middle class prompted him to give his sovereign approval fairly regularly to petitioned requests (shares).

As Parliament became progressively more influential, the royal tendency to centralize English military organization was again taken up by Edward I. This was in keeping with his personal desire for greater administrative standardization and efficiency. One of Edward's most significant acts was the Statute of Winchester (1285), which dealt in part with the military organization of the realm. The statute reenacted the Assize of Arms, requiring every man under sixty to arm himself at his own expense for the defense of the kingdom and the maintenance of internal order. Sheriffs were to make regular inspections of arms and, for the first time, maintain muster rolls of those liable for service.

During much of his reign, Edward needed all the military resources he could gather in order to pursue the conquest of Wales, gain control over the Scots, defend his fiefdom in Gascony, and suppress dissent among barons disaffected by his heavy and arbitrary taxation. Although the barons were able to pressure Edward into reaffirming the principles of Magna Carta, he subsequently used every device he could to circumvent his obligations. As distrust built up, the barons began to suspect all royal actions and prerogatives. This distrust of the monarchy was carried over into the reign of Edward II, who was deposed eventually in favor of his son, Edward III.

During the long reign of Edward III (1327–77), knights and burgesses in Parliament began to use petitions and their revenue resources with regularity and skill in bargaining with the king. In preparation for negotiating sessions, knights and burgesses began to meet in a common place apart from the others, that is, in "the commons." These meetings eventually became the lower house of Parliament.

Edward III launched the Hundred Years' War against France in 1337. This brought further changes in English military policy and organization. For example, Welsh spearmen were the first English troops to be dressed in uniform (1337), an important symbol of national identification. Archers and the longbowmen were given special prominence in the infantry. Cannons were used for the first time. The army was organized into units of relatively uniform size under officers at each level: units of twenty led by a vintenar, a hundred by a centenar, and a thousand by a millenar. The king, at the top of the hierarchy, had two principal staff officers: a high constable or adjutant and a marshall or quartermaster.

Edward III not only hired mercenaries, but also inaugurated a contract system whereby subjects could agree to raise troops for him (incumbencies) in exchange for a stipulated sum from the royal treasury (commodities). This gave the urban middle class an opportunity hitherto available only to the nobility; namely, the right to raise military forces for their king. It also gave the king further independence from the constraints placed on him by a Parliament dominated by the nobility. Edward's statute on contracting provided that men could not be forced to sign military service contracts, that men chosen to serve abroad would be paid by the Crown from the time they left the country, and that contracts that were against "all right and reason" could be cancelled. English kings of the fifteenth century managed to evade these constraints, usually on grounds of national emergency (Cruickshank 1966, 5).

Edward's victory at Crécy in 1346 and his subsequent successes in France kept the English involved on the Continent until the middle of the fifteenth century. However, domestic strife during the rule of Richard II (1377–99) forced a reduction in the scope of these involvements.

In 1397, after twenty years of constitutional rule and almost at the end of his reign, Richard II suddenly embarked upon a policy of domestic repression. He had tried for treason the author of a parliamentary petition criticizing royal household expenses. (Personal immunity was not yet a parliamentary privilege.) He then packed successive sessions of Parliament with his own adherents, conducted numerous treason trials, imposed arbitrary imprisonments, and the like. Richard's breach of the Magna Carta led to a joint baronial-popular uprising. The leader of the uprising was Henry of the House of Lancaster, who became King Henry IV as soon as Richard was forced to abdicate.

English ventures on the Continent were climaxed in the Treaty of Troyes (1420), under which England's Henry V married Catherine, daughter of Charles VI of France. Their heirs were to become dual monarchs ruling over England and France, but allowing each nation to retain its separate institutions. By 1453, however, the English were driven from France, ending the Hundred Years' War.

Henry VI was dethroned in 1461, restored in 1470, and deposed again in 1471. This in part reflected the disintegration of the English royal military establishment and an intensification of domestic rivalries and internal wars among the English nobility. Entire baronial families and their allies chose sides as they carried on the War of the Roses. Those of Lancaster lineage, including King Henry VI, were arrayed against the House of York. Civil war lasted thirty years and concluded with the accession of Henry VII, first of the Tudors, in 1485.

The representative composition and policy prerogatives of Parliament continued to expand throughout the fifteenth and sixteenth centuries. Great conflicts over the succession and competition for influence within the royal court were manifest by changing alliances among baronial families on the battlefield, in the House of Lords, and in liaisons with the increasingly wealthy mercantile families. The competing aspirations of Catholic and Protestant clergy further complicated the crisscrossing elite struggles.

The development of the nation's most representative institution, the House of Commons, proceeded, but less dramatically. As early as Henry VI's reign (1399–1413), the burgesses and knights, particularly the latter, explicitly traded their contributions to royal revenues in exchange for royal concessions on policy. The House of Commons, representing merchants, was especially persistent in asking the king for full public accountings of tax moneys granted him. Commons also urged the appointment of royal advisers (incumbencies) who also met with Parliament's approval (shares), an early formulation of the doctrine of ministerial responsibility to Parliament.

These demands and transactions were evidence of successful coalition-formation among the burgesses and knights of Commons. This reflected the fact that the mercantile classes in the constituencies were increasingly active in politics. Merchants and manufacturers were becoming aware of their stake in national tax policy and the disposition of military forces for the protection and expansion of overseas markets. They therefore made themselves influential participants in the selection of the membership of Commons. In doing so, they joined the company of landed gentry and county politicians who had previously comprised the principal constituents of Commons.

By the time the Tudors came to the throne in 1485, mercantile representation had become ascendant in Parliament. As a consequence, the Tudors conducted their royal administration in a businesslike fashion, opposed monopolistic trade practices at home and abroad, expanded the export market for English goods, and built a navy that could protect trading ships on all seas.

As Henry VIII prepared for the wars of 1538–47, his revenue needs grew, and he was increasingly solicitous of Parliament's goodwill and support. For its part, Parliament acquired a strong sense of its prerogatives. Statutes came to be described as actions of the king "in parliament," that is, joint acts of Lords and Commons, approved by the king. The English monarchy was becoming a constitutionally more power-sharing institution even as Continental monarchies were becoming more absolutist.

Military Enterprise under Constitutional Monarchs: The Tudors

The House of Tudor ruled from 1485 to 1603: Henry VII (from 1485 to 1509); Henry VIII (1509–47); Mary I (1553–58); Elizabeth I (1558–1603). During the Tudor reign, the affluent English middle class was busily buying up the lands of bankrupt nobles and the recently confiscated monastic property of the Catholic church. Through land ownership, business connections, and intermarriages, the ambitious mercantile elite bought its way into the offices at royal disposition and into membership in Parliament. Class interests were fairly explicit and respected. The leaders of manufacture and trade were of sufficient renown, and royal policies were widely enough supported, so that Parliament and crown enjoyed extremely cordial relations.

Having derived so much of their resources from Parliament, the Tudors endorsed practices close to the hearts of the middle-class representatives in that body. Under the Tudors, the cherished liberal principles of immunity from arrest, freedom of speech, and assurance of access to the king through the Speaker became established privileges of members of Parliament. Henry VIII took special pains to remain personally popular in Parliament and among the general citizenry. Consequently, when he separated himself and the church of England from papal suzerainty, he did so with enthusiastic Parliamentary approval (the Reformation Parliament, 1529–36). His move was a victory for English Protestantism, although English Catholics pursued the religious struggle for nearly two centuries more.

In the military realm, changing military organization and tactics continued to flow from the technological innovations of the fifteenth century. Artillery became increasingly important as the War of the Roses progressed; for example, gunnery specialists acquired officer status, receiving commensurate wages. Siege artillery sealed the doom of castles, whose walls crumpled under their cannonballs. The handgun came into use, at first little more than an iron tube closed at one end, with a hole into which powder was poured and ignited. Over the next half century, handguns would render the armor-clad knight and horse obsolete.

Henry VIII took special pride in the work of his royal foundry, which produced large bronze cannon with several technical innovations. Handguns—arquebus, carbine, and petronel, as the different types were known—received his special attention. Henry also introduced the practice of supplying uniforms for all royal soldiers (Curtis 1943, 14).

The Tudors made war against the Scots, the French, and the Spanish. The international machinations of Henry VII were specifically designed to promote English commerce. To support this objective, he developed a system of taxation and audit that tripled royal income over the short period of two decades. Henry VIII was therefore able to begin his reign with a costly war against the French and the Scots (1512–14). The wars were popular, but the requisite taxes were not. Many political leaders also recognized that the Henrys had constructed a royal military machine that could all too readily be used as an instrument of repression when not engaged in foreign wars. Defense preparations and several foreign wars (1538–47), however, kept the king dependent upon Parliament for money. After Henry VIII ended papal jurisdiction over the Church of England, many of these wars took on a religious character. The possible elevation of a Catholic to the throne of England became one of the principal issues of the English civil wars of the next century.

Sixteenth-century English armies were not very large forces. In 1557, the first unit to be called a regiment was created and consisted of one thousand cavalry and four thousand infantry. This regiment was sent by Queen Mary to help her Spanish husband, Philip, against the French. When the Spanish Armada threatened England in 1588, Elizabeth's general muster of the national militia activated only sixty thousand men who, in the actual event, never had to fire a shot (Curtis 1943, 14). The sixty thousand, it appears, were merely 10 percent of the names on the muster rolls maintained by the sheriffs (Fortescue 1899–1930, 1: 133). Elizabeth's largest expeditions to France and the

Low Countries never numbered more than about twenty thousand men (Cruickshank 1966, 15–16).

After the short and tumultuous reigns of Edward VI and Mary I, Elizabeth I assumed the throne in 1558. She gave strong royal direction once again to the development of English commerce, the conduct of foreign wars (the Spanish Armada was defeated in 1588), and the maintenance of a substantial military force to defend the empire. It has been estimated that the wars between 1585 and 1602 cost about 4 million pounds, a large sum for that era. When the queen died, she left her country burdened by debt and the taxes needed to pay for its military expenditures.

Before Elizabeth's reign, the condition of the English army had already seriously deteriorated. This was common knowledge throughout Europe. The loyalty of her royal troops was doubtful. Mutinies were common. Fraud was widespread among officers. According to one student of the period, "though the muster-rolls of the army in Scotland showed eight thousand men for whom the Queen paid wages, but five thousand were actually with the colours, and the pay of the remaining three thousand went of course into the captains' pockets." Captains were the principal managers of their units and exploited this for personal advantage, for example, by encouraging men to buy their way out of service, selling the equipment of dead or discharged soldiers, and often colluding with suppliers of military goods. Elizabeth, parsimonious and ambivalent about the military, did little to improve matters (Fortescue 1899–1930, 1: 128; Cruickshank 1966, chap. 9).

The Privy Council, particularly the six members of its subcommittee on military affairs, shared with Queen Elizabeth responsibility for military administration. The full council, made up of about a dozen advisers to the Crown plus administrators of the royal household, had acquired under the Tudors the substantial authority over general government policy, sharing with Parliament many regulatory and legislative duties. For example, despite the English predilection for the longbow and the inefficiency of the handguns of the day, the Privy Council in 1597 substituted "weapons of fire" for the bow as the requisite weapon of the infantry. It was the council that struggled unsuccessfully to improve the methods of recruiting and maintaining the army.

The council gave strong encouragement also to the development of the navy, which was now a principal source of English military glory. By 1600, the English had gained substantial skill in combined army and navy operations. There were also many proposals for reorganizing the national militia; that is, the ancient fyrd. None, however, suggested a national standing army, a concept that was to be at the center of contention throughout the seventeenth century (Cruickshank 1966, 286).

One Elizabethan military effort that would have particular importance a century later was the private recruitment in 1572 of an expeditionary force to aid the Protestant Low Countries in their war against Catholic Spain. It began with a parade for the queen, conducted by London troops leaving service. Following the parade, financial subscriptions were solicited by Protestant interests in the city. Enough money was contributed to organize a company of three hundred veterans of wars in Scotland, Ireland, and France to assist the Dutch. Under Captain Thomas Morgan, this company was the first of some fifty to one hundred thousand English volunteers who fought for Dutch independence over the next seventy years. It also, in many respects, paved the way for Parliament's call to William of Orange in 1688 to save the kingdom from the excesses of James II. By then, the Dutch people and William had been the beneficiaries of several generations of English volunteers and some of England's best military talent.

Despite the legacy of taxes for military purposes, the Tudor period ended with a "golden age" of prosperity and expansion under Elizabeth. At the time of her death in 1603, the country and Parliament were self-confident and pleased with royal leadership. Policy negotiations among factions in Parliament and between Parliament and royal ministers often followed practices common among modern party politicians. The negotiations were facilitated by the mutual respect and trust between Parliament and crown that was particularly prevalent under Elizabeth. The political parties as organizations, however, did not emerge until a century later.

The highly arbitrary royal style of Elizabeth's successor, James I came therefore as a shocking change for Parliament and England's political leaders. The shock grew to rebellion as Parliament's newly acquired constitutional prerogatives, economic interests, and religious concerns became the targets of royal hostility and manipulation. Thus, most of the seventeenth century under the Stuart kings experienced revolutionary turmoil as well as the aftermath of war debts left by Elizabeth.

Political Parties and Revolution

The period 1603–1714 has aptly been called the Century of Revolution. It was certainly a time of critical transition among England's key political institutions. Parliament took control of the armed forces away from the king, and the emergent party system gained control over Parliament.

Only recently at war with each other, England and Scotland in 1603 were reconciled by the ascension of James VI of Scotland to the English throne as James I, the first of the Stuart kings. Peace was established in Ireland, and friendly relations with Spain were renewed. With James came his belief in the divine right of kings, a philosophy then widely held on the Continent.

Uneasy with a foreign-born king, Parliament began to react negatively to James's divine-rights theories, his preference for religious conformity, and the closer ties he sought with the recently hostile Scotland. His views and behavior triggered a century-long struggle between king and Parliament over royal prerogative, revenues, control of the military, and civil rights.

Confronted with Elizabeth's war debts, James quickly convened Parliament in order to request a grant of taxes. Parliament, using its well-established petition procedure, took the opportunity to ask for redress of several grievances, including discontinuation of archaic feudal dues, and an end to purveyance (royal seizure of goods at an arbitrarily appraised value); debate ensued also over the king's recent levy of impositions (import duties) without Parliament's consent. To deal with these issues another great contract in the tradition of Magna Carta was under negotiation in 1610 between court representatives and parliamentary leaders when James, asserting his presumed absolutist prerogatives, dissolved Parliament. Popular and parliamentary distrust of the foreign king now turned to active resentment.

James again convened Parliament in 1614 (the Addled Parliament), but could get nothing done; he dissolved it within two months, and arrested several of the most vocal opposition members. The situation worsened in 1616 with the king's dismissal of Sir Edward Coke, chief justice of the king's bench. Coke, long a champion of the precedence of common law over royal and parliamentary prerogative, had refused to respond to a royal command *not* to hear a case without prior consultation with the king. Coke's dismissal left the courts of England devoid of authority and prestige until the departure of the Stuarts in 1688.

Meanwhile, a crisis was beginning to surface in the nation's military. In contrast to the navy, the English army at this time was in poor repute and ill-repair. Following a practice pursued under Elizabeth, James I recruited many English foot soldiers directly from local jails and from among the unemployed. Corruption and ineptitude were rampant among the royal units. Although there was a growing literature in England on military subjects, none recommended the development of new forms of military organization, least of all a standing army such as those becoming common on the Continent.

A standing army, a new concept in that era, was an official national military force established on a permanent basis and maintained even in peacetime. It was a mode of organization quite different from the English militia, which was locally recruited, casually trained, and called into service only on an emergency basis—usually in times of invasion. The more permanent English military components consisted largely of mercenaries, contract units, and the king's household guards.

In 1612, James's Privy Council began to deliberate on the problem of strengthening the militia. It created a Council of War to coordinate the army and navy. It took measures to train soldiers and provide modern weapons. James's critics saw these policies as first steps toward the creation of a standing army and an English tyranny. The English distrusted professional soldiers and, more so, kings who sought to train citizens to be professional soldiers (Schwoerer 1974).

The Thirty Years' War broke out on the Continent in 1628, pitting Protestant German princes and nobles against the Catholic church, France, and their allies. James turned over the management of England's participation in the war to his son, Charles I and George Villiers, the Duke of Buckingham. The king's Council of War estimated that an army of twenty-five thousand infantry and five thousand cavalry would be needed for Continental service. When Parliament resisted raising taxes for such a large army, James resorted increasingly to forced loans, arbitrary imprisonment for those who refused to make loans, quartering of troops in private households, martial law to be applied to mutinying soldiers and any civilians associated with their misdeeds, and enforcement of these royal practices by county lieutenants (who much earlier had replaced sheriffs as the king's local military agents) or specially appointed commissions.

These practices were continued on a grander scale when Charles I came to the throne in 1625. Every royal tactic failed to win Parliament's financial support during its sessions of 1625, 1626, and 1627 (Schwoerer 1974, chap. 2; Firth 1962, 1). From mid-1624 to early 1628, about fifty thousand men—an estimated 1 percent of the total English population—had been conscripted into the army and arbitrarily billeted in homes in many parts of England. Officers, according to Privy Council rules, were billeted in the homes of the well-to-do; soldiers elsewhere. In short, all classes were involved, and the outcry against this practice was universal. Protests against Charles's measures originated in the counties, were taken up in Parliament, and led to the Petition of Right in 1628.

The petition condemned the levying of taxes without the approval of Parliament, billeting of soldiers in private households, arbitrary imprisonment, the excessive use of martial law, and the use of the county lieutenant as a royal agent for intervening in local affairs. Charles assented reluctantly to the petition, which had been supported by both houses of Parliament, and then proceeded to ignore its provisions. He did not again call Parliament until 1640, when an unexpected rebellion in Scotland compelled him to raise an army to restore order there.

A large number of the representatives elected to the 1640 Parliament were members of the dissident Puritan sect against which James I had exercised particularly repressive measures. Parliament met and refused to respond to the royal request for resources until grievances had been redressed. Unwilling to negotiate such conditions, Charles dissolved the Short Parliament within three weeks.

Unable to raise funds for an army, Charles was soon having to deal with the occupation of the northern counties of England by the Scots. When the Scots refused to agree to an armistice unless it was ratified by Parliament, Charles was forced to convene another Parliament. This one sat for thirteen years. The Long Parliament voted a "Brotherly Assistance" of three hundred thousand pounds to the Scottish force to help pay for its subsistence until it could disband. The practice of using foreign allies—Scottish, Dutch, and the like—to help defeat England's royal armies would be repeated in the subsequent struggle of the Glorious Revolution.

In its first year, the Long Parliament voted in favor of six royal subsidies and a poll tax (commodity currency) in exchange for which Charles acquiesced to the following eight statutes (mainly shares currency):

1. The period between parliamentary sessions could never be longer than three years.

2. Consent of both houses (shares) was required for any dissolution within fifty days of a first session.

3. Special courts, such as the Court of Star Chamber, instruments of imprisonment under Stuart tyranny, were abolished.

4. The Court of High Commission, used for ecclesiastical persecution by Charles, was abolished.

5–8. Arbitrary and abused levies, such as tonnage duties, levies of ship-money, forest fines, and fees for compulsory knighthood, were to be illegal if instituted without parliamentary consent (shares).

Military Centralization and Critical Transition

Parliament was by this time a numerous body. Some forty-five counties and two-hundred boroughs were represented in Commons, seating a total of 504 members. During the first half of the sixteenth century, to lend continuity to its discussions and actions, each house began to maintain a journal. By the time the Stuarts came to the throne, ambitious local leaders were attracted by the opportunity to serve in Parliament. During the reigns of James I and Charles I, the first manifestations of political party formations in Parliament began to emerge, usually as an opposition to the king. Small factions rallied around particular leaders, and coalitions of factions comprised voting majorities. The modern English party system had its beginning in these early years of the critical transition.

In 1641, an army was needed to quell a rebellion in Ireland. Unwilling to give Charles an army that could be turned against itself, Parliament, particularly the radicals led by John Pym, voted funds (commodities) for an eight-thousand-man army with the stipulation that the king appoint only ministers approved by Parliament or else relinquish control of this army to Parliament (shares). Pym's motion passed, 151 to 110. The vote reflected the fact that the factional coalitions had become relatively evenly matched.

Infuriated, Charles invaded Commons in an unsuccessful attempt to arrest five of the radical leaders. This breach of the constitutional immunities of the House enabled the radicals to mobilize enough votes to pass a Militia Bill requiring approval of both houses of Parliament for future appointments of commanders of the militia. The critical question now was how civilians would share in control of the nation's military forces.

Charles refused to approve the statute and departed for Nottingham to wage war against Parliament. For its part, Parliament used the Militia Bill as the basis for raising its own army. In doing so, it enacted a law without royal consent for the first time and, also for the first time, created an independent parliamentary army. This precedent of parliamentary participation in the organization and command of England's armed forces would later be confirmed in ARTICLE VI of the Settlement of 1689 wherein a professional standing army without the consent of Parliament was forbidden. In implementing the principle, Parliament created Oliver Cromwell's New Model Army during the Interregnum (1642–60) and the standing armies of Charles II and James II thereafter.

In 1642, the constitutional issues raised by the Militia Bill were debated in many forums by leaders of all persuasions; the subject was the single most difficult issue of the day. Civil war seemed the only way to resolve the problem (Schwoerer, chap. 3). As civil war began, each side found itself building an army practically from scratch. Both sides tried to make use of the extant military organization of the country: local agents for summoning the militia; attempts to seize munitions and equipment stored in county magazines; and calls for volunteers.

Experienced officers were available on both sides, but trained and disciplined men were not. In fact, impressment and mutinies had been a common problem for both Charles and Parliament. Although each side raised from sixty to seventy thousand men, no more than twelve to twenty thousand were ever in one place for major engagements. The royal forces prevailed until 1644. Then, Parliament took steps, at the behest of William Waller and Oliver Cromwell, to reorganize its forces along radically new lines. Cromwell's own troop of two thousand Ironsides had gained a favorable reputation for discipline, skill, and victories; it became the prototype for the New Model Army.

The creation in 1644 of the New Model Army, made up mainly of Independent Puritans (favoring freedom of worship), under the leadership of Oliver Cromwell, put Cromwell at the head of the radical Independent faction in Parliament. The Presbyterian radicals (favoring the establishment of a Presbyterian Church of England), led by John Pym, Denzil Holles, and William Waller, became the majority coalition at about this same time. The Cavaliers were the royalist party, having become a minority in Commons after some two hundred of their number had earlier departed, but continuing as a majority in the House of Lords.

Cromwell's Independents wanted a statute creating a New Model Army of twenty-one thousand regularly employed soldiers supported by monthly assessments of the counties. The Presbyterians, for their part of a legislative bargain, wanted a Self-Denying Ordinance that forbade any military commander from holding a seat in Parliament (a transaction consisting of incumbency currencies). The ordinance was passed and compelled numerous members of the House of Lords, many of whom happened to be incompetent military leaders, to resign from the military because their noble status did not allow them to leave their Parliamentary seats. The ordinance also forced the resignations of Cromwell and many of his followers, clearing the way for Presbyterian control of Parliament.

Initially, the New Model Army was one of many armed forces in the service of Parliament. In time, the other armies disappeared or were absorbed into the New Model Army. By 1649, the Commonwealth's army consisted of forty-four thousand soldiers. By 1652, this had risen to nearly seventy thousand. Toward the end of Cromwell's Protectorate, the number was reduced to about forty-two thousand. In 1660, it was eighteen thousand.

Impressment of recruits into the New Model Army was necessary until 1651, after which county quotas could be filled by voluntary enlistments. Discipline was strict. Training was thorough, particularly in the use of the newest weapons, cavalry, and artillery tactics. Organization was symmetrical (regiments of comparable size and function), hierarchical (all England, for example, was divided into eleven military districts, each under a major-general), and centralized. Promotion from the ranks on the basis of ability was one of the radical new policies. Tenure was full-time. Uniforms were standardized and attractive. Morale was high. Cromwell succeeded to an unequaled degree in centralizing the nation's military institution.

All this was unprecedentedly expensive. In 1645, Parliament estimated that the New Model Army of 21,000 men cost about 585,000 pounds a year. By 1649, the budget for a larger force was estimated at 1,560,000 pounds a year; two years later, this estimate rose to 2,041,000 pounds per annum, probably the maximum for the period

(Firth 1962, 183–84 and passim). This cost was, for the most part, paid for by the monthly assessments of the counties.

Cromwell's army very quickly became a political machine. Levelers and radical civil libertarians enlisted voluntarily, encouraging political activism on the part of the soldiers. The chaplains preached about the army's high *political* purposes. The eleven major-generals expanded and intensified the exercise of their authority in their respective districts. Wary of just this kind of politicization of the New Model Army, the Presbyterian majority in 1645 passed the Self-Denying Ordinance described above.

During 1648, as the New Model Army won new victories on the battlefield, King Charles's armistice negotiations with Parliament remained inconclusive. Charles did his best to exploit differences between Independents and Presbyterians. The latter, as the majority in Parliament, responded by taking steps to disband the New Model Army. Cromwell and his followers refused to go along with this maneuver, insisting that the army be a distinct party to any settlement between the king and Parliament.

In December 1648, Parliament passed a Militia Ordinance that again asserted its ultimate civilian authority over the military. Four days after this bill was passed, a detachment of Colonel Pride's army troops prevented nearly 200 Presbyterian members of Parliament from taking their seats, leaving in place a "Rump Parliament" of only ninety members in a body whose official membership numbered 504, diminished by some 200; that is, the Cavaliers who had departed six years earlier to align themselves with the king. Charles was then taken into custody by the Rump, which set up a commission to try him. The king was executed in January 1649. The Rump proceeded to abolish the House of Lords and the monarchy, declaring England a Commonwealth to be governed by an executive council appointed annually by Parliament.

The Rump ruled until 1653, at which time Model Army radicals convinced Cromwell to dissolve Parliament entirely and establish a temporary military dictatorship with himself as Lord Protector. Very shortly thereafter, however, Cromwell found that he could not avoid summoning Parliament in order to raise revenues. The first Parliament of the Protectorate was returned in September 1654. Among its new members were many Presbyterians and Republican representatives opposed to a standing army. When this Parliament voted in January 1655 to reassert its ascendancy over the military, Cromwell preemptorily dissolved it.

Among the supporters of parliamentary supremacy were some of the leading military men of the army itself. To head off dissension within the army, Cromwell took steps to organize a "new militia" under the eleven district major-generals whose duties now included authority to suppress rebellion, combat crime, assess and collect certain real and personal property taxes, license trade, and encourage "godliness and uprightness." Reaction was intense throughout the country; England resounded with antimilitary feeling and charges of tyranny.

In 1656 and 1657, Cromwell again summoned Parliament to request revenues, and again the effort was fruitless. Cromwell died in 1658, and his son, Richard, succeeded him as Lord Protector. Richard did little more than preside over a group of squabbling army officers. Dissatisfaction with the New Model Army, the eleven major-generals, and the county lieutenant system now swept across class lines and included a substantial number of military leaders.

James Harrington's *The Commonwealth of Oceana,* published in 1656, offered a timely and classic analysis of the relationships among military, economic, and social elements in society, in which he stressed how important a balance of property distribution was for the organization of the military. In brief, his theories made the argument that the military were obligated to the landed gentry and to the people rather than to the nobility. Harrington's analysis stimulated public debate and helped the opponents of the New Model Army bring matters to a head in Parliament's sessions in January 1659, immediately after Oliver Cromwell's death.

Distrust of the military led to disbandment of the New Model Army, but not before General George Monck, who led the army's troops in Scotland, declared himself in favor of a free Parliament and civilian control of the military. Monck marched on London, restored the members of Parliament who had been excluded in 1648 by Pride's Purge, arranged for a newly elected Commons, and urged Parliament to negotiate with Charles II for a restoration of the Stuarts to the throne.

Before the parliamentary invitation, Charles II, at Monck's suggestion, issued the Declaration of Breda offering to pardon all rebels except those Parliament might designate (incumbencies); leave the restoration of lands to royalists for Parliament to decide (commodities and shares); pay the army's wages (commodities); and leave the religious settlement up to Parliament (shares).

Parliament responded by making Charles II's tenure on the throne (incumbency) retroactive to 1649, thus maintaining unbroken the lineage of the monarchy; levying permanent taxes (commodities) intended to yield a large and regular annual income; placing a small standing army under Charles' command (incumbencies and shares); and assuring the king a lifetime annual income (commodity). Charles also agreed to retain all the reforms of 1640–41, which were reaffirmed by Parliament. The transaction was successful, albeit involving a complex set of political currencies.

The religious settlement was not accomplished at this time, although Charles, who was something of a Deist, preferred greater toleration of rebels, Catholics, and Dissenters than the strictly Anglican Parliament was willing to bestow. Charles II entered London in May 1659. The Model Army was disbanded in September 1660, receiving all back pay due its soldiers. A force of five thousand men was retained as the king's guard.

In the enthusiasm over the Restoration and the disbanding of the New Model Army, advocates of parliamentary supremacy over the military neglected to give sustained attention to the new policies. Several plots against the king, together with a number of relatively small domestic uprisings, caused a general feeling that the country needed a well-led army to maintain domestic order. In response, a 1661 Militia Act stated, without qualification, that the king alone was to have overall command of the militia. Day-to-day military management was returned to the local county gentry. The king was given assurance that any attempt by Parliament to raise soldiers or make war against the Crown would be considered illegal.

Charles II promptly sought to re-establish the county lieutenant as the influential local royal military agent. A second Militia Act of 1663, however, went into detail regarding county lieutenant powers in a way that restricted the king in his command functions and strengthened the county gentry (Schwoerer 1974, chap. 5). As he rebuilt the military, Charles gave elevated stature to the navy, establishing the admiralty office under his brother, the Duke of York.

Before long, Charles II aroused the suspicions of Parliament by adopting a pro-Catholic policy and embarking upon an intense friendship with France's Louis XIV, most absolutist of the monarchs on the Continent. Initial distrust resulted from Charles's efforts to raise an army for the Second Dutch War of 1665–67. More serious, however, was the discovery of his plot to restore Roman Catholicism in England at the behest of Louis XIV, for which the French monarch would provide Charles with a personal annual pension. To carry out this plan, Charles issued a 1672 Declaration of Indulgence suspending the operation of penal laws against Catholics and Protestant dissenters. Parliament convinced Charles to withdraw the declaration by also offering him a large subsidy. Instead, Charles accepted a Test Act that required all civil and military officials to take the Anglican sacraments. The outcome was further deterioration of relations between crown and Parliament.

Charles appointed as his chief adviser the Earl of Danby, a strong advocate of royal prerogative. Before long, Danby's followers in Parliament were called, disparagingly, "Tories," a term previously applied to Irish papists. An opposition coalition, lead by the Earl of Shaftesbury, consisted of those favoring Parliamentary supremacy and religious toleration for Protestant dissenters. Shaftesbury's following came to be known as "Whigs," after the Whiggamore, members of a Scottish group that marched to Edinburgh in 1648 to oppose the court party. England's party system was now taking full form, its major parties having acquired names, leaders, and basic programs.

In 1678, the Whig party made much of rumors of a "Popish Plot" to assassinate Charles and place his Roman Catholic brother, James, on the throne. The parliamentary election of 1679 was fought along party lines and returned a Whig majority. The Whig-dominated Parliaments of 1679 and 1680 passed bills to exclude not only James from succession to the throne, but also his Protestant daughters, Mary and Anne, as well as Mary's Protestant husband, William of Orange, king of The Netherlands. With the help of a four-hundred-thousand pound annual subsidy from Louis XIV and various domestic political maneuvers, a Tory majority came to power at the next Parliamentary election, enabling Charles to undo some of the restrictions and arrange the succession of his Catholic brother, James II, in 1685.

James's religious policies were immoderate and his method of governance arbitrary. He promptly doubled the size of the army and demanded 1,200,000 pounds from Parliament to support it; he received 700,000 pounds. Between 1686 and 1688, the army grew from thirteen thousand to fifty-three thousand officers and men. Many of the commands were given to Catholics, as were a growing number of civil offices. James also issued a Declaration of Indulgence and refused to rescind it despite substantial pressure from Parliament.

When a son was born to James's Catholic wife in 1688, the prospect of a Catholic succession prompted seven of England's most distinguished statesmen and religious leaders, both Tory and Whig, to invite William of Orange and James's daughter, Mary, to send an army to save England and redress popular grievances. William landed unopposed with his army, which included several English regiments heir to the glory of the English volunteers who aided The Netherlands during the previous century. Most of James's army, unhappy with its Catholic officers and arrears in pay, either joined William's forces, withdrew, or mutinied (Fortescue 1899–1930, vol. 1, 333–50).

A Convention Parliament met to reorganize the government. It declared that James had abdicated, and it bestowed the throne on the joint sovereigns, William and Mary (Schwoerer 1974, chap. 7). Parliament and the new sovereigns wrote a lengthy contract known as the Settlement.

A Second Great Transaction: The Settlement of 1689

In view of the facts that Parliament had not been called by the required royal writ of James II and that the declaration of a vacancy on the throne was an informal act in Parliament's role as a convention, the Settlement gave Parliament full control over its own sessions as well as the right to remove a king who was acting unconstitutionally. The Settlement also delineated the following statutes, most of which were enacted into law after 1689.

1. Appropriation bills were limited to expenditures for one year, thereby assuring annual meetings of Parliament.

2. Parliamentary approval of a standing army was required.

3. All sects except Catholics and Unitarians were allowed to worship freely.

4. Duration of Parliamentary sessions was limited to three years, to prevent repetitions of the Long Parliament.

5. Persons accused of treason were to be permitted examination of the indictment, retention of counsel, and confrontation with two witnesses of the overt act, thus diminishing the king's capacity to try political opponents.

6. Judges could be removed only with the assent of both houses of Parliament.

7. All executive business of the kingdom would be carried on by the resolutions of the Privy Council (made up mainly of royal ministers). This provision led to the cabinet system under Queen Anne (1702–14) and strengthened Tory/Whig two-party control of Parliament (Mansfield 1964, 935–36).

The military provisions of the Settlement were particularly significant. Because many public and private papers of this period were deliberately destroyed for reasons that are not clear, only indirect evidence suggests that, with the exception of ARTICLE VI, the provisions were heatedly debated (Schwoerer 1974, 147–54). Although the House of Commons unanimously approved various militia provisions in an early draft of the Declaration of Rights, these were withdrawn to avoid disagreement with the House of Lords. In the final Bill of Rights, the trade-off was an arrangement to share control of the military.

ARTICLE VI, in keeping with the Militia Acts of the Restoration, designated the king as sole commander of the army and the militia in war and peace. Parliamentary control of the army in peacetime was merely asserted in a general way. The king could no longer recruit as many soldiers as he wished in peacetime. "Article VI marked a genuinely revolutionary change. . . . The power of the monarch had been broken in its most essential feature." Its language was quietly negotiated and, on this article, debate seems to have been studiously avoided (Schwoerer 1974, 152–53, 189).

In subsequent statutes, Parliament attended to other aspects of military centralization. A Mutiny Act sought to strengthen army discipline through a uniform system of penalties for mutineers and deserters. This act established martial law as distinct from civil law. Mutiny, sedition, and desertion were subject to capital punishment. Parliamentary approval of any standing army was required every six months at first, every year later. Billeting of troops in private households was forbidden (Code 1869, 1: chaps. 5 and 6). The Settlement's creation of a standing army coincidentally introduced the concept of national debt as an aspect of military finance (Code 1869, vol. 1, 110).

From the beginning of the reign of William and Mary in 1689, England was beset by military engagements. The country was at war with its recent monarch, James II, and his ally, Louis XIV. Rebels in Scotland and Ireland had to be contained. The English Channel had to be brought under control. The fleet was sent to the Mediterranean to protect English trade from French raids. English armies had to fight in The Netherlands. Parliament felt a need to be assertive about its new prerogative of annually authorizing the continuance of the army and providing its support.

Louis XIV, abandoning James II, accepted the Treaty of Ryswick in 1697, thus ending England's war with France. This promptly raised the question what to do with King William's army of ninety thousand men. William would have been satisfied with a force of thirty-five thousand. He proceeded to argue for it discreetly, but antiarmy sentiment was still strong in Parliament. ARTICLE VI of the Settlement was therefore put to test.

In January 1698, Parliament voted an army of only ten thousand, with native-born officers, of which there were about fifteen hundred, to be retained as reserves on half-pay. Stunned, William disbanded the army so slowly that by December there were still thirty thousand under arms, whereupon Parliament voted to reduce the force even further to seven thousand. Four months later, Parliament refused to include the king's Dutch Guard in this force.

There was heated debate and much pamphleteering during the 1697–99 deliberations. The arguments had consequence for English and American military institutions well into the eighteenth century. In this way, Parliament firmly asserted its new power to determine the existence and size of the nation's central military organization. Although this was not the last test of this prerogative, it was perhaps the most precedent-setting (Schwoerer 1974, chaps. 8 and 9).

Civilian control of England's military establishment was thus settled. The principal powers rested with Parliament, where the nation's most important political elites, including the king, carried on their contests for power and made their decisions about such vital matters as the purpose, size, and support of the army and navy. The command prerogative was the king's, but even this was removed by Parliament in the next century by the War Office Act of 1870. This act required that royal military powers be exercised by a Secretary of State for War, who, as a member of the cabinet, was responsible to Parliament.

During the first half of the eighteenth century, the English peacetime army was extremely small compared to those on the Continent. The English usually had about 20,000 men in service, whereas the French had upwards of 133,000. Further, the army was a source of substantial royal and Whig patronage; hence military corruption during this period was a subject of much antiarmy literature and oratory (Schwoerer 1974, 192; Haswell 1975, 40). On the other hand, the exploits of the English army in the Continental wars during the reigns of William and Mary and their successor, Anne (1702–14), were a source of great national pride. The Peace of Utrecht (1713–14) brought most of the army home. A force of 8,000 was maintained in England and 11,000 overseas, mainly at Gibraltar and in the colonies.

The development of the party system took another step forward when Anne discontinued use of the royal veto. This represented full royal acquiescence to cabinet government. The cabinet during her reign consisted of a small group of key ministers within the Privy Council who served as her principal advisers. Thereafter, changes in executive policy were accomplished by changes in cabinet membership rather than by the veto. Further, the cabinet itself became dependent upon the balance of party membership in the Commons, where support by the majority was necessary to implement cabinet recommendations.

Cabinet unanimity also began to appear during Anne's reign. It was developed further under Robert Walpole, the first minister of George I (1714–27). Thus, by the mid-eighteenth century, the major policy-making powers of the English nation were, for all practical purposes, transferred from the crown to the party leaders in the nation's representative assembly.

The death of Queen Anne in 1714 precipitated the last significant split in the nation's leadership, requiring that the armed forces be used to resolve the issue of succession. George I, a Protestant elector of Hanover and great-grandson of James I, was supported by the Whig party. An election for a new Parliament at this time returned a large Whig majority to the Commons. Numerous Tory extremists, hostile to George because of his foreign origins and bitter over recent Whig vindictiveness (impeachment of leading Tories), supported the pretensions of the son of James II in what came to be known as the Jacobite Rebellion.

James, a Catholic, had substantial support in northern England, Scotland, and France, but when he invaded Scotland, he was unable to win further domestic support. Despite their preference for James, most Tories were unwilling to destroy the Settlement or revive the religious issue. By the end of 1715, James was back in France, and the brief rebellion ended. George I assumed the throne and appointed a cabinet made up almost entirely of Whigs. England's elite was now clearly wedded to partisan rather than military methods in the conduct of their disputes.

Tory party fortunes, stigmatized by the Jacobite Rebellion, declined rapidly thereafter. The rebellion was the last attempted civil war in England. Thereafter, George I and George II were content to leave English governance in the hands of their Whig cabinets and prime ministers. The English critical transition had been negotiated successfully. From 1714 to 1820, under the Hanoverian kings—George I, George II, and George III—the English party system developed rapidly.

Although the Whig-Tory competition continued, severe factionalism existed within each party, a condition exploited by George III in his efforts to have his policies adopted. The first decade of George III's reign was a particularly unstable period until, in 1770, he appointed Lord North as his prime minister. North promoted parliamentary reform, sought economy in the armed forces, and dealt with the American Revolution in a conciliatory manner in the hope that this would eventually lead to a settlement.

During the eighteenth century, the British army was mainly preoccupied with disarming the Scottish clans, the War of the Austrian Succession (1740–48), the Seven Years' War (1756–63), and a number of colonial wars, usually against France and in alliance with Spain, Holland, or Prussia. Officer commissions were granted by purchase. Enlisted men continued to be recruited from the poorest strata of English society and subjected to rigorous training and discipline. Tight infantry and cavalry formations were de rigueur on the Continent, but loose, guerrilla-like formations were used on the colonial battlefields. Muskets, bayonets, bullets, and grenades made each infantryman a veritable arsenal.

At the time of the American Revolution, all British forces numbered about 90,000. They were reduced to 17,000 with the arrival of peace in 1793, then greatly expanded to 246,000 during the period of the campaigns against Napoleon. For many years after Waterloo, the standing army remained at about 72,000 men.

The American Revolution, the French Revolution, and the rapidly changing industrial and commercial technologies of the day gave rise to demands for further English institutional reform. The heavy cost of the Napoleonic Wars added to popular disenchantment with the system of government. These dissatisfactions led to the Reform Bill of 1832, which extended the suffrage, reconstituted Parliament, and thoroughly tied the parliamentary party system to the electorate.

These institutional modifications were the outcome of a millennium of transactions involving a variety of political currencies. In the beginning, among primitive kings, competing armies were the principal instruments of elite conflict, the system of representation was weak, and the party system was nonexistent. England progressed through a critical transition during the period between the Cromwellian Protectorate in 1648 and the establishment of the Hanoverians in 1714. During this transition, a national standing army was reluctantly accepted as a permanent institution, control of the military establishment was shared between the crown and Parliament, and the ongoing contests among English political elites were conducted through parliamentary, later electoral, parties rather than by military combat.

Thus, by the eighteenth century, the loom of English history had produced a centralized national military establishment, a system of representation in Parliament that controlled the military establishment, and a vigorous and stable party system within which the nation's leaders carried on their disputes. The century also saw an end to England's long history of internal wars.

Chapter 4

Lessons from the English: The American Case

The United States has had only one major internal war, the Civil War of 1861–65. This was the bloodiest and most devastating war experienced by the civilized world to that date. Ostensibly, the United States was a well-organized nation at that time, operating under a unique constitution adopted three-quarters of a century earlier. American military, representative, and party institutions, fashioned in large measure after eighteenth-century English practice, had presumably already become stable and enduring.

Closer examination reveals that these assessments are not entirely accurate. The national military organization of the United States at mid-century was in fact weak and decentralized. The constitutional arrangements for representative government were under severe strain, challenged by states' rights advocates, sectional coalitions, and competing slave-property interests in the west of the country. The national political parties were loose coalitions of congressional and sectional factions and had yet to become stabilized as a two-party system.

A critical transition among U.S. political institutions began some time after the Civil War, probably during the 1870s. At that time the federal army began to exercise new authority over state militia, the operation of representative government returned to normal with the withdrawal of federal occupation forces from the South and renewed southern participation in Congress and the electoral college, and the Democratic and Republican parties became the principal extragovernmental organizations in national politics, sufficiently influential to forestall a threatened second civil war arising out of the disputed Hayes-Tilden election of 1876.

America's English Institutional Heritage

American military attitudes were largely drawn from seventeenth-century English debates about standing armies and from the provisions of the Settlement of 1688–89. American military experience was first acquired from service in the English colonial forces of the eighteenth century. Much was also learned from colonial contact with native Indians, particularly in the area of individual and small-group self-defense in the colonial environment. As a consequence, Americans were reluctant to support standing armies and held a deep-rooted reliance upon personal possession of weapons for self-protection.

Anglo-French colonial wars were among the major military engagements of the eighteenth century. The English, using mixed forces of imperial red-coated regulars and colonial troops, tended to deploy in close formation. The French and their Indian allies exploited the cover of forests, engaging in what today would be called guerrilla tactics. Thus, in 1755, when General Braddock marched toward the French stronghold of Fort Duquesne, he and a thousand of his men were killed by a force of half their numbers. Some of his troops successfully escaped under the leadership of a colonial officer, Major George Washington. This disaster brought a radical modification of English formations and tactics; that is, the use of smaller formations, lighter equipment, and light cavalry. The lessons were not lost on colonial officers such as Washington. Their skills and tactics developed into a distinctive mix of European military formalism and North American bush fighting (Curtis 1943, 26).

Colonial defense was administered from England through royal governors and royal captains-general. Colonial assemblies, however, insisted upon being consulted about the funds, materiel, and men that they were indirectly providing from taxes levied upon them by the distant crown. The assemblies were representative institutions in the English tradition. With the exception of Pennsylvania, each of the colonies had a bicameral legislature that mirrored the structure of the English Parliament. Members of the upper houses, similar to the House of Lords, were usually appointed by the king, the royal proprietor of the colony, or the lower house, with the consent of the king's colonial governor. By mid-eighteenth century, representatives to the colonial lower houses were, without exception, elected by the qualified voters. As in England, the elected representatives formed cliques and coalitions in the assemblies, the beginnings of colonial legislative party systems.

Going beyond English practice were the efforts of colonial representatives and their constituency friends to come together to nominate candidates behind whom they could unite and campaign. The object was to increase factional voting power in the colonial legislature and place friends into local community offices. Suffrage laws allowed only substantial property-holders to vote; hence elections involved relatively few citizens and were often conducted viva voce. In time, the introduction of paper ballots permitted more independent voting, but also required more careful factional coordination and electioneering.

As disagreements between the English crown and the colonists grew in scope and intensity, the tiny electorate (less than 3 percent of the population) and its representatives in the colonial assemblies began to organize themselves into Court and Country parties. The latter were precursors of many of the committees of correspondence that mobilized the American Revolution.

In these ways, colonial military, representative, and party institutions, from their beginnings, set organizational and developmental patterns that would endure beyond the formation of the new republic.

At the end of the French and Indian War in 1763, the crown began to discuss plans for a unified defense organization for all the colonies, with a projected standing army of ten thousand to be supported and quartered by the colonies. To pay for these new military expenses, Parliament levied the Stamp Act of 1765, enacted without consulting the colonists and causing deep resentment among them. In 1770, Benjamin Franklin argued that the support of a colonial standing army without the consent of the colonial assemblies was contrary to the

British constitution. He was referring to the provisions of the Settlement of 1688–89 (Kriedberg and Henry 1955, 1–2).

From the early 1720s, literature about the Glorious Revolution, with its strong antimilitary themes, circulated in the colonies. Thus, arbitrary actions by royal military governors, enforced quartering of English soldiers, taxation without colonial participation in the levy, and related issues became well-argued colonial grievances. Colonial leaders such as John Adams and Thomas Jefferson spoke and wrote that a standing army in peacetime was a threat to liberty, destructive of a balanced constitution, susceptible to corruption, and morally indefensible. These leaders unanimously considered the defense of the colonies a matter best left in the hands of the colonial militia, that is, able-bodied freemen called up by their colonial assemblies in time of emergency: shades of the ancient English fyrd and the more recent English county militia (Schwoerer 1974, 196–97).

Colonial militia were mandatory forces. Each able-bodied male from sixteen to sixty, with certain exceptions, was required to own a firearm, usually a musket, and stipulated amounts of powder, flint, and bullets. All were carried on muster rolls. Training took place at least once a month. Over six hundred colonial laws pertained to militia regulation. Indians were excluded for fear that they might use arms for uprisings. Negroes were excluded on grounds that service could be required only of freemen. Various systems of sounding alarms were used for routine or emergency mobilizations.

The American penchant for elections was early manifest in the way most militia officers were chosen. Generals, however, were appointed by the royal governors, usually after consultation with the colonial assemblies. With growth in population, local militia regimental organizations came into being, often made up of volunteers interested in certain kinds of field service. There was an early inclination to impress those reluctant to serve. Colonial assemblies tended to be penurious about providing pay and supplies. During the period 1765 to 1770, following the French and Indian War, popular interest in and legislative support for colonial militia declined appreciably, causing some concern for colonial security.

Despite lack of attention, the problem of colonial self-defense did not go away. The more politically astute colonial leaders and assemblies began to call for preparedness measures. In 1773, the Virginia House of Burgesses urged the other colonies to gather military supplies: munitions, engineering equipment, provisions, etc. In 1774, a Massachusetts Committee of Safety was established and proceeded to reorganize the Massachusetts militia, constitute the minutemen as alert units, vote funds for military expenditures, purchase military supplies, and plan a New England army (Kriedberg and Henry 1955, chap. 1). Such an army could, of course, be employed not only in defense against Indians, but also in rebellion against the mother country.

The Stamp Act and the general approach of the king to relations with the colonies spread a sense of political mistreatment among the colonists, nurtured by the Country party caucuses in several cities and legislatures. Samuel Adams's Boston Committee of Correspondence, established in 1772, was in touch with scores of similar committees in Massachusetts and other colonies by 1774. On May 23, 1774, the New York committee circulated a recommendation that a continental congress be convened to discuss colonial grievances. Shortly thereafter, the First Continental Congress, whose delegates were selected by a mix of colonial legislatures and committees of correspondence, gathered to issue a Declaration of Rights, in which they cited their constitutional rights as Englishmen.

The Second Continental Congress, by now the new nation's principal governmental institution, was somewhat more formally structured and more representative. It met in 1775, composed the Declaration of Independence, carried forward the War of Independence, and served as the republic's representative assembly until the Articles of Confederation, written by it, went into effect in 1781. Its members were chosen by other representative bodies, namely, the colonial legislature turned state legislatures. The predominance of the legislative bodies was appropriate to the political climate of the day, which was antimonarchical and antiexecutive.

The complaints of the Declaration of Independence were clear. The king had imposed a standing army in peacetime upon the unwilling and unconsulted colonists. Troops had been quartered in the homes of unwilling civilian subjects. Unconstitutional actions implied that the colonial military were superior to civilians. Despite the clarity of their case, it took the colonial leaders sixteen months after the first battles at Lexington and Concord to agree upon the declaration. It took another year to write a constitution, the Articles of Confederation.

Although the Articles gave the Continental Congress the power to declare war, make treaties, control and issue currency, and borrow money, they never authorized Congress to raise an army, levy taxes, regulate commerce, or enforce its own laws. There was no central executive machinery to run either the national government or the continental war. At most, Congress created a five-member Board of War, with a paid secretary who functioned until replaced by a Secretary of War in 1781.

In the conduct of the war, there were few indications of national solidarity. Not only did state militia stay home, Pennsylvania farmers sold produce to the English in Philadelphia even as Washington's men suffered hunger and death in nearby Valley Forge. "Everywhere in the military, political and commercial sectors, loyalties rarely transcended the defense of home and hearth, and in some cases were totally subordinated to the demands of a good profit" (Ellis 1974, 53–55).

In October 1775, the Second Continental Congress appointed Washington commander in chief of the Continental Army and authorized him to recruit twenty thousand men from quotas it assigned to each of the states. The states never filled their quotas even though, a year later, Congress offered higher pay, a twenty-dollar bounty, and a hundred acres of land to all who enlisted for a three-year period. By 1778, the Congress was offering newly recruited officers half-pay for seven years after the cessation of hostilities.

There were few takers at any rank. State assemblies were reluctant to do anything about national army needs because they preferred to conserve their manpower and resources for local defense. Although Congress authorized an army of seventy-six thousand at the end of

1776, in March 1777, Washington still had only three thousand men under his command. Three or four months later, the British had an estimated thirty thousand troops in the colonies and Washington had only eight thousand.

The official military establishment of the United States thus began with General Washington's minuscule army, whose average size was twelve thousand regular troops from among a colonial population of slightly more than 3 million. This little army—a guerrilla force by present-day standards—continually suffered shortages of arms, ammunition, clothes, food, and medicine.

Washington never had more than twenty thousand men assembled in one place at one time, although for particular battles state militia were able to put this many and more into the field for local combat. The British had artillery and artillerymen whose skills carried over from colonial wars, whereas Washington was particularly shorthanded and ill-equipped in artillery. He also lacked trained staff, such as had been available to him under the British in earlier years (Ellis 1974, 48–49; Kriedberg and Henry 1955, 17; King 1897, 116).

In the summer of 1776, nearly a quarter of the colonial troops had no arms, and the Second Continental Congress did little to improve their supply. The army of the new nation in the years between 1776 and 1779 fluctuated between ninety thousand troops in 1776 and forty-five thousand in 1779. These figures included the state militia, about which Washington wrote: "The militia come in, you cannot tell how, go out, you cannot tell when; consume your provision, exhaust your stores, and leave you at last in a critical moment." During the course of the War of Independence, another ninety thousand men rendered service at sea, mostly on privateers.

At the end of the War of Independence, Congress almost completely disbanded the Continental Army. Only a nominal military force was retained: eighty enlisted men and a few officers to guard military stores at Fort Pitt and West Point. When troops were needed in the northwest to deal with Indian raids into Pennsylvania and Kentucky, these states had to depend completely upon their own state militia. Congress called for 700 men to be furnished from quotas assigned to Connecticut,

New York, New Jersey, and Pennsylvania. All but New York eventually complied. A similar call for 1,340 men went out in 1786 in response to Indian unrest in western Massachusetts. Fortunately, the British did not vacate their northwestern posts until 1796, otherwise the region would have been grossly unprotected by the small and unfilled American troop quotas (Kriedberg and Henry 1955, 23–24).

The Articles of Confederation established the precedent of military decentralization by prescribing that "every State shall always keep up a well regulated and disciplined militia, sufficiently armed and accoutred, and shall provide and constantly have ready for use, in public stores, a due number of field pieces and tents, and a proper quantity of arms, ammunition, and camp equipage." Although no state could engage in any war without the consent of the United States "in Congress assembled," the organization and the financing of the common defense remained primarily the responsibility of the states. All officers of the rank of colonel or lower were the appointees of state legislatures. Taxes for defense were levied by the state legislatures. Furthermore, all "charges of war and all other expenses that shall be incurred for the common defense . . . shall be defrayed out of a common treasury which shall be supplied by the several States, in proportion to the value of all land within each State granted to or surveyed for any person, and such land and the buildings and improvements thereon shall be estimated according to such mode as the United States in Congress assembled shall from time to time direct and appoint."

In Number XXIII of *The Federalist Papers,* Alexander Hamilton observed how ill-founded and illusory were the Confederation's expectations that such an organization of the national defense would work. He declared, "We must discard the fallacious scheme of quotas and requisitions. . . . The Union ought to be invested with full power to levy troops; to build an equipped fleet; and to raise the revenues which will be required for the formation and support of an army and navy."

Decentralized Constitutional Institutions

The framers of the new federal Constitution provided for a relatively coherent national military organization, retaining, at the same time, a decentralized framework of federal government. Under the Constitution, Congress was authorized to

a. declare war, grant letters of marque and reprisal, and make rules concerning capture on land and water;

b. raise and support armies, with a two-year limit on moneys appropriated for this purpose, a lesson well-learned from the English Settlement

c. provide and maintain a navy;

d. make rules for the management of land and naval forces;

e. call up the state militia to execute the laws of the Union, suppress insurrections, and repel invasions; and

f. provide for organizing, arming, and disciplining the state militia and for governing that part of the militia employed in the service of the Federal government, reserving to the states, respectively, the appointment of officers and the authority to train the militia as prescribed by Congress.

To assure civilian supremacy over the military, the president was to be commander in chief of the army and navy as well as of the state militia when called into national service. Thus, the Constitution placed congressional, presidential, and state hands on the nation's military machine.

During the ratification debates, the Antifederalists pressed for a bill of rights. Paramount among these was a provision that, when adopted in 1791, became the Second Amendment: "A well regulated Militia, being necessary to the security of a free State, the right of the people to keep and bear Arms, shall not be infringed." Here was a proposition that seemed to best characterize the decentralized military structure of the Revolutionary Period, at the same time harking back to the English fyrd. A rifle or two in almost every colonial household was, after all, the principal weapon of standing armies of the day (Agar 1950, 28–29; Jameson 1926, 103).

Alexander Hamilton, again in Paper Number XXIII of the *Federalist*, objected to military decentralization either to state militia or to the people. "Is there not a manifest inconsistency in devolving upon the federal government the care of the general defense, and leaving in the state governments the *effective* powers, by which it is to be provided for? Is not the want of cooperation the infallible consequence of such a system? And will not weakness, disorder and undue distribution of the burdens and calamities of war, an unnecessary and intolerable increase of expense, be its natural and inevitable concomitants" (Riker 1957, chap. 2)?

In *Federalist* Number VII, on the other hand, Hamilton acknowledged the risks inherent in the creation of powerful military establishments. "The violent destruction of life and property incident to war; the continual effort and alarm attendant on a state of continual danger; will compel nations the most attached to liberty, to resort for their repose and security to institutions which have a tendency to destroy their civil and political rights. To be more safe, they, at length, become willing to run the risk of being less free."

Hamilton did not expect this to happen in the new Union. He noted that the great powers of Europe were quite distant and, therefore, the Union enjoyed "an insulated situation." Further, a small army would be "utterly incompetent to the purpose of enforcing encroachments against the united efforts of the great body of the people."

Together with decentralization of its military arrangements, the new nation also established a system of dispersed political power rare, if not unique, in world history. After fumbling their way through extreme disunity under the Confederation, leaders in the thirteen states acknowledged, reluctantly, a need for a stronger structure of national coordination. Their new Constitution's design was and still is masterful in its dispersion of power. The device to accomplish this was a system of representation that constructed various and overlapping electoral constituencies.

The powers of the three branches of national government were separated. Each branch was given its distinct constituency, particular functions, and independent prerogatives. A hierarchy of governments was built that consisted of a federal organization, the thirteen states, and "the people." The arrangements produced a novel combination of traditional and radical principles of representation, the most radical being the direct election by the citizenry of their representatives in the lower house of Congress.

The political party system—what little there was of it—was initially as decentralized and informal as the military and the representative institutions. Party alignments were first portrayed as personal followings: in the Congress, for example, Jeffersonians versus Hamiltonians. One outgrowth of the post-Revolutionary demobilization and the dire economic circumstances into which many veterans fell was the emergence of the first veterans' organizations: the Society of the Cincinnati, made up chiefly of former officers, and the Society of St. Tammany, comprised of former enlisted men. Both provided organizational networks that facilitated the development of the parties in and among the principal urban centers.

The Federalists, also known in Congress as Hamiltonians, denied that they were a political party, and disappeared doing so. The Jeffersonians became Democratic-Republicans, then Jacksonians, then Democrats. The Democrats struggled valiantly during the 1840s and 1850s to hold together their Southern and Northern wings. The National Republicans appeared and disappeared, followed by the Whigs, and then the modern Republicans.

The 1850s witnessed severe fragmentation of the national political parties. Whigs scattered in several directions. The Free Soil party gained strength. Know-Nothings appeared. The new Republican party began to build its platform from the splinters of others. The Democrats were the only truly national party, yet barely able to unite behind the Pierce and Buchanan tickets in 1852 and 1856, respectively, failing entirely in 1860.

Party lines were often determined entirely by the personal followings of such men as Madison, Jefferson, Hamilton, Clay, Jackson, and Van Buren. When personalities were lacking, "dark horses," such as Polk and Pierce, and military heroes, such as Harrison and Taylor, served as temporary and fragile links among the factions. The parties had no national organizations until the Democrats took steps to create a national committee in 1848.

Yet, despite these evidences of political disunity, the national parties and their leaders continued to serve as the principal proponents of whatever national unification was taking place. It was Jefferson, in his inaugural address, who asserted that "we are all republicans; we are all federalists." Jackson and his Democratic colleagues managed to pave the way for the inclusion of the new western states and the newly enfranchised urban workers as significant participants in the nation's politics. The westward movement's Great Compromises between slavery and abolitionism were the work of Clay and other moderate partisans. On the other hand, the battles for "Bleeding Kansas" and similar struggles for control of new states were in large part managed by leaders of competing parties. All this factional and party movement verged on chaos at the time of Lincoln's election in 1860.

In the realm of military organization, the First Congress retained the Department of War that had been established at the close of the Revolutionary War. Secretary of War Henry Knox was made responsible not only for supervision of the army and navy but also for land grants and Indian affairs. Congress authorized an army of 840 men; 672 were actually on duty at the time. By 1791, after numerous Indian troubles, the authorization was raised to 2,000 (Kriedberg and Henry 1955, 26–27).

The Militia Act of 1792, in a first step toward coordinating the new nation's several military systems, provided that all able-bodied white male citizens, ages eighteen to forty-five, were to be enrolled for state militia duty, each to provide his own musket, bayonet, belt, spare flints, knapsack, pouch, and cartridges. Enrollment, training, and organization into operating units were left entirely to the state and local militia commanders.

It was, of course, unrealistic to expect *all* citizens liable for service to supply themselves to this extent. Nor was it likely that authorities in the weak state governments could implement the organizational requirements. In effect, this system of self-supply imposed the equivalent of a special tax on all white males from eighteen to forty-five because money was never appropriated to pay militiamen. Realizing this situation, Congress in 1798 enacted a permanent annual appropriation of $200,000 to buy muskets for distribution among the states in proportion to their militia enrollments. This was the first federal grant-in-aid to the states.

The militia system remained an out-and-out failure for the next six decades. Called upon to provide counts of men, officers, and equipment on an annual or semiannual basis, local and state militia officers complied irregularly, usually with inflated figures, according to accounting procedures that varied from state to state. At times this was owing to neglect of duty, at others it represented practically the complete abandonment of a state's militia organization and responsibilities.

The poor reporting meant that states were deprived of their allotments of muskets, but this was a consequence that seemed to be of little importance to political leaders. From 1802 to 1860, there was a gradual decrease in the number of states submitting militia returns, until, on the eve of the Civil War, "only a few states were interested in or capable of reporting." The indifference of the states destroyed the militia system. This indifference arose from lack of citizen enthusiasm, poorly organized state governments, and limited state financial resources. Only Massachusetts, Connecticut, New Hampshire, Maine, and Rhode Island in New England, New York in the North, and Virginia in the South maintained, with any integrity, the rudiments of militia organization during these years (Riker 1957, chap. 3).

The nation's territory was doubled by the Louisiana Purchase and so, too, were its security needs. In addition to frontier security, war with France, Spain, or England was a threatening possibility throughout Jefferson's administration. In 1803, and again in 1806, Congress authorized Jefferson to call up eighty thousand militia and appropriated the very substantial—for that day—sums of $1 million to $2 million to pay militia expenses. The president did not exercise his authority on either matter. In 1808, however, Jefferson asked Congress to increase the regular army by six thousand men, which it promptly did. This brought the army's enrollment up to ninety-nine hundred men.

President Madison, on the other hand, took steps to reduce both the army and the navy. When the newly elected "War Hawks" came into Congress in 1811, and war with England became a reality in 1812, demobilization was reversed. By the time war was declared, the president had been authorized to raise the regular army's strength to 35,603 officers and men, call up 100,000 state militia, and mobilize 30,000 volunteers, for a total of 166,000.

Inept War Department administration, sectional differences over the merits of the war, and a reluctant citizenry resulted in a mobilization far short of its goals. In 1813, there were available no more than 19,000 regular army men, 5,000 volunteers, and a number of state militia impossible to estimate. The final official total of troops enrolled throughout the War of 1812 was 527,654, but this included 147,200 serving terms of less than one month and 317,275 who served from one month to a year.

Not only was turnover in the enlisted ranks excessive but trained officers were few. The new military academy at West Point had graduated only eighty-nine officers since opening its doors in 1802. Searching for a better recruitment system, Secretary of War Monroe offered four plans to Congress, one of which included the first proposal for a national draft. The proposal called for a draft administered by county courts, county militia officers, and other persons appointed for this particular purpose. This was an attempt to circumvent the state governments and militias.

Congress did not accept the draft plan. Training programs and camps were practically nonexistent. Equipment was lacking or shoddy. The burning of Washington by the British could have been carried off by any small band of arsonists. From a military point of view, the War of 1812 was an embarrassment to both sides (Kriedberg and Henry 1955, 45–53; King 1897, 122–23).

After the War of 1812, there was another near-complete demobilization of the regular army. By 1821, a force of only 6,183 was authorized by Congress, mainly as an Indian-fighting constabulary. A half-dozen recruiting centers were set up in several cities and succeeded in the limited recruiting goals set for them. Even after Mexico broke diplomatic relations with the United States over Texan independence in March 1845, army recruitment goals remained modest. By June 1845, a tiny "Army of Observation" of fewer than 1,500 men in twenty-five undersized companies was assembled in western Louisiana under General Zachary Taylor. A slow build-up continued until, by the third of October, 3,860 troops, more than half of the regular army, were concentrated in Louisiana. To accomplish this the army stripped posts of their manpower along the Atlantic coast, the Gulf of Mexico, and the frontiers.

Not until 1846 did Congress authorize a total strength of 8,619 men for the regular army and a call for 50,000 volunteers for one year's service. This procedure made it unnecessary to deal with the state militia. The Mobilization Act of May 13, 1846, also required volunteers to furnish their own uniforms, clothes, horses, and horse equipage, with reimbursement to be made by the army for uniform and clothes. Officers were to be chosen according to state militia laws, which meant election by the troops. In short, recruitment, training, leadership, procedure, equipment, and tactics were still of eighteenth-century vintage.

Between May 1846 and July 1848, some 116,000 men passed in and out of military service as regular army recruits or volunteers. The level of troop strength at any particular moment was highly variable and often militarily frustrating. General Taylor never had more than 10,000 troops for his campaign in northern Mexico, General Winfield Scott never more than 9,000 for the advance on Vera Cruz, and Colonel Stephen Kearny barely 2,000 for the conquest of California. Halfway between Vera Cruz and Mexico City, for example, General Scott had to send home 3,700 men, one third of his force, because their year's enlistment had ended. Victory came to the Americans largely because the Mexican military was even more primitive.

The Mexican War over, the regular army and its volunteers were again disbanded. On January 1, 1861, the eve of the Civil War, the regular army of the United States had only 16,367 officers and men on duty to defend a national population of 32 million. Military decentralization remained the order of the day up to the Civil War and may have been a major consideration in the South's decision to risk secession.

Civil War and Centralization

In 1860, certain state militia were better armed than the federal government. New York and Massachusetts in the North and Virginia and Louisiana in the South possessed the major military forces on opposing sides. The 16,367 officers and men in the national regular army were distributed among 198 companies or similar-sized units, of which 183 were widely dispersed along the frontiers. This put some 4,300 men in Oregon and California, 6,000 in New Mexico and Texas, and 2,900 in the Midwest and Great Plains. Only fifteen companies— approximately 1,200 men—were posted along the Atlantic coast and the Canadian border, hardly an adequate force to defend the nation's capital or suppress a rebellion.

Available records describing the size of the state militia leave the impression that in the North some 2,471,000 men were on hand for service and in the Confederacy only 692,000. Unfortunately, the reports upon which these figures were based dated back, in some cases, to 1827. For all practical purposes, neither side had substantial state militia in being in 1861.

Before secession, the federal army was under the command of distinguished military talent, nearly all southerners. Jefferson Davis of Kentucky, later president of the Confederacy, was President Buchanan's secretary of war. Key positions in the national general staff were held by southern military men. Little wonder that southern political leaders believed they could, with minimum military effort, establish a separate nation. Led by the militia of Virginia and Louisiana and by the nation's most talented military men, the South seemed to have every military advantage. Four years of war proved their expectations wrong and produced a new national concern about centralizing and strengthening the military establishment of the federal government.

In April 1861, President Lincoln called up 75,000 militia to suppress "the insurrection," as he called it. A month later, with Congress still in recess, Lincoln, by presidential proclamation, increased the size of the regular army by 22,714 men, called for 42,000 volunteers, and invited enlistments of 18,000 seamen for the navy. Later, Congress vigorously debated the legality of these presidential actions, but eventually approved them. In addition, Congress authorized Lincoln to call up 500,000 volunteers for service of six months to three years. Quotas were apportioned among the states according to population. The president was authorized to appoint general officers, but company and field officers were to be commissioned by state governors, subject to removal by presidential military boards if unqualified.

Between January 1861 and May 1865, the Union Army expanded from 16,367 to 1,000,516. At one time or another during the war more than 2,690,000 men served in the Union forces. New York furnished 446,000, Pennsylvania 338,000, Ohio 311,000, Illinois 258,000, and so it went down the roster of twenty-five states and the District of Columbia. These enlistments were in response to the quotas assigned to them. Most New England states, the District of Columbia, Ohio, Illinois, Tennessee, Arkansas, and North Carolina oversubscribed their quotas.

Although Congress initially placed responsibility for raising troops squarely upon the state governors, the Enrollment Act of 1863 established the principle that every male citizen was obligated to defend the nation and that the federal government had the authority to impose that obligation directly on the citizen without involving the states (Kriedberg and Henry 1955, 94–97, 108).

The South was not without its resources. Four men who had served as national secretaries of war between 1849 and 1860 were from the South; in 1861, all four elected to join the Confederacy. When Jefferson Davis, one of the four, became president of the Confederacy, he was probably the most informed person on either side regarding the condition and disposition of the United States Army. Of the 1,098 officers in the regular army in 1861, 313 joined the Confederacy. The first calls for southern militia and volunteers were oversubscribed. The secession effort was expected to be brief and successful.

The principle of military decentralization was, surprisingly, maintained by the Confederacy almost to the end of the war. For example, General Lee was not appointed general in chief of the Confederate armies until February 1865. Up to that time, the southern governors insisted on having the final word as to the disposition of troops raised in their respective states. Not until February 1865 also, did the Confederate government at Richmond have authority to control the railroads for military purposes (Agar 1950, 440).

President Jefferson Davis, however, consistently stood for military centralization. He received from his Congress extraordinary wartime powers. As losses were suffered, the Confederate Congress enacted in April 1862, a Conscription Act authorizing Davis to draft all white males between eighteen and thirty-five years of age for a three-year term of service. Despite the South's states' rights philosophy, here was the first American national draft law, almost a year before the North took similar steps.

Official estimates set the number serving in the Confederate army, navy, and marines during the period 1863 to 1866 at between 600,000 and 1,500,000, of whom 134,000 were killed. The total for the Union forces between 1861 and 1865 (computed somewhat differently from those above)—army, navy, and marines—was 2,213,000, with 365,000 fatalities. Given a total national population, North and South, of 31,440,000, these enlistment and casualty figures are a dry indication of the degree to which this war was an all-out mobilization and a frightening introduction to modern warfare. The world had never seen such a blood feud.

Reconstruction, Critical Transition, and the Transaction of 1876

State governments, both North and South, played the major role in recruiting and equipping troops at the outset of the Civil War. By the end of the war the two national governments had become the dominant agencies for raising and maintaining armies. The principle of direct citizen military obligation to the national government was firmly established, circumventing the state militia. Whereas 88 percent of the total American force in the War of 1812 came from state militia, the latter made up only 12 percent of the national force in the Mexican War. Even fewer—less than 2 percent—were state militia in the Civil War (Riker 1957, 41).

Civil War politics played a major role in the selection of military leaders, particularly in the Union armies. Since successful generals almost automatically became candidates for president or other high office, state governors and political party bosses were highly motivated to influence, obstruct, or limit President Lincoln's appointment options. Lincoln was particularly harassed by the Radical Republican leadership in Congress. Inexorably, however, military need compelled national coordination and presidential ascendancy, and this gave new impetus to the long-term trend toward nationalization of the military.

Growth in the organization of industry and finance accompanied military centralization, particularly in the munitions industries in the North. The South, an agricultural economy, had to resort to large-scale blockade-running in order to obtain its arms and other supplies from Europe. In time, the Confederate government either established or took over factories to produce munitions and other supplies, but only to the extent necessary to fill their normal military requirements. Very little of southern munitions manufacturing survived the war. The converse was the case in the North where war industries and economic expansion hastened the American industrial revolution. Northern manufacture of munitions was accompanied by the building of railroads, which in turn stimulated the extractive industries in the west. The expansion led to unprecedentedly large-scale financial operations.

Most northern munitions were bought in Europe during the first two years of the war (some 1,165,000 rifles and muskets), but, by the end of the second year, American production had expanded to the point of meeting all the needs of the Union armies. At the Springfield, Massachusetts, armory, small-arms production increased from 800 muskets a month to 10,000. During the second year of the war, this armory produced 200,000 muskets while private contractors produced half a million. Among the famous-name munition-makers were Colt's armory, Sharp's rifle works, Remington, Burnside, and the Alfred Jenks Company. Because this was for the most part an infantry war, more than 4 million muskets were issued to the Union armies, but only 7,892 cannon (Davis 1973, 64, 106).

By the time the war was over, the North had become a challenger to the English in world munitions manufacture. There was also a domestic consequence; the "military-industrial complex" of that day gave the national government clear military and economic ascendancy not only over the South but also over the previously semi-independent state militia. Occupation and demobilization of the South by federal forces removed most obstacles to further nationalization of the military establishment.

The nation's representative institutions also evolved as a consequence of the stresses of the period. Undergoing change were the relationships of the national and state governments; that is, the structure of the federal system; the relative power of the Congress and the presidency; the relative importance of the Senate vis-à-vis the House of Representatives, and, on the extra-constitutional side, the role of the political parties in national affairs. Before the Civil War, these relationships were placed under stress by the economic and philosophical antagonisms between North and South, further complicated by the expanding influence of the West. The trauma of the Civil War hastened the changes.

A principal change related to federal-state relations. From the founding of the Republic, the South had played a highly influential role in national politics. Virginia, as the most populous state in the new Union, gave the country its first president. The influence of the states was sufficient to embolden John C. Calhoun of South Carolina, Andrew Jackson's vice-president, to resign his office to lead the fight for the principles of concurrent majority and states' rights. The latter argued for the right of a state to nullify federal statutes with which it disagreed. In response, President Jackson alerted the army and navy to prepare for whatever demonstration of force would be necessary to compel Calhoun's South Carolina to abide by federal law.

Thus, precedents were set for President Lincoln's response to the secession ("rebellion") of the Confederacy. Following Jackson's declaration, a decline in state influence in the federal system began, accelerated by several other factors: expansion of the role of the presidency; admission of new states, thereby diluting southern voting power in the Senate and House of Representatives; an increasingly determined abolitionist movement in the North; a losing fight to carry the slave economy westward. The trend was speeded by events following the Compromise of 1850 and by the outcome of the Civil War.

The Compromise of 1850 was Henry Clay's last great contribution to national unity. In the transaction that became the Compromise, the North succeeded in having California admitted as a nonslave state and the slave trade abolished in the District of Columbia. The South won a promise that stricter Federal statutes would be enacted to require the return of runaway-slave property. Although a Fugitive Slave Act was passed by Congress, the South viewed continued support by northerners of the "underground railroad," which helped slaves escape, as a breach of contract.

Southern distrust of northern intentions was translated into military action in the battles for control of Kansas and Nebraska, two territories that had become eligible for statehood. A proslavery minority in the Kansas Territory proposed a state constitution—the Lecompton Constitution—which, despite President Buchanan's support, failed to win acceptance in the antislavery Congress of 1858. The days of southern dominance in national politics were numbered.

The final straw was the inability of southern delegates at the 1860 Democratic national convention to prevent the nomination of Stephen A. Douglas, whom they considered to be an abolitionist. The southerners bolted the party and thereby broke the last bond of national unity, precariously held together by the Democratic party during the 1850s. The national parties no longer had nationwide constituencies and could no longer serve as a representative body or as an arena for nonviolent competition among leaders.

Later, President Lincoln's great achievement as a party leader was his ability to put together a governing coalition of Republicans and "War" Democrats. Southern Democrats and Southern Whigs were, of course, excluded from national party politics during the war. The "Peace" Democrats of the midwest tended to isolate themselves from party affairs as they flirted with subversion and treason in expressing their sympathies for the South.

After Lincoln's assassination, the political problem confronting the Radical Republican leadership in Congress was how to prevent a former Democrat, President Andrew Johnson, from leading his old party back to national power. The Radicals began by crippling all attempts to bring the South back into the normal representative arrangements of the nation during Reconstruction. Part of this strategy included impeaching and nearly convicting President Andrew Johnson of a breach of law.

Once they destroyed Johnson as a national political figure, the Republican Congressional cabal succeeded in electing a war hero, General Ulysses Grant, to the White House. Frustrated, liberal Republicans bolted their party, adding to the confusion in the party system during the 1870s. The confusion reached a climax in the disputed Hayes-Tilden presidential election in 1876, carrying the nation once again to the brink of civil war.

Political interest in the nation's military system remained at the end of the Civil War. Nevertheless, the South, in its defeat, was disarmed and demobilized. The North also followed the usual custom of disbanding its military forces. A year after the end of the war, Congress authorized an army of only 54,302 men. By 1876, the year of the Hayes-Tilden election crisis, army enlistments were reduced to 27,272, thought to be sufficient for Indian fighting on the frontiers as well as occupation duties in some parts of the South.

At the same time that it was reducing military manpower, Congress was also giving thoughtful attention to various military issues, including reorganization of the War Department, military training at land-grant colleges, and the revival of deteriorating state militia. With respect to the latter, only an estimated twelve states were believed to have anything approaching trained companies and systematic coordination of statewide militia activities (Riker 1957, 46).

Of concern during the Hayes-Tilden crisis was the reactivation of old and the rise of new secret, quasi-military organizations among the citizenry. These clandestine political societies had thrived mainly in the midwest during the Civil War and were thought to be composed mainly of Peace Democrats opposed to Lincoln's war effort. The societies took such names as Knights of the Golden Circle, Order of American Knights, and Sons of Liberty. The Judge Advocate General of the United States reported that some 340,000 of the half-million members of these organizations were persons trained or in training for military action. As the Civil War proceeded, pro-Union citizens and War Democrats took up their own arms by organizing themselves into Loyal Leagues.

As part of southern remobilization during Reconstruction, Southern Republican leaders enlisted large numbers of former slaves into southern state militia. Unhappy with this practice, many southern whites organized "rifle clubs" and secret societies such as the Ku Klux Klan, Knights of the White Camellia, and White Leagues. By 1870–73, the terrorism of the Klan societies had become so outrageous that most were outlawed or disbanded, but not forgotten. In the southern election campaigns of 1874 and subsequent years, white rifle clubs were again activated in large numbers and succeeded in electing white Democratic candidates with similar racial attitudes. By 1876, the only southern states remaining under Republican control, with the protection of federal troops, were Florida, South Carolina, and Louisiana (Vann Woodward 1956, 2, 7–8, 210; Carter 1959, 197–229).

The presidential campaign of 1876 between Democrat Samuel J. Tilden and Republican Rutherford B. Hayes was hotly contested. Republicans waved "the bloody shirt," declaring the Democrats responsible for the Civil War and hence incompetent to govern. Democrats blamed Republicans for the depressions of 1873 and 1876 and for preventing a more positive southern reconstruction. At the polls, Tilden received 250,000 more popular votes than Hayes. In the electoral college, however, where 185 votes were needed to win, the Democrats could be certain of only 184. Voting returns were disputed in four states: Louisiana (eight electoral votes), South Carolina (seven votes), Florida (four votes), and Oregon (one vote).

Negotiations between Democratic and Republican party leaders in and out of Congress took place in the nation's capital from election day in November to inauguration day in March. Meanwhile, in communities throughout the nation, and particularly in the South, rifle clubs, partisan groups, and secret societies were tense and arming. President Grant, refusing to protect Republican state administrations any longer with federal troops, but prepared to take military action to keep the peace, placed responsibility for a nonmilitary solution squarely on party leaders in Congress.

The candidates, Tilden and Hayes, were extremely cautious, avoiding inflammatory statements or acts. Their supporters in Congress and elsewhere were far less restrained. Could the presidential election be settled without force, that is, without a second civil war? A reading of the press of that day and the memoirs of leaders who lived through the crisis strongly suggests that another civil war was in the making. Only the determined negotiations of party politicians, mainly in Congress, forestalled the catastrophe. The party system, in contrast to its inadequacy in 1860–61, was now able to provide an institutional alternative to war.

A special fifteen-member bipartisan Electoral Commission was created by Congress. The negotiations that resolved the dispute involved an exchange of political currencies. The Commission awarded the twenty disputed election returns (shares) to the Republicans, giving Hayes a one-vote majority in the electoral college (incumbency). In return, Republicans agreed to withdraw Federal troops from the South (commodity), in effect leaving the government of that section (incumbencies) to the Democratic party.

Thus, the political parties, evenly matched and well led by astute brokers, carried off a successful negotiation. The trade-off resolved the election crisis, prevented civil war, and enabled the nation's political institutions to continue on through their critical transition. The principal representative institution, Congress, once again reflected all of the nation's significant constituencies and reasserted civilian ascendancy over the military. The military institutions continued on their way toward nationalization.

Nationalization: Representative, Partisan, and Military

As noted earlier, Congress had become an unfriendly environment for southern interests during the late 1850s, as seen in congressional rejection of the proposed Lecompton Constitution. During the Civil War and most of the Reconstruction era, the eleven states of the Confederacy were entirely unrepresented in the electoral college, the Senate, the House of Representatives, the major national parties, and the federal bureaucracy. By 1880, the Reconstruction era appeared to be over, and the major organs of national government once again included all sections and constituencies in the nation.

Congress in particular began to assert its revived influence by assigning major prerogatives to the speaker of the House and by renewing senatorial activism in the presidential selection process. No longer crippled by the exclusion of the South, the extremism of the Radical Republicans, and the divisive issue of slavery, Congress of the 1880s could now claim to be a comprehensive and relatively efficient representative institution.

The two-party system also achieved stability by the end of Reconstruction. Despite the clustering of one-party Republican states in the northeast and one-party Democratic states in the Solid South, the overall outcome was a close two-party balance in the electoral college and the Congress. A major blemish, however, was the emergence of a virulent racism in the South that excluded or distorted the electoral influence of black citizens for the next eighty years.

Since the mid-1870s, most voters have cast their ballots for either the Democratic or the Republican tickets, with occasional aberrations resulting from such large-scale defections as the Populists in the 1890s, the Roosevelt Progressives in 1912, the LaFollette Progressives in 1924, the Wallace Progressives and the Dixiecrats in 1948, the Wallace American party in 1968 and 1972, and the Anderson Independents in 1980. The two major parties have survived these defections only to face in recent decades a more insidious form of defection, namely, the rise in the number of voters who consider themselves unaffiliated "independents." In the 1980s, about one-third of the active electorate classified itself in this nonpartisan way.

Another party trend has been evident since the 1960s, namely, the nationalization of party organization. With urban and rural local party machines only a memory in most places, the national organs of the parties have been expanding their functions and strengthening their control over the management of party affairs. The national party conventions have given much attention to matters of party self-governance. The national committees have become oversized executive councils. Party mechanisms in Congress, though still poorly coordinated, have added partisan considerations to such traditional influences as seniority, personal reputation, committee specialization, and so on.

Despite the growing influence of the media, the intensive lobbying of organized interest groups, the increase in voter independence, and repeated forecasts of the party system's demise, very few serious aspirants for public office seek office without nomination by the Democratic or Republican party. Few believe that the American parties are about to disappear. The Democratic party continues to be one of the longest-lived human organizations in history. Even with the tragedy of Watergate, the Republicans demonstrated great resiliency by soon gaining a majority in the Senate and control of the White House. There are even a few observers who predict that within the next decade or two the major parties will perfect their respective national organizations to the point of enabling them to serve their constituents more directly.

The nationalization of the military establishment of the United States has progressed more slowly than apparent at first glance. As noted earlier, the most powerful military force in the world in 1865; that is, the Union Army, was reduced to a mere 27,472 by 1876. The state militia would probably have been similarly disbanded had there not been special circumstances; namely, the controversial role of labor unions in industrial development during the late 1870s.

The largest union of that period was the Knights of Labor. From only five thousand members in 1877, this union grew to about fifty

thousand by 1879. Because of the extreme hostility of corporate, political, and media leaders, the Knights conducted their affairs in secret.
Secrecy created the impression, widely held, that the union was another armed, quasi-military group and a threat to corporate enterprise.
The state militia were called upon to deal with the threat.

In July 1877, a railroad workers' strike led to the call-up of forty-
five thousand state militiamen in eleven states to suppress the strike
and protect railroad property. The regular army was also alerted. In
the inevitable violence, about 100 strikers were killed and several
hundred wounded. Thus began a practice of employing state militia
for strike-breaking. According to testimony before a House committee
in the Fifty-second Congress, between 1877 and 1892 strike duty was
the principal activity of state militia. Thus began a renewed concern
for state militia as military organizations (Riker 1957, 47–52).

In ensuing years, the more active state militia reduced the attention
they gave to strike duty, social functions, athletic events, parades, police work, and similar activities. Instead, they intensified drill, summer
camps, and other types of training of a more strictly military character.
In their search for financial support for these new programs, militia
officials acquired impressive lobbying expertise; initially, at state legislatures and, later, before Congress. State military codes were revised
to modernize militia organization. By 1896, state militia—now called
the National Guard—collectively had about 115,000 men enrolled and
were receiving state appropriations totaling $2,799,549 (Derthick
1962, 198).

Congress studied the problems of national military organization almost continuously between 1865 and 1898, the year of the Spanish-
American War. The state militia became an important source of volunteers in that war; entire militia enlisted as a body in some instances.
As a consequence, the Dick Act of 1903 made major provision for the
nationalization of the state militia by authorizing federal funds for
militia organization, training, and utilization under the supervision of
the United States Army (Riker 1957, chap. 5). At the same time,
Congress took other actions that contributed to military nationalization, namely, the establishment of the Army War College in 1900 and

creation of the General Staff Corps in 1903. This was the beginning of a process that led to the National Guard legislation of 1933, by which the state militia were fully nationalized (Riker 1957, 83–84, 141, 144, chap. 6).

The sheer numbers of Americans in the military service during the Spanish-American War and World Wars I and II required previously unimagined degrees of command and management centralization. The Spanish-American War brought 307,000 Americans into the armed services. The number serving in World War I reached 4,703,000, rising to an astronomical 16,354,000 in World War II. The customary rapid demobilizations took place at the conclusion of each of these wars. The World War II demobilization, however, ground to a halt in the late 1940s as the cold war began. The nation's defense forces were then nationalized on a permanent basis.

At the end of World War II, the United States found itself in the unique role of nuclear superpower, policeman for the world, and self-appointed guardian of the Western democracies. Consequently, and with great trepidation, the nation entered the company of those countries that maintained standing armies. The army was stabilized at about 1.5 million soldiers, the air force between 750,000 and 900,000, the navy between 600,000 and 750,000, and the National Guard at about 500,000. The three services and the Marines were unified under a single Department of Defense. The defense budget soared to more than one-fourth of the total national budget. The North Atlantic Treaty Organization became the world's leading military alliance, with the United States as its best-armed member. An arms race with the Soviet Union began. The United States became the leading supplier of weaponry to other nations.

A permanent national military force has not been seen as a gratifying possession by many Americans. The traditional suspicion of standing armies remains. Some recall Alexander Hamilton's warning; namely, that nations, to be more safe, become willing to be less free. A general-become-president, Dwight D. Eisenhower, cautioned his countrymen about the excessive influence of the "military-industrial complex" and its insatiable appetite for military appropriations.

The constitutional power of Congress to declare war has become obfuscated by the need for prompt presidential military judgments in moments of crisis, most recently in Korea and Vietnam. The age of nuclear weaponry, intercontinental ballistic missiles, and undeclared wars tends to debilitate civilian control of military decisionmaking. The pressures of the arms race seem to have weakened the congressional grip on the nation's military purse strings. Although the political parties are the principal managers of representative government in Congress, and although Congress continues to be in civilian charge of the military, there are those who worry that the growing influence of the military-industrial complex may be weakening this system of control.

Although civilian control of the military has always been a lively public issue in the United States, the content of the argument has changed appreciably over the past two centuries. At first a states' rights issue, the discussion now highlights executive-legislative relations in disputes over military strategy, budgets, weapons systems, and the power to declare war. There is concern about military-industrial political collaborations regarding the development and purchase of weapons systems, and the like. There is also a new dimension added by the fact that constraints on the military often come from foreign rather than domestic controls; that is, the obligations of arms limitation agreements, military alliances, and peacekeeping commitments to the United Nations.

In sum, the development of the military, representative, and party institutions in the United States began with a decentralized military structure, a Congress that was ascendant among the branches of national government, and a nascent party system focused around a few national leaders. The initial minuscule military force has since become a highly centralized and bureaucratic Department of Defense. The Congress has been a comprehensive and politically efficient institution since the end of the Reconstruction period. By the 1880s, the party system also stabilized and provided the principal channel of leadership recruitment and elite competition in the nation. The United States appears to have completed its critical transition.

Chapter 5

Mexico: The Peace "Machine"

Mexico's last major civil war was the Revolution of 1910–17, in which an estimated 1 million persons died. During the preceding century, internal warfare was commonplace. Attempts to incite civil war occurred after 1917, particularly in connection with the presidential elections of 1924 and 1928. Since then, civil strife has taken the form of occasional riots and demonstrations, but not civil war. During the several crises in the 1920s and 1930s, civil war was averted in large measure by successful political transactions between the nation's party and military leaders. These events placed Mexico's critical transition between 1920 and 1936, during which time the nation's representative, military, and party institutions achieved relative stability.

When Hernán Cortés began the Spanish conquest in 1519, some 6 million Indians of various tribal origins inhabited the land now called Mexico. In 1821, when Mexico gained its independence from Spain, the population, still 6.5 million, was 54 percent Indian, 18 percent Caucasian, and 27 percent Mestizo, or mixed blood. The difference reflected three centuries during which Spanish settlers created a caste society—New Spain—based on race. The total population remained fixed in numbers through constant decimation by smallpox, influenza, syphilis, and imperial exploitation.

Increases in population began during the nineteenth century. There were 15 million Mexicans at the time of the Revolution of 1919 and over 80 million by the end of the 1980s. Race continues to be socially and politically significant. It is estimated that the current population is two-thirds Mestizo, one-fourth Indian, and about 10 percent Caucasian.

Under strict imperial control, New Spain maintained an enforced peace for over three centuries. Following independence in 1821, however, the country was involved in recurrent civil war, climaxed by the Revolution of 1910–17. The Revolution presumably ended with the adoption of the Constitution of 1917, at which time a critical transition began. Unlike the critical transition experienced by England, however, Mexico's took place during a century in which military organization was sophisticated, representative institutions were no longer rarities and came in various designs, and political party systems were universal among nations. Thus, many available models should have facilitated Mexico's critical transition, but did not.

Mexico's Colonial Institutions

Cortés arrived in the Yucatán with fewer than five hundred men, sixteen horses, and ten brass cannon. His military equipment and tactics were typical of the sixteenth century: cavalry in mail armor, small cannon, firearms, and steel swords. Against these, the Indians fought with bows and arrows, javelins, slings, and wooden swords bladed with obsidian. Most of Cortés' military operations involved raiding parties of from five hundred to six thousand men, often mainly Indian warriors. A combination of weapons, wiles, massacres of Indians, and shifting alliances with competing tribes brought all of Mexico under the control of Cortés within a decade.

What perhaps most impressed the Indians were the Spanish horses, animals never before seen in Mexico and believed by the Indians to be supernatural creatures (Parkes 1960, 40–42). European guns did not come into the possession of Mexican Indians until the seventeenth century, and then by way of Canada and the North American plains. The French colonizers of Quebec traded with the plains Indians, who in turn raided or traded with the Mexican tribes to the south.

After the conquest, the Holy Roman Emperor, Charles V, turned the governance of New Spain over to members of his court rather than to Cortés, much to the latter's disappointment. Between 1535 and 1821, the Spanish crown administered New Spain as an integral part of its empire. Some sixty-two royal viceroys ruled the imperial territory. Most were despots, a few were enlightened. Change came slowly to New Spain's political institutions; that is, the military, representative, and party organizations.

New Spain was a highly centralized administrative structure, divided into provinces for administrative convenience. Each province was managed by a governor. Despite tight viceroyal control, the provinces eventually acquired small degrees of autonomy, which provided the basis for a federal republic in the nineteenth century.

A rigid social caste system grew alongside a feudal economy. Indian peons were at the bottom and Spanish-born royal officials, or *gachupines,* at the top. The gachupines dominated the imperial bureacracy. At a second level were the native-born Caucasians, or Creoles, and below them the Mestizos of mixed white, Indian, and Negro blood. The Creoles held subordinate salaried positions in the bureaucracy, but were mainly employed as owners and operators of mines and haciendas or as lay bureaucrats in the Catholic church.

For nearly two centuries the only permanent troops in New Spain were the viceroy's personal guard and two companies of royal palace troops. There were also troops—mainly native Mexicans—along the northern frontier for defense against Indian attacks from the North American plains. During the mid-eighteenth century there were some three thousand troops on frontier duty. The only other organized military forces in New Spain before 1700 were small regiments maintained by merchant societies in the cities, primarily for the protection of trade. Serious steps to organize a sizable army were taken only after the Spaniards had reason to fear attack by the English (Lozoya 1970, 16).

The military needs of New Spain were eventually defined by the encroachments from other imperial powers: the English during the mid-sixteenth century and the Dutch several decades later. In the seventeenth century, English buccaneers operated against New Spain from Jamaica, the French from western Haiti, and the Dutch from Curaçao.

By the eighteenth century, the English had settled the eastern coast of North America as far south as Spanish Florida, France controlled Louisiana on the northern coast of the Gulf of Mexico, and the Russians were moving down the western coast of North America from Alaska. In time, the most serious threat to Spanish imperial interests in Mexico and the Caribbean came from the United States, the chauvinistic and rapidly expanding new nation to the north. To make matters worse, the United States was not only a land-grabbing neighbor, but also a revolutionary model.

These external threats increasingly affected military organization in New Spain. During the sixteenth and seventeenth centuries, small royal military forces were under gachupine command. Toward the close of the eighteenth century, native components were added to the royal units as reinforcements against possible English invasions. The officers of the native Mexican units were Creoles; the rank-and-file soldiers were Mestizos, who would not become significant members of the elite structure until the following century. At all times the Indians remained confined to the bottom of the caste system.

In keeping with mercantilist philosophy, Spain exploited its colonial possession in every way that Spanish gachupines, merchants, landowners, clergy, and miners could devise. Colonial upper-class opulence grew at the expense of the native population. The church, an early arrival after the conquest, grew wealthy in property holdings and through its system of tithes and fees. In the class structure, the church hierarchy was second only to the gachupines; the archbishop was next in social rank to the viceroy. By the eighteenth century, there were from five to six thousand priests and from six to eight thousand members of church orders in Mexico. The clergy and the military were set apart from the rest of the population by separate legal and judicial systems, which eventually became a major source of friction between gachupines and Creoles (Parkes 1960, 105, 117).

Not unlike military organizations elsewhere, New Spain's colonial army had a dual composition from the outset. Permanent troops were differentiated from the emergency militia. The regular army was kept few in number and limited in equipment lest it become the target of local agitations aimed at the mother country. The ultimate responsibility for the defense of New Spain fell to the emergency militia; that is, native troops called up for short periods of crisis duty.

From the beginning, militia units were organized solely in wealthy urban centers such as Mexico City, Vera Cruz, and three or four others. In the provinces, units were composed of peasants, often organized on the model of the infantry regiments of Castille. Thus, certain features of Mexican military mobilization were well established long before the twentieth century: distinct urban and provincial units, a military class structure comparable to that of the rest of society, and short-term enlistments for crisis situations.

The officer class was largely made up of Creoles, but the highest military authority usually rested with the gachupines. There were no funds for equipment. Training programs were nonexistent. With weapons, uniforms, and other equipment usually in short supply, most militiamen brought their own daggers and machetes. During the eighteenth century, militiamen rarely had an opportunity to familiarize themselves with contemporary weapons or equipment.

Confronted by a growing need for a well-organized and stable military establishment, eighteenth-century gachupines, themselves untrained and undisciplined, became thoroughly overwhelmed by the administrative and technical requirements of military organization. For example, they arbitrarily determined military salaries and prices for supplies. They lacked trained officers and were unable to enlist recruits largely because the populace was wholly disinterested in military service. Like their counterparts in England and elsewhere, the peasants of New Spain resisted militia service on grounds that they were needed to raise crops so as to pay imperial taxes and other tributes; some even feigned illness or took refuge in convents. Evasion of this sort led to the practice of forced enlistments, which in turn brought a disproportionate number of prisoners, outlaws, and outcasts into military service. These men were hardly the raw material for a disciplined army. Desertion rates were extremely high, loyalty to officers low.

Corruption in military administration was another pervasive condition, already common in the sixteenth and seventeenth centuries. Funds allocated for military expenditures tended to end up in the pockets of local Spanish functionaries and, later, military officers. The pattern of military graft persisted well into the twentieth century, and, to some extent, became the device for retiring caudillos in the years after the 1910 Revolution.

There were significant social and political consequences of these military conditions. In the popular mind military service was viewed as a royal and bureaucratic imposition rather than as a necessary defense of home and country. In the absence of glorious battles and victorious wars, there was a dearth of national military heroes; economic achievement was the principal criterion of status and social esteem. The wealthy were interested in military positions chiefly for the pomp and circumstance. The military themselves were interested in their salaries, retirement benefits, and legal exemptions and privileges; for example, military personnel could not be sent to debtor's prison.

On the eve of independence in the early years of the nineteenth century, there were no more than nine or ten thousand men in New Spain's regular army. Urban and provincial militia added another twenty-two to twenty-three thousand. These were small forces for the defense of a territory of such vast expanse. Fortunately, the expected attack by the British never materialized, and the Mexican armed force of that time never had to face a test of its capacity (Lozoya 1970, 18–21).

Incipient Parties and Internal Wars

The rigid hierarchy of New Spain's government was matched only by that of the Catholic church. Roman Catholicism was the only form of religion permitted. By the end of the colonial period (1700–1800), church organization was far-reaching: one archbishopric, eight bishoprics, and 1,793 parishes in a population estimated to include about 3 million Indians, 2 million Mestizos, and eight hundred thousand Creoles and gachupines. There were more than 250 convents maintained by different orders and more than ten thousand churches. The church exercised exclusive control over education, cultural affairs, and political orthodoxy, the latter through its powers of censorship.

Toward the close of the eighteenth century, the Creoles were increasingly offended by the social privileges of the clergy and the gachupines. Creoles resented having to remain politically impotent despite their personal fame or fortune (Turner 1968, 26–27). In reaction to these restrictive circumstances, Creole and Mestizo intellectuals became fascinated by the philosophy of eighteenth-century English liberalism, particularly as it had been implemented in the American War of Independence. They also turned to the French Revolution's call for liberty, equality, and fraternity as welcome slogans against the hated gachupine class.

The inability of the Spanish crown to prevent the United States from acquiring Louisiana from the French in 1803 and Florida in 1819 exposed the weakness of the royal military forces. Creole leaders began to be concerned about their own security against predatory neighboring states. Security debates became mingled with discussion of the possibility of independence from the mother country, a possibility openly discouraged by England and the United States (Parkes 1960, 28–29).

Napoleon invaded Spain in 1808 and placed his brother, Joseph Bonaparte, on the Spanish throne when Charles IV abdicated. Repercussions were felt immediately in New Spain. Creole leaders now found it convenient to affirm their loyalty to Charles IV and to demand New Spain's independence from the Napoleonic empire. The Creole effort was endorsed by King Charles's viceroy. The gachupines, fearful of burgeoning Creole influence, opposed independence, seized the viceroy, and suppressed the rebels.

Two years later, in 1810, Miguel Hidalgo, a parish priest supported by a small group of Creoles, Mestizo intellectuals, and military leaders, gathered a small army of his Indian parishioners and proclaimed Mexico's independence. Hidalgo assumed the title of general and moved his army from place to place in the guerrilla fashion of George Washington's Continental Army. The army grew in numbers and passion until Hidalgo had a force of eighty thousand men, poorly organized, but large enough to defeat the seven thousand well-armed Spanish troops.

Hidalgo established his government in Guadalajara. His undisciplined soldiers, having survived their short-term enlistments, began to return to their homes. It was only a matter of months before the Spanish forces recovered, defeated what was left of the insurgents, tried and shot Hidalgo, and ended the rebellion. Or so it seemed.

Others carried on Hidalgo's mission. José María Morelos and Vicente Guerrero put together a new type of military force—the insurgent soldier—that quickly came into its own in modern Mexico. This force was separate from the regular army and the emergency militia; in organization and tactics it was essentially a guerrilla force. Most of its troops were rustic Mestizo farmers and peasants (Lozoya 1970, 22). Morelos's insurgent army consisted of nine thousand men. Guerrero led a smaller force in the south. When Morelos was captured, others retreated to the mountains and carried on guerrilla warfare from there. For the next century, the insurgent soldier was a major element in the evolution of Mexico's military institutions.

In Spain, meanwhile, the son of Charles IV, Ferdinand VII, accepted the liberal constitution of 1812 and succeeded to the throne. Mexico's gachupines saw this as a threatening development because it seemed to encourage the liberal rebellion of the Creoles and Indians. One liberal Creole landowner and former officer in the royal army, Agustín de Iturbide, managed to put together a coalition of Guerrero's southern rebels, the clergy, and the Creole leadership in general. Having done so, in 1821 Iturbide called for Mexican independence under his Plan of Iguala.

In addition to independence, the plan proposed equal rights for gachupines and Creoles, continuation of Catholicism as the official religion, and full protection of property. After several military skirmishes, Iturbide was able to convince the newly installed Spanish viceroy to submit to the independence movement. On September 27, 1821, Iturbide led a triumphant army into Mexico City.

The new government was immediately in trouble. Iturbide's army of eighty thousand had to be paid, but the national treasury was empty.

Creoles expected prompt appointments to the national bureaucracy, but the colonial administrative structure had to be radically reorganized before it could be assigned national duties. Meanwhile, gachupines, encouraged by Ferdinand VII's refusal to recognize Mexican independence, were plotting a Spanish reconquest.

Iturbide created a council of five regents and declared himself its president. He also designated himself generalissimo and high admiral. A Congress dominated by wealthy Creoles but entirely inexperienced in representative government, was elected. Most proved to be hostile to Iturbide. Thus, in May 1822, Congress began to consider ways to reduce the army of eighty thousand to twenty thousand as an economy measure. It also sought to prohibit members of the regency from holding military commands, following the English principles of separation of army and state and of civilian supremacy over the military. Iturbide rejected this proposal. Then, claiming that he was responding to popular demand (represented by a parade staged by the army's Mexico City garrison!), Iturbide declared himself emperor of Mexico. With more than half of its members abstaining, Congress voted, 67 to 15, to confirm this declaration (Parkes 1960, 183–84).

Iturbide's empire lasted about ten months. Some thirty-five thousand soldiers continued to be unpaid. Wealthy Creoles became alarmed when Iturbide began to print paper money. When the commander of the Vera Cruz garrison, Antonio López de Santa Anna, proclaimed a republic, regiment after regiment in other cities, financed as they were by local commercial oligarchies, joined the rebellion. When Iturbide abdicated, Congress outlawed his return. A new Congress in 1823 declared Mexico a federal republic.

Institutional Inadequacy: Congress and Army in a "Federal" System

The states of Mexico, as noted earlier, originated as subordinate administrative units in a highly centralized colonial system rather than as independent colonies in the manner of the United States and other federal systems. Weak provincial governments, under royal governors, enabled many local caudillos (military chiefs with personal armies) to become state and regional political bosses. A well-organized Catholic church was also a beneficiary of weak provincial (later, state) governments.

The new national government of Mexico consisted of an executive, a bicameral legislature, and a judiciary, based on a federal system of provinces converted into states. The national government was to draw its main military strength from a national army, although there was not yet an army to speak of. Nor did the system of representation directly include two organized centers of power: the church and the provincial caudillos.

The argument against making Mexico a federal system was aptly put by Father Servando Teresa de Mier, a Dominican who had been a leader in the struggle for independence and later became an advocate of a centralized unitary system of government. "Federation is a system for unifying what is asunder, and for that reason has been adopted by the United States. Their entire colonial history makes a federal pact imperative, as the only possible way to cement a new nationality. Here [Mexico] it would be tantamount to dividing what is already unified, at a time when our crying need is to make the new Mexican nation firmer and more compact" (Sierra 1969, 190).

The federal principle, poorly applied in the Constitution of 1824, was adopted by a coalition of reformist liberals, Iturbide followers, and urban oligarchies. The liberals were enthusiasts of the United States model. The Iturbide group were long-time proponents of decentralization and regionalism, which would leave political power with landowning and commercial interests. The urban oligarchies saw federalized states as a compromise between a centralized national system and the localism that they really preferred.

The constitution's system of elections favored the development of state and local political and military machines. The president and vice-president of Mexico were to be elected by vote of the nineteen state legislatures. Each state's legislature and governor were to be elected by the people. The people consisted of a very limited electorate: urban laborers subject to the influence of local commercial-military (mainly Creole) oligarchies and rural peasants subject to the guidance of the church, landowners, and leaders of rural militia. The system provided only indirect representation of church and caudillos and encouraged irresponsibility on the part of the unrepresented.

Ironically, the incipient political parties of the first days of the new republic tended to favor institutional arrangements that were disadvantageous to themselves. Conservatives—former royalists, wealthy landowners, church leaders, and the military—were centralist and authoritarian, resentful of any system of popular elections, which, in fact, they could and eventually did easily manipulate. Liberals—antichurch and pro-mercantile—were decentralizers, wedded to popular democracy in every form and to federalism as the great American-style disperser of governmental power (Parkes 1960, 189–190). Liberals had neither the constituency bases nor the party organization necessary for mobilizing the dispersed centers of power into governing majorities.

The Congress was a bicameral assembly organized to accommodate the federal principle. Senators were to be elected to four-year terms by the state legislatures, which in effect further decentralized power to local church, landowning, military, and commercial oligarchies. Each member of the Chamber of Deputies represented eighty thousand people in the states and was to be elected by popular vote for two-year terms. Without experience in representative government or the development of electoral parties, Mexico's popular elections soon proved meaningless.

The political parties that did emerge consisted mainly of congressional factions and pressure groups representing the church, landowners, merchants, former agents of the Spanish crown, and similar interests. The parties were legislative, not electoral, as in the early stages of party development in the English Parliament. Organized labor and organized peasants were not among the politically significant electoral constituencies until a century later.

Thus, Congress merely mirrored and rarely mobilized the party constituencies of the day. For the first quarter-century of the republic, party alignments were chiefly liberal-federalist or conservative-centralist in orientation, with a few independent moderates devoted primarily to the preservation of the constitutional system. Coalition formation was largely the work of ambitious military leaders.

From the outset, the military budget was a critical factor in the politics of the republic. In 1825, the revenue of the Mexican national government was approximately 10 million pesos. The Congress nonetheless appropriated over 18 million pesos for the operation of the government, of which more than 12 million pesos were for the army alone. Rather than tax the church and landowners or reduce the size of the army, the president and Congress inaugurated the risky policy of borrowing from abroad, largely from the British (Parkes 1960, 189–90). Soon conservatives in Congress were receiving political as well as financial support from the British. For their part, the liberals were busy developing close ties with Americans. These external relations tended to aggravate centralist-federalist policy differences.

Following independence, the regular army continued to be the basic organization for national defense. In 1823, a military academy, the Colegio Militar, was established to train officers who presumably would be professionals loyal only to the constitutionally chosen civilian officers of the new nation. In 1827, however, Congress, in a federalist move once again imitative of the United States, created a civic militia—the National Guard—with a decentralized organizational structure. Units of the civic militia were placed under the jurisdiction of the states. All males were obligated to serve in the civic militia whenever the nation required.

The distinction between militia and regulars added another dimension to the contest between federalists and centralists. The president of the republic was the commander in chief of the regular army. Its commanding generals were supposed to carry out his orders. Throughout the nineteenth century the reverse was usually the case. Presidents were generals or civilians who deferred to the generals, or, more precisely, to coalitions of generals. Often, the general best able to put together a military coalition became president. Otherwise, the president had no organizational or institutional infrastructure—a strong political party, a coalition of organized interest groups, well-organized unions, or a network of corporations—that could challenge the military and thereby maintain civilian supremacy.

Commanding generals of the civic militia and their troops were appointees of the states. They therefore had no special obligation to the national government except when serving as part of a military coalition controlling the president. In an unusual practice, generals had authority not only over personnel on active duty but also over retirees.

Even though state generals received funds from the national treasury, they were not required to render accounts to the national treasury. The corruption so prevalent in the colonial armies reappeared under the new republic. Generals kept as much as they could for their personal use and thoroughly exploited their soldiers in the process. Cheating on ration and uniform purchases, for example, was widespread. These corrupt conditions were well known and contributed to the difficulties of recruitment and to high desertion rates. Under these conditions, local generals and political chiefs—caudillos—became the principal actors in a decentralized system of political and military organizations.

Several other factors supported military decentralization. The geographical isolation of most states and regions enabled local and regional caudillos and political machines to become powerful. Often a rich landowner and his peons were able to constitute themselves as a militia unit, unchallenged by any public authority because none was present. Military leaders at both local and national levels were nonprofessional, depending largely upon personal charisma, courage, wealth, and similar sources of leadership influence. Even the principal national military officials were, for the most part, lacking in professional training or experience, having risen to their national eminence on the basis of regional or coalitional success. Officers trained professionally at the Colegio Militar were few in number, limited in competence, and little esteemed by their noncareer colleagues.

There were thirty turnovers in the presidency between 1824 and 1848. All of them involved some degree of military action and reflected changing alliances among the generals. One of the principal coalition builders was General Antonio López de Santa Anna, commander of the Vera Cruz garrison that overthrew Iturbide in 1823. Santa Anna was party to a substantial number of these turnovers. He himself occupied the presidential chair from 1832 to 1836 (retiring upon the secession of Texas), from 1841 to 1844 (when he was removed), and from 1853 to 1855 (when he was again removed).

The first nonmilitary transfer of presidential office took place in 1851. The first serious attempts to reduce the size and budget of the military were initiated by Presidents José Joaquín Herrera (1848–51) and Mariano Arista (1851–53). The generals would have none of it, and reinstalled Santa Anna in 1853, with dictatorial powers.

From Institutional Reform to Dictatorship

The coalition that overthrew Santa Anna in 1855 was led by liberal generals who called for a new federal constitution and further military and church reforms. The minister of justice in the provisional government from 1855 to 1857 was Benito Juárez who promulgated the Ley Juárez (Law of Juárez) ending the traditional privileges and legal immunities of the military and the clergy.

The new constitution made numerous other fundamental reforms. Simultaneous military and civilian officeholding was prohibited, a move to separate army and state. The Catholic religion was not mentioned as the only official religion, an unspoken separation of church and state. Ecclesiastics were specifically prohibited from serving as deputies or presidents, a further move to separate church and state. Religious corporations could no longer own or administer real property except in places actually used for public worship. Communal property, especially land from the sale of church holdings, was to be held in public trust for those persons actually working the land, a major but unsuccessful effort to enable Indians to become landholders.

From a distance, Pope Pius IX, concerned about the role of the church in Mexico, condemned the new liberal policies. Conservative military leaders took the cue in order to embark upon a War of Reform that lasted three years (1858–61). The Liberal Army—the coalition of generals supporting Juárez—occupied the capital on Christmas Day 1860. Under the Constitution of 1857, an electoral college similar to the one in the United States nominated and the new unicameral Congress duly elected Juárez to be president. With the exception of ministerial and military appointments, all presidential actions now had to be submitted for congressional approval. This attempt to make president and Congress more truly representative of the nation was, however, doomed to failure largely because of the decentralized character of the military establishment and the inclination of Mexican presidents to resort to the use of force.

The war with the United States (1846–48) cost Mexico nearly half its territory and laid bare the inadequacy of the Mexican military establishment as a defense force. The regular army was poorly organized, hardly trained, without weapons or supplies, and led by grossly incompetent officers. The civic militia was no better—widely scattered and significant only in domestic politics. Therefore, the return of the Liberals to power under Juárez in 1861 held promise of progress in military and church reform. The promise was frustrated by Mexico's debt problem.

The costs of the War of Reform were high and compelled Juárez to suspend debt payments to Great Britain, France, and Spain. With the collusion of Mexico's conservative leaders, these European powers agreed to make a show of military force at Vera Cruz as part of a joint demand for repayment. British and Spanish units withdrew after a brief display of might. Napoleon III's troops stayed on, in part to carry out his plan to use Mexico as a base for aiding the Confederacy in the Civil War in the north. He also intended to govern Mexico through a European prince: Archduke Maximilian of Austria.

Juárez and his Liberal Army resisted the French. Napoleon sent reinforcements and became too preoccupied with Mexico to provide much aid to the Confederacy. At the end of its own Civil War, the United States, invoking the Monroe Doctrine, sent assistance to Juárez. More than three hundred thousand Mexicans died in this conflict. Maximilian was deposed in 1867. Juárez returned to office and was twice reelected, contrary to the Constitution's limits on number of terms. His chief opponent in both reelections was General Porfirio Díaz.

With Liberals in command of the nation's military forces, generals loyal to the republic were selected as state governors. These were political generals. After fifty-eight years of officer training at the Colegio Militar, only two of its alumni became division generals in 1882. This reflected the political weakness of the official military establishment. Over the quarter-century from 1872 to 1897, for example, only 334 of the army's 2,600 lieutenants were graduates of the Colegio Militar. In view of this imbalance, military professionalism was given renewed attention. At the same time, the army was reduced in size; only 26,000 of the 65,000 soldiers who fought against the French were retained in service (Lozoya 1970, 26–28).

Juárez died in 1872. He was succeeded by Chief Justice of the Supreme Court Sebastián Lerdo de Tejeda. Contrary to the Constitution, Lerdo sought reelection in 1876. With the support of almost the entire army, Porfirio Díaz led a revolt and installed himself as president and dictator. He ruled with an iron hand until 1910, much of his durability deriving from his consummate skill as a political broker. He understood how to distribute political currencies to those who supported his coalition.

The Díaz period brought growth in industrialization, internal order, and relative political balance among the competing interests within the country. To the better educated and wealthier Creoles, Díaz gave office (incumbencies) and prerogative (shares) in the formulation of economic policy; many in this constituency came to be known as *científicos* (scientists) for their positivist economic views. Díaz catered to the anticlerical constituencies by appearing to enforce the laws of the Reform, that is, suppression of religious orders, closing of monasteries, and the like. In practice, he usually warned church authorities (shares) before making moves against them and gradually allowed the church to increase its landholdings (commodities). To the military loyal to him, Díaz awarded public offices (incumbencies) and outright bribes (commodities), thus placing most of his generals in public office and high-style living. By 1891, eighteen of the twenty-seven state governors were generals allied to Díaz (Lozoya 1970, 29).

Díaz took particular precautions to keep the generals in line. This tactic usually produced some further nationalization of the military establishment. He frequently rotated the commands of officers who showed signs of ambition or were otherwise troublesome. Countryside bandits were given employment as rural police and became a pro-Díaz counterforce to the regular army.

Because the army's principal function had more to do with internal policing than with defense against external attack, Díaz divided Mexico into ten military zones, three military commands, and fourteen prefectures for the purpose of maintaining internal order and heading off any political agitation occurring outside the normal governmental machinery. This mode of organization facilitated hierarchical control from the top. Each state's mounted police and rural militia were headed by chiefs responsible directly to the state's governor, who in turn was a Díaz loyalist.

With Díaz catering to their special interests, Liberal politicians and Creole leaders paid less and less attention to the military and to the oppression and brutality increasingly practiced by the Díaz military machine. Cruelty and corruption once again prevailed in Mexico's military forces. Although Díaz sought to modernize the Colegio Militar's programs along German and French models, including impressive uniforms and modern weaponry, few rich or middle-class youth were attracted to military careers. It was common knowledge that Colegio Militar graduates never rose to influential positions in the Díaz army.

Díaz Starts the Revolution

At the age of eighty, Díaz let word go forth that he would not seek reelection. The year was 1908. The office of vice-president had been created four years earlier, with its incumbent, Ramón Corral, in place as the prospective successor. During the three decades of the Díaz dictatorship, practically all semblance of party organization had dis-

appeared. Instead, economic development had stimulated the organization of interest groups: labor, industrialists, mining interests, small
farmers, peasants, the professions, and so forth. Thus, it came as a
surprise that, in announcing his retirement during an interview with
Pearson's Magazine, Díaz suggested that Mexico was ready for democracy and that he would welcome the emergence of an opposition
party.

Within two years, three parties came into the field to contest the
succession. The Reelectionists favored Vice-President Corral, who had
the support of the Creole cientificos; the latter occupied most of the
senior positions in the national bureaucracy. The Democrats backed
General Bernardo Reyes, perhaps the most efficient of Díaz's governors
and a former secretary of war. Both men had been Díaz's colleagues,
but the president declined to indicate a preference between them.

Anti-Reelectionists were the third political party, led by Francisco
Madero. Madero was a member of a wealthy Creole family in the state
of Coahuila. He achieved national fame in 1908 by writing a book
about the problem of presidential succession. The book assumed
Díaz's reelection, urged a popularly elected vice presidency, and made
a strong plea for political freedom. As a candidate, Madero organized
local political clubs, founded a newspaper, and toured the country
making speeches. He attracted increasingly larger audiences. When
some thirty thousand Anti-Reelectionists demonstrated outside the
National Palace, Madero was blamed and imprisoned for plotting an
insurrection. Released on bail, he crossed the border into the United
States.

The 1910 presidential election was hardly free or fair. Díaz removed
Reyes from his military command, and the latter departed for Europe.
Madero's campaign had to be conducted from across the border. Díaz
and Corral were reelected.

Madero issued a call for revolution. The popular response was immediate. Francisco Pancho Villa in the north, Emiliano Zapata in the
south, and others throughout the nation took up arms. Peons and
Mestizos flocked to the call and the insurgent soldier once again became a living force. Caudillos led volunteers. Revolutionary officers

and their enlisted men maintained informal and brotherly relations. Centuries of oppression and decades of brutal dictatorship made ideology unnecessary. The major political demands of the revolution were modest: redistribution of the land and greater attention to the needs of capital and labor in an industrializing country.

Most of the divisional generals in Díaz's federal army were over seventy years of age. More than half of the twenty thousand federal troops were illiterate Indians; the rest were criminals, beggars, and other outcasts. Their European weapons regularly malfunctioned. Each month the National Arms Factory produced only a half-day's supply of munitions. The federal army was hardly ready for serious fighting.

Calling for an end to the rule of the generals, Madero promised promotions to all federal troops defecting to his Ejército Libertador. He also authorized the leaders of volunteer forces to assume the military rank corresponding to the number of troops under their command, promising to confirm these ranks when the revolution was won. The revolution ran its full course between February and May, at which time the Díaz regime collapsed (Lieuwen 1968, 7–12).

Under the Treaty of Ciudad Juárez (May 21, 1911), Díaz resigned from the presidency, Madero renounced any claim to the provisional presidency, and Díaz's foreign secretary, Francisco de la Barra, was designated provisional president. In a precedent-setting clause, the treaty required de la Barra to organize his cabinet to include representation for the revolutionaries; that is, appointments to three of the eight cabinet posts. The other five were carryovers from the Díaz cabinet. In view of the inadequacies of the Mexican Congress as a representative assembly, this arrangement established the presidential cabinet as the principal institution of representation. This mechanism of oligarchic rule was employed for at least the next two decades. In later years, the one-party system replaced it.

With Díaz and his generals removed, Madero considered the principal objective of the revolution to have been accomplished. He agreed to the disbandment of the Ejército Libertador, with the exception of those forces that wished to continue as part of a new rural corps. Maintenance of internal order was once again left primarily to the federal army. The treaty reneged on Madero's promise to give revolutionary officers permanent military rank. De la Barra endeavored to sweeten the demobilization by offering six million pesos in discharge bonuses and pensions for the wounded. When a number of revolutionary generals angrily demanded permanent rank, Madero berated them for insubordination to civilian authority. De la Barra decreed that those who resisted discharge would be considered bandits.

As of August 1911, the federal army consisted of sixteen thousand troops. The Ejército Libertador had twelve thousand troops, half of whom were about to be discharged. There were serious problems in the administration of bonus and pension payments. Above all, several revolutionary forces, particularly the Zapatistas in the south, refused to lay down their arms. Fighting broke out. Madero interceded to prevent bloodshed and, trying to be evenhanded, criticized General Victoriano Huerta for his federal army operations against the Zapatistas.

At one point Zapata agreed to surrender arms if the de la Barra government withdrew all federal troops from the State of Morelos and redistributed land to the peasants. De la Barra agreed, but, as Zapatista troops began to give up their arms, federal troops moved in to seize towns in that region. Over Madero's protest, de la Barra gave orders to fight Zapata, a move that generated enough distrust to poison all future peace negotiations.

Madero was elected president in 1911. In 1912 a conservative majority was elected to the Senate and a revolutionary majority to the Chamber of Deputies, producing a divided government. Despite the continuation of civil war throughout his tenure, Madero favored disbandment of the Ejército Libertador, including the Zapatistas. He also wanted to reduce the size of the appropriation of national funds going to the state militia.

Still in full operation were the regular army built by Díaz and the local forces of the Zapatistas. Zapata again offered to suspend hostilities if federal troops were withdrawn from Morelos for a period of forty-five days, some five hundred Zapatistas were incorporated into the rural police force under an acceptable chief, the governor of Morelos was replaced, and land redistributions were enacted into law. Exasperated, Madero rejected the demands and asked Congress for enough money to defeat the revolutionaries.

Zapata responded by issuing the Plan of Ayala. This plan ended his support of Madero and recognized General Pascual Orozco as chief of what remained of the Ejército Libertador. Orozco's was the army that gave Madero his first revolutionary victories. In response to Zapata's declaration, Madero brought the federal army to a strength of sixty thousand in order to engage Orozco. When some of the federal forces suffered initial defeats, Madero sent other forces under General Victoriano Huerta, who succeeded in defeating Orozco.

Meanwhile, retired generals of the Díaz regime were busily plotting a coup. Felix Díaz, nephew of the former dictator, put together a coalition of cientificos and followers of the self-exiled General Reyes. With a small army, Díaz began a march from Vera Cruz to the capital. President Madero called in General Huerta to defend the capital.

When Huerta returned from the victory over Orozco to conduct the defense of Mexico City, he was startled to learn that the forces assigned to him had been reduced. Angered, Huerta decided to join the Díaz coalition and proceeded to arrest Madero and his vice-president, Piño Suárez. This action delighted the landowners, the church, and most business interests.

At this point, the American ambassador, Henry Lane Wilson, intervened. Wilson had lost confidence in the unstable Madero regime and was interested in bringing order to the torn country. Huerta, Díaz, and Wilson met at the American embassy to conclude the Pact of the Embassy. This agreement supported Huerta's assumption of the provisional presidency on condition that his cabinet would assure a wide representation of Mexican constituencies (incumbencies); the names of specific cabinet members were stipulated. Huerta and Díaz pledged themselves to oppose the restoration of Madero (incumbencies). Within a few days, presumably on Huerta's orders, Madero and Suárez were assassinated during an alleged attempt to escape from the city. This coup threw Mexico into a period of civil war that lasted from 1913 to 1920 (Lieuwen 1968, 13–18).

Both sides viewed the war as a battle to the death. Brutality and atrocities were universally practiced, although Huerta spoke of the federal army as the most virtuous institution in the country. His force of 40,000–68,000 men, which included regulars, state militia, and rural police, came to be known as the *federales*. A weak force, the federales relied heavily on the forced recruitment of criminals, vagabonds, and beggars, and was further debilitated by mutiny and desertion.

In contrast, the revolutionaries who had supported Madero were a well-organized and highly motivated force. They were led by Venustiano Carranza and other military amateurs of middle-class origin. Carranza, governor of Madero's home state of Coahuila, shared Madero's goal of establishing civilian supremacy over the military and creating an army loyal to all constitutional regimes. Although he called himself *primer jéfe* (first chief), Carranza refused to take a military title and insisted upon wearing only civilian clothes. His goal was to replace the federales with a new democratic army (Lieuwen 1968, 19–23).

Governor Carranza and Coahuila's state legislature proceeded to authorize the creation of an army. On March 26, 1913, one hundred newly appointed officers declared Huerta's coup illegal, formally established the Constitutionalist Army, appointed Carranza as primer jéfe, and nominated him for the provisional presidency upon achieving victory. The movement spread rapidly. Bandit chief Pancho Villa and others volunteered. Zapata would not recognize Carranza as primer jéfe, but he cooperated in the battle against Huerta's federales.

The Constitutionalist Army was a hierarchical and unified organization, with Carranza as its civilian head. There were three major commands under different generals: Alvaro Obregón as commander of the northwestern corps, Pancho Villa in the northern corps, and Pablo González in charge in the northeast. Zapata operated independently in the south.

Obregón was a former rancher, González a miller, and Villa a bandit. The obvious lack of military experience typical of revolutionary generals from 1913 to 1920 did not prevent them from winning many brilliant battlefield victories. As amateurs, they also found it easier to discard their military status to return to civilian roles after the revolution was over.

Despite the organizational integrity of this army, the five principal leaders tended, for a variety of reasons, to distrust each other. This was particularly true in the relationship between Carranza and Villa. The relationship grew increasingly tense as the Constitutionalist forces approached Mexico City. Villa captured a town that Carranza had specifically ordered not to be attacked. Angered at Villa's insubordination, Carranza terminated Villa's supply of ammunition and coal.

The squabbling allies reached a truce in the Pact of Torreón. Villa agreed to continue to recognize Carranza as primer jéfe (incumbency). Carranza kept Villa in command of the Division of the North (incumbency), resumed delivery of ammunition and coal (commodities), and gave Villa freedom of action within his own area on condition that he report all actions to Carranza for "rectification or ratification" (shares). Both agreed that Carranza, upon assuming the provisional presidency, would choose his cabinet from the list drawn up at Torreón (shares and incumbencies), which was equally divided between Carranza and Villa supporters.

The Constitutionalist Army was able to acquire standard uniforms and modern weapons, such as the Winchester carbine and the Colt machine gun, but could not match the superior artillery of Huerta's federales. Constitutionalist tactics were a mix of conventional and guerrilla fighting; there was a decided preference for operations requiring rapid hit-and-run movement. The revolutionaries used war cries and musical instruments for morale as well as communication. Zapata's troops followed the ancient Spanish "two-fifths system" of manpower management: for every five militiamen, two were to be in active battle, two tilling the soil, and one protecting soldiers' families. The more modern Constitutionalist Army was the first in the world to use the airplane for military purposes, in this case to attack Huerta's warships (Lozoya 1970, 37; Turner 1968, 157–62).

In the spring of 1914, Huerta's federales suffered a major blow when President Woodrow Wilson lifted a United States embargo on arms shipments to Mexico, an action that favored the Constitutionalists. Huerta and most of his ministers resigned and fled the country in July. The entire federal army of about 40,000 men at this time surrendered and was demobilized by the Carranza forces, now about 150,000 strong. Old-style military tactics in Mexican politics seemed ended at last. The facts were otherwise. It required another quarter-century to install the new-style constitutional army envisioned by Carranza.

Instead of declaring himself provisional president as agreed at Torreón, Carranza called a special convention, presumably to pave the way for his own election as a full-term president. He invited all the leading revolutionary chiefs, with the exception of Zapata, to attend. Obregón and Villa became wary of Carranza as soon as he failed to abide by the Pact of Torreón. They also objected to the exclusion of any faction from the convention, particularly Zapata's. Carranza responded to these objections by severing all rail connections between Villa's division and Mexico City. Villa promptly withdrew his recognition of Carranza as primer jéfe. A transition from military maneuvers to peaceful negotiation eluded the Constitutionalist coalition.

On October 1, 1914, Carranza's followers conducted their convention and nominated Eulalio Gutiérrez for president. Meanwhile, Obregón, representing a number of revolutionary factions, made an effort to placate Villa, even at the risk of offending Carranza. The Obregón group and Villa arranged to hold a separate and more inclusive convention on October 10 in Aguascalientes. Villa and Obregón sent delegates; Zapata sent "commissioners."

Although Carranza refused to acknowledge the authority of the Aguascalientes meeting, this convention eventually agreed that Gutiérrez was the best compromise for the presidency. Before the convention concluded its business, Villa's troops moved in, the Obregón faction withdrew, and the nominating convention was transformed into a military conference between Villa and Zapata supporters. These convencionistas then joined forces to embark upon a military struggle against Carranza.

By December 1914, Carranza retreated to Vera Cruz. Obregón joined him as part of the Constitutionalist campaign against the Conventionists. In Mexico City, President Gutiérrez sought to appease the Villa and Zapata interests by including in his cabinet individuals sympathetic to their views. In the end, Gutiérrez was compelled to flee the capital, taking with him some of the principal government bureaucrats and most of the national treasury.

The two hostile camps now consisted of the armies of Villa, Zapata, and others arrayed against the armies of Carranza, Obregón, and Gonzáles. The seventy-two thousand villista troops outnumbered the fifty-seven thousand carrancista at first, but were seriously lacking in munitions and political skill. The carrancistas were better organized and able to obtain supplies from foreign sources. Obregón led the carrancista armies in the field. Carranza kept him well supplied with munitions and replacement soldiers.

1917: A New Constitution and a New Role for Labor

After months of limited battles, Obregón lured Villa into several major confrontations and defeated him resoundingly. By August 1915, the carrancistas recaptured Mexico City and reestablished the normal federal agencies. Villa and Zapata retreated to the countryside and carried on guerrilla warfare for another four years. Villa even declared war against the United States for recognizing Carranza's government. When Villa raided Columbus, New Mexico, in 1916, the United States sent ten thousand troops, led by General John J. Pershing, into Mexico on an unsuccessful punitive expedition. Zapata was eventually killed in 1919 by Carranza agents.

With Mexico City reoccupied, Carranza made a broad appeal for popular support. He promised land to the peasants. To labor he promised reforms, fair treatment in confrontations with employers, and help in organizing unions. Obregón became Carranza's representative and negotiated an agreement with the Casa del Obrero Mundial, the principal labor organization. The Casa was founded during the years when unionization was first encouraged under the Madero presidency. It operated as both a trade union and a Marxist propaganda movement.

In exchange for Carranza's pro-labor policies, the Casa del Obrero Mundial agreed to: support the Constitutionalist cause, particularly through its propaganda; for every town in which the Casa had a branch, draw up a list of members who were ready to join the Constitutionalist Army; organize members locally to act as military reserves capable of holding territory captured by the Constitutionalist Army, and enter active service in the Constitutionalist Army in distinct units called Red Battalions.

Obregón had the help of six Red Battalions during the civil war. The Red Battalions established the first workers' component of the civic militia. Since these worker battalions were organized directly by a national body, the Casa del Obrero Mundial, Obregón did not have to deal with intermediary caudillos, local chiefs, state governors, or regional generals. In an indirect way, this arrangement was an important step in the centralization of the Mexican military establishment (Clark 1934, 29–30; Turner 1968, 109).

Despite the warfare that dragged on throughout his presidency, Carranza called for the election of a constitutional convention. The convention began to meet in 1916 and produced the Constitution of 1917. Carrancistas dominated the convention numerically, but a more radical and more cohesive element was backed by General Obregón. One observer reported the ideological and military complexion of the convention membership as civilian: Left 78, Right 81, Moderate 71; military: Left 33, Right 11, Moderate 1.

Although the military were fewer in number, they had greater political resources and were more radical in their advocacy of worker and peasant interests. This had important consequences for the economic provisions of the constitution.

The military provisions were standard for a modern democratic constitution and were adopted without debate. They included the following: No armed assembly has the right to deliberate (shares). Soldiers could not be quartered in homes without the consent of the homeowner (shares). No candidates for Congress or president on active military duty three to six months prior to election day could be eligible for public office (incumbencies). No military official may, in time of peace, be engaged in any but military duties (incumbencies). In a decentralizing provision, a national guard force was created in which officers in each locality were to be elected by their troops (incumbencies and shares) (Lieuwen 1968, 40–45, 48).

The new constitution drew upon Indian and Spanish traditions as well as socialist doctrines. The nation was authorized to limit and regulate property rights generally (shares and commodities). All land and waters were to be owned exclusively by the nation, which was also empowered to expropriate property upon payment of compensation. Foreign investors, large landowners, and the church were the principal property-holders to be subjected to government control in this way. The communal property of the villages was to be divided eventually into plots for the individual use of peasants. Labor, whether agricultural or industrial, was to be guaranteed an eight-hour day, minimum wage standards, abolition of child labor, abolition of peonage, the right to organize unions, and the right to strike (shares and commodities). The latter provisions recognized that labor was a new political force in Mexican politics, a fact that was not lost on General Obregón. The political and economic activities of the Church were limited strictly (shares and commodities).

Obregón's role in the development of the constitution and in the Carranza government was significant. He served as minister of war during Carranza's provisional presidency and assumed the difficult task of drastically reorganizing the Constitutionalist Army. The army had grown to over two hundred thousand troops commanded by fifty thousand officers, of whom over five hundred claimed the rank of general. It had become a decentralized force; generals who had recruited their own troops treated them as private property. Soldiers, attached to soil and family, were reluctant to leave their region.

Obregón began by reducing the army to 125,000 troops and 20,000 officers. The 30,000 officers discharged were permitted to join a newly created Legion of Honor of the National Army at full rank and full pay. Those who declined to do so voluntarily would have the basis for their rank investigated and could be reassigned at half pay. (Unhappy with their forced retirement, many of the surplus officers and enlisted men were among the principal recruits for the 1920 military uprising against Carranza.)

To further the professionalization and centralization of the army, Obregón established a General Staff Academy for advanced training of officers. The Colegio Militar, closed by the Revolution, remained closed until 1920. An interim officer-training school, however, had seventy cadets in its first class.

All this effort notwithstanding, the army remained a costly and disorganized force throughout Carranza's presidency. Military governors and local chiefs ignored War Department orders. Muster rolls continued to be padded; of the 125,000 troops listed, perhaps only 50,000–60,000 were ever on duty. Villistas and Zapatistas continued to harass national military forces and local staff of the federal bureaucracy. The military budget escalated astronomically. In 1914 the Constitutionalist Army appropriation was 31 percent of the nation's total governmental budget. By 1917, the military portion went up to 72 percent of the budget. In 1919, it still constituted two-thirds of the national budget.

With the encouragement provided by the new Constitution, Mexican labor began to organize energetically. However, Carranza did relatively little to implement his bargain with Casa del Obrero Mundial, and his relations with the unions worsened steadily. During strikes in 1915–16, Carranza hardly supported labor's organizing effort and actively suppressed a street railway workers' strike against the government. Previous to this, Obregón had resigned from the Carranza government, thereby remaining politically untarnished by the government's actions. Obregón was later favorably remembered by labor and agrarian leaders for having worked closely with them.

In May 1918, the governor of Coahuila convened a conference of labor leaders to establish a national federation of unions, the Confederación Regional Obrera Mexicana (CROM). CROM was modeled after the American Federation of Labor on a craft-union basis. Luis Morones, leader of the Casa del Obrero Mundial, became head of CROM. A secret Grupo Acción of representatives of eighteen member unions directed CROM's activities. The following year the Grupo Acción organized the Mexican Labor Party. Morones was the architect of the party's endorsement of Obregón for the presidency. Thus, the cordial relationship between Obregón and labor, begun in 1915, came to full bloom.

President Carranza, with a candidate of his own for the succession, did what he could to obstruct Obregón's campaign. He refused to accept Obregón's resignation from the army, which was constitutionally required of all military men running for public office, and he removed Obregón supporters from military and bureaucratic offices.

Leaders of the state of Sonora were at the forefront of the opposition to President Carranza. They included General Plutarco Calles, commander of the federal troops in Sonora, and Governor Adolpho de la Huerta. When Carranza ordered federal troops to break a railroad strike in Sonora, the state declared its independence from Mexico and dispatched its militia down the Pacific Coast toward the capital. Local armies and other military personnel, particularly the forced retirees of the Legion of Honor, joined the rebellion. Calles and de la Huerta issued the Plan of Agua Prieta as their platform. Their actions favored the Obregón candidacy.

The plan called for withdrawal of recognition of Carranza as chief executive, removal of his appointees in state and municipal offices, designation of de la Huerta as supreme chief of a Liberal Constitutionalist Army, and an early election for a provisional president. As the pro-Obregón forces marched into Mexico City, Carranza, as happened to others before him, was assassinated, ostensibly while fleeing the city.

Mexico's Critical Transition

Obregón was elected president in 1920. From 1920 to 1924, under his leadership, Mexico experienced a period of institutional development comparable to England's from 1688 to 1715 or that of the United States from 1865 to 1880. Significant steps were taken to nationalize Mexico's military establishment. The president's cabinet, by incorporating the major political interests of the country, remained the oligarchic equivalent of a representative assembly. A relatively stable party system emerged. It was true that many of the habits of sixteenth-century New Spain also remained.

President Obregón continued to work closely with his allies in the labor movement. He cleared the appointment of a minister of commerce, industry, and labor with the leadership of CROM. He tried to promote the growth of the Mexican Labor party. The principal opposition to the Obregón administration was the powerful Partido Liberal Constitucionalista.

In an attempt to strengthen Congress as a representative institution and to give it parliamentary ascendancy over the executive, the Liberals proposed to have Congress control selection of the cabinet and the preparation of the budget. This was a threat to Obregón's program and coalition. Several parties—the Mexican Labor party, the National Cooperative party, and others—joined together as a National Revolutionary Confederation to defeat the Liberal proposals. The Confederation captured the executive committee of the Congress and defended the appointment of a strongly pro-Obregón cabinet. By 1922, the National Cooperative party, successor to the Confederation, became the majority party in Congress. The episode was a victory for the president and the party over the legislature. Not long thereafter, party rather than Congress became the effective representative institution in Mexican politics.

To balance his dependence on labor, some elements of which were less than cordial to him, Obregón began to nurture his relations with numerous agrarian groups. One step was to conclude an agreement with the Zapatistas, who, even without their late charismatic leader, were still active in the south and in control of the state of Morelos. A Zapatista general was placed in command of federal troops in Morelos (incumbency). Zapatistas were appointed to positions in the national Department of Agriculture (incumbencies).

A second step was to make progress with land redistribution. By the end of Obregón's administration, some 1.2 million hectares had been distributed to the peasants. He also supported the establishment of a National Agrarian party, with a Zapatista at its head.

Obregón's promotion of political-party development was accompanied by substantial efforts to gain control of and centralize the military. His appointment of a Zapatista general, noted above, was a step in this direction. Even before his inauguration; that is, during de la Huerta's provisional presidency, Obregón arranged for the dismissal of carrancista generals from the federal army. Military governors and chiefs were replaced by Obregón supporters. To speed Pancho Villa's "retirement," a 200,000-acre hacienda was purchased and awarded to the former bandit. Similar arrangements were made for other generals. Where military conspiracies against the Obregón regime continued, many of the generals involved were courtmartialed and executed.

To bolster any sagging loyalties among his own generals, Obregón incorporated them into the regular army at full general's pay and privileges. He also transferred local army officers from state and local payrolls to the federal payroll, a major step in the nationalization process. To weaken the opposition of other local officers, he allowed unit enlistment records to be loosely documented, thereby enabling officers to inflate their unit payrolls, keeping for themselves the salaries of personnel already discharged. Obregón appointed CROM leaders to directorships at the Federal Military Factories, positions with substantial patronage. He reopened a number of professional and technical military schools, particularly the Colegio Militar for officers. Obregón was intent upon creating a new generation of professional soldiers loyal to the nation's constitutionally elected officials.

The Obregón administration gradually reduced the size of the regular army from one hundred thousand to sixty thousand men, a process that required three years. Obregón understood and was sympathetic to the frequently forgotten employment needs of military personnel; he made arrangements to facilitate their return to civilian occupations. Officer and enlisted retirees were given an opportunity to purchase, at low interest rates, parcels of land in military-agricultural "colonies" for which the government provided tractors and other equipment. Some thirty thousand officers and men, including many villistas and Zapatistas, joined together in eight such colonies (Lozoya 1970, 44–46; Lieuwen 1968, 67–72).

In further moves toward nationalization of the military, Obregón diminished the size of military districts. This increased their number and made it more difficult for any military opposition to organize a large force within a single district command. He appointed very few military men to public offices, thus underscoring separation of the military from the state. As noted earlier, he was a strong advocate of military professionalism and encouraged improvement of the Colegio Militar teaching staff. Schools of military medicine and engineering were opened. Standard uniforms were provided and required to be worn. In addition to their military training, some nineteen battalions were assigned various productive duties such as roadbuilding, irrigation development, and railroad repair.

Obregón continued Carranza's policy of reducing the military component of the national budget. This is best assessed from comparisons in the accompanying table of rates of military expenditure from 1916 to 1963 (Wilkie 1967, 102–3, table 5–1). Carranza had managed to keep the official federal expenditures below the amounts requested by his generals, but he also authorized them to raise funds in whatever way they could. It was Obregón who systematically reduced the real federal expenditure, with the exception of the period of the 1923 rebellion. Subsequent presidents continued the budget-reduction policy.

Reductions notwithstanding, the military were able to win substan-

Table 5.1. Military Expenditure as Percentage of National Budget

Years	President	Maximum/Minimum Percentages During Presidency
1917–1920	Carranza	69.6/47.4
1921–1924	Obregón	53.0/33.6
1925–1928	Calles	32.3/29.8
1929–1930	Portes Gil	37.3/30.9
1931–1932	Ortiz Rubio	29.9/28.8
1933–1934	Rodríguez	24.6/22.7
1935–1940	Cárdenas	20.9/15.8
1941–1946	Avila Camacho	19.1/14.3
1947–1952	Alemán	12.9/ 7.2
1953–1958	Ruiz Cortines	9.3/ 7.3
1959–1963	López Mateo	6.5/ 5.4

tial budgets well into the 1930s. Between 1935 and 1939, President Cárdenas succeeded in once again speeding the rate of reduction substantially, at the same time diminishing the political influence of the military. Another significant reduction of the military budget was achieved during the presidency of Miguel Alemán (Wilkie 1967, 105).

The election of a new president in 1924 presented Obregón with the choice of endorsing either former Sonora governor Adolpho de la Huerta or General Plutarco Calles. The two men had supported the railroad workers' strike in Sonora and had launched the movement to overthrow President Carranza, thus paving the way for Obregón's election to the presidency. Obregón favored Calles. Calles also had the support of a majority in CROM and in the National Agrarian Party. De la Huerta, as Obregón's treasury minister, claimed that he had been given to understand that he would be the successor. As anti-Obregón generals began to coalesce around de la Huerta, Obregón warned them that political activity was forbidden among the military on active duty under ARTICLE 545 of the General Orders of the Army and that such activity could lead to severe punishments. Despite the warning, the opposition generals resorted to force in August 1923.

The rebel forces included 102 generals, nearly 3,000 other officers, over 23,000 regular army troops, and 24,000 civilian volunteers. Obregón had only 35,000 troops on active duty, but immediately called up recently discharged reservists. He also was able to recruit thousands of volunteers from workers' and peasants' militia. Poorly led, the rebel forces were quickly defeated. Obregón then acted on his earlier warnings—discharging, executing, or driving into exile the 102 rebel generals and promoting junior officers loyal to the national government to take their places (Lieuwen 1968, 76–78; Lozoya 1970, 44–45).

When General Alvaro Obregón marched into Mexico City in the spring of 1920 at the head of a rebel army of forty thousand, it marked the sixth time in nine years that the central government had been overturned by force. Largely because of the political reforms of Obregón, this never occurred again. He was the first to visualize and to implement successfully an entirely new set of control techniques. These essentially involved a broadening of the base of support for the central government. Obregón achieved this by curbing the local military chieftains and by developing labor and peasant counterpoises to the military. By playing various power groups off against one another, Obregón greatly enhanced the strength of the central government in general, and that of the president in particular (Lieuwen 1968, 57).

As Obregón's term ended in 1924, the Mexican army was well on its way to becoming a nationalized, professional military establishment entirely under civilian control. By 1928, President Calles's minister of war, General Joaquín Amaro, completed the process. Amaro required all generals to justify their claims to the rank, placed a moratorium on all promotions, put a 55,000-man ceiling on the army's enlistments, reduced the military portion of the federal budget from 36 to 25 percent, and won congressional approval for new statutes to govern the armed forces. One of the new statutes dealt directly with the issue of loyalty. "A career in arms requires that a soldier, in the fulfillment of his duties, sacrifice all personal interests to the sovereignty of the nation, to loyalty toward its institutions, and to the honor of the National Army" (Lieuwen 1968, 87).

Convinced that the older political generals and senior officers would never be able to fulfill a professional role, Amaro embarked on a program to prepare the next generation of officers. He sent his most competent younger captains and lieutenants to military academies in France, Spain, Italy, and the United States and assigned military attachés to Mexico's embassies so that they could observe the more advanced armies of other nations. Amaro also began rebuilding the physical plant, curriculum, and faculty of the Colegio Militar along modern lines. Its professionally trained graduates were systematically assigned to regiments of doubtful loyalty to the national government.

President Calles followed the tactics of his predecessors by making it worthwhile for the older political generals to retire. He helped many of them become millionaires through outright bribery, low-interest loans from the national treasury, and gifts of land and property. The lives and pesos saved by retiring or removing men who benefited from rebellions seemed well worth the immediate monetary and ethical costs.

Calles continued most of Obregón's policies. He rewarded his friends in the labor movement and speeded up the redistribution of millions of hectares of land to small farmers. His administration introduced the first Mexican income tax and achieved a major refunding of the nation's foreign debt. The domestic debt was significantly reduced in size and funding cost.

But the Calles regime did not escape serious military disturbances. As he began to enforce the laws limiting the prerogatives of the Church, armed bands calling themselves Cristeros organized and engaged in terrorist acts. The Cristeros had as many as 12,000 men in the field during 1927–28. The rebel forces were vigorously suppressed by the National Army, which engaged in its own acts of terrorism in the process.

A more serious confrontation occurred in October 1927, in connection with the presidential succession. Initially, Calles considered supporting Luis Morones, his ally at the head of CROM, for the presidency. A coalition of generals opposed to having *any* civilian in the presidency was particularly concerned that Morones might organize workers' militias again to challenge the ascendancy of the army. To add to the confusion, former president Obregón announced that he would seek another term despite the constitution's single-term clause. In support of Obregón, Calles had the constitution amended to permit reelections, extending the term to six years instead of four. Obregón also had the support of most of the political generals as well as the new National Agrarian Party.

Two generals, Arnulfo Gómez and Francisco Serrano, both former Obregonistas, became opposition candidates. By September 1927, these two decided to resort to force. Anticipating the rebellion, Calles had all its leaders arrested and shot, ending the enterprise within a month. The regular army remained loyal; the rural reserves, which were alerted, were never needed. Obregón was easily reelected, only to be assassinated by a religious fanatic two weeks later, creating an unusual succession crisis.

The political generals, a great many of whom were Obregonistas, convened in the capital to hear President Calles's message to Congress regarding the crisis and to demonstrate their active interest in the issue. Calles urged the generals to stand aside and let the Congress, also dominated by Obregonistas, handle the succession in a constitutional manner. He then carried on a series of secret meetings with the generals during which he recommended that they find a candidate for provisional president upon whom they and Congress could agree in advance of the congressional proceedings.

Typically, several of the generals considered themselves presidential timber, making it impossible to find a candidate among themselves around whom they could unite. Instead, they chose Emilio Portes Gil, the civilian minister of government, who was unanimously elected by Congress on September 25, 1928. Most of the generals apparently were unaware that Portes Gil was one of the most loyal of President Calles's colleagues.

The Callista Party Machine

The succession crisis again displayed the weaknesses of the Mexican Congress. The military still believed they could take over the selection of a president. This convinced President Calles, the Congress, and others that the time had come to reform certain Mexican political institutions.

For more than a decade, the president's cabinet had been the nation's principal representative institution. Congress had become an arena for the rise and decline of volatile political parties and factions, but it was hardly competent for the onerous tasks of serious legislative work or major conflict management. The succession crisis confirmed the need for an improved system of representation. Calles, a beneficiary of political-party organization, sought the answer in the party system.

About to end his term as president (1928), Calles and a number of other prominent political figures signed a declaration founding an "official" National Revolutionary party (Partido National Revolucionario, or PNR). Calles explicitly hoped to establish a party structure and process that would end for all time the recurrent crises associated with presidential succession, lend legitimacy to the selection process, and make obsolete the military intrusions into contests for that high civilian office.

PNR was organized to provide political representation from each state, territory, and the Federal District. This structure paralleled the existing state party organizations, which were usually headed by local military leaders. To manage the new party, representatives in PNR selected a national "directive" committee which in turn chose a powerful seven-member national executive committee (Comité Ejecutivo Nacional, or CEN) (Lieuwen 1968, 102).

During the provisional presidency of Portes Gil, PNR organizational work proceeded with great haste. The National Executive Committee (CEN) created branches in many states, endorsed candidates for governorships and state legislatures, and became actively involved in their campaigns—usually victorious. In a very short time, a PNR endorsement became an indispensable prerequisite for success in winning public office.

A major immediate task before PNR was the nomination of a candidate for president. Some 900 delegates attended the first PNR national convention in March 1929. Three major interests—labor, peasants, and the military—had relatively equal voting strength. Only the military were sufficiently cohesive to dominate the proceedings. Calles was able to win their support for his choice, General Pascual Ortiz Rubio, who eventually won the election and succeeded the provisional president, Portes Gil.

Once again, a faction of generals condemned the proceedings and launched a rebellion. This was a strong movement, supported by about one third of the officers and thirty thousand troops of the regular army. This time, CROM and other labor organizations refused to lend much support to the government's cause. President Portes Gil appointed Calles as war minister to deal with the problem. Calles mobilized the rural militia, directed the campaign against the rebels, defeated the political generals, and again purged the army of its dissident officers. The uprising was the last serious attempt at civil war. The job completed, Calles "retired" to the position of Supreme Chief of the Revolution, a title specially created for him.

With the election of Ortiz Rubio to the presidency, PNR, under the control of callistas, became the directive force in the government. From his retirement, Calles became the main force of PNR. In short, Calles assumed the role of party boss, exercised not only through his influence in PNR, but also through an informal committee he set up consisting of five powerful military leaders: "The Big Five."

In addition to Calles, the committee included War Minister Amaro, military governors Saturnino Cedillo and Lázaro Cárdenas, and Minister of Public Works Juan Almazán. In effect, the Big Five was a domestic military oligarchy with resources capable of maintaining internal order. The Big Five dominated the national government throughout the presidencies of Portes Gil (1928–30), Ortiz Rubio (1930–32), and Abelardo Rodríguez (1932–34).

Calles served again as war minister under Ortiz Rubio. Cárdenas succeeded Calles in this position under Rodríguez. Whenever plots to launch military coups were discovered, and there were several, they were quickly suppressed by the Big Five.

While the Big Five found it difficult to dispense with military approaches to problems of domestic order, they were also uneasy about the power of the electorate being nurtured by PNR. When Ortiz Rubio became president, Calles arranged for provisional president Portes Gil to become head of PNR. Disputes soon arose between the Ortiz Rubio and Portes Gil factions. When Portes Gil, as head of PNR, began dedicating the organization to broader popular participation in party affairs, he was unceremoniously sacked by Calles and the Big Five. Calles then recommended Cárdenas as a compromise successor at PNR.

At the head of PNR, Cárdenas labored to strengthen callista control of the party and the Mexican Congress. Anti-CROM elements among the unions became allied with and dependent upon the Calles leadership. When PNR was reorganized along more hierarchical lines in 1932, the callistas terminated the regional agrarian confederations, thereby reducing peasant influence. Officeholding in government and the party tended to overlap, with the military dominant both in the executive branch and on the PNR executive committee.

When President Ortiz Rubio tried to pursue independent policies, the Big Five forced him to resign. He was succeeded by Abelardo Rodríguez, and this put the callista party machine almost completely in control of the government. In 1932, a peaceful campaign led to the election of General Cárdenas to the presidency for a six-year term. In this way "Calles emerged the full-fledged caudillo he had said Mexico would be well rid of. The chief difference between himself and Obregón was that he had the backing of a highly organized and united political party, which he ruled with an iron hand. He became, in short, the modern political machine boss so familiar in American politics" (James 1963, 246).

Although much of their power base was in the military as well as the PNR, the callistas continued the policy of military reform. The national military budget was reduced. Public works projects were assigned to the army. The military training programs that were expanded were those contributing to professionalization: literacy and technical training for enlisted men; a general staff college for young officers; more officers sent to foreign military academies; more stringent accountability for military finances.

The concluding years of the Mexican critical transition took place during the Cárdenas administration. The one-party system now had a powerful party that also served as the major institution of representation. Military interests were well represented in the PNR, yet civilian control of the national military forces was fully established. The military were no longer the instrument of adversary elites, but rather the institution for maintaining internal order and preserving the rules for elite competition.

The callista machine grew conservative, but President Cárdenas became increasingly interested in further economic change. He undertook a large-scale distribution of some 45 million acres of land to the peasants and improved agrarian lending facilities. Unions were once again permitted to conduct strikes. Employment was increased through an extensive program of school, hospital, railroad, and highway construction. Tense relations between government and church were eased. When foreign-owned oil companies refused to raise the wages of their workers, Cárdenas nationalized the petroleum industry. This liberal program, particularly the program for arming the peasants, eventually led to serious disagreements between Cárdenas and his mentor, Calles.

After only a few months in office, Cárdenas began to consider proposals for arming the peasants and strengthening radical elements in the labor movement, then under the leadership of Vicente Lombardo Toledano. Some of the older and more conservative generals were deeply disturbed by these developments. Returning from a medical trip abroad, Calles publicly called on Cárdenas to end labor strikes and agrarian violence, pointedly recalling the resignation of President Ortiz Rubio the last time the PNR leadership split on policy issues. At the same time, the callista majority in Congress began to adopt resolutions supporting Calles's criticism of Cárdenas.

Outside the halls of Congress, declarations of support for Cárdenas, inspired upon the initiative of former president Portes Gil, flowed forth from large numbers of prominent labor and agrarian leaders. Cárdenas issued his own statement expressing his intention to pursue his own policies and requesting the resignations of the callista members of his cabinet.

Cárdenas's firm actions precipitated a large-scale shift to his side in PNR and Congress. He promptly arranged for the election of Portes Gil to the presidency of CEN, the PNR executive committee. Cárdenas then continued to remove callistas from positions in the officer corps, PNR, the unions, and the agrarian organizations. Military commanders known to be sympathetic to the callistas were transferred. Before long, it was generally accepted that the Calles challenge had been met and overcome.

Working through CEN, President Cárdenas directed the organization of peasants into political leagues. Eight such leagues were established by the end of 1935 and were armed as rural militia. In time, over one and a half million peasants were mobilized into these agrarian units. Peasant loyalty to Cárdenas was, of course, in part a consequence of his aggressive land-redistribution program.

Before long, several members of Congress were unseated on charges of engaging in seditious activities. In April 1936, Calles and Luis Morones, the leader of CROM, were arrested and advised to leave the country, which they did. Thus ended the last threat of civil war in Mexico.

Meanwhile, Cárdenas pressed forward with military reform and the nationalization of the military establishment. Officership was made full-time employment. A merit system was established for promotion and other purposes. Enlisted men were provided life-insurance programs and education for their children. The military budget dropped to 19 percent of the national budget. In addition to the regular army, now comprised of fifty-five thousand men, a system of obligatory military training was established on a lottery basis for all men over eighteen. A rural defense corps, trained for guerrilla and antiguerrilla warfare, was developed, and this agrarian corps grew to eighty thousand cavalry and forty thousand infantry (Lieuwen 1968, chap. 5; Lozoya 1970, 71).

Taking advantage of the favorable political momentum, Cárdenas called for a special convention to reorganize PNR into a more functionally relevant and more thoroughly representative institution. The convention created the Party of the Mexican Revolution (Partido de la Revolución Mexicana, or PRM). It was the occasion for implementing a different principle of political representation.

PRM established four sections within the party, reflecting the major occupational interests: army, labor, agrarian, and popular. As of March 30, 1938, there were 2.5 million members in the agrarian section, 1.25 million workers in the labor section, fifty-five thousand active duty soldiers in the military section, and the entire general citizenry (through the party's local and state officials) in the popular section. The apportionment was a triumph of numerical tactics: the military were clearly overrepresented, but also readily outvoted, three to one.

Presidential nominees were to be selected in a national assembly in which all four sections would cast equal votes. Similarly, in state races for governor or senator, each of the four sections would hold its own nominating caucus and then cast equal votes at the state convention. The same kinds of procedures were applied to the nomination of federal and state legislators. The section structure assured that peasants and workers would never go unrepresented in the government. The military section assured that competition among military leaders would be in terms of votes rather than armies.

One general—Saturnino Cedillo—resisted the new party apportionment plan, but his effort to start a rebellion was crushed in a matter of weeks. When a workers' militia of over one hundred thousand was organized, Cárdenas warned reactionaries among the military that they would have to fight this militia if they persisted in trying to overthrow his regime. By 1940, the military were so fully incorporated into the party politics of the nation that PRM was able to abolish its military section without incident.

The 1940 presidential election was the last in which the generals played a role. Several generals took leaves to pursue their respective candidacies. Although three opposition parties prepared to contest the election, the real choice was to take place within PRM, three of the four sections having to agree on a nominee. After much negotiation, the nominee was Defense Minister Manuel Avila Camacho. The callistas, led by General Amaro, considered Camacho unacceptable, as did other noncallista generals. General Juan Almazán was the principal opponent to Camacho, supported by thirty-four generals and a large number of junior officers.

On May Day 1940, a workers' militia of 30,000 paraded in support of Camacho. Election day rioting was commonplace, with twenty-seven dead and 152 injured. When a plot for a post-election coup became known, Cárdenas condemned the opposition parties' activities as subversive, took certain leaders into custody, and brought sixty thousand peasants to the capital for the inauguration. One month later the conspiracy was crushed by the army wherever Almazanistas started disturbances in various parts of the country. Faced with the risk that their property holdings would be confiscated, Almazán and other generals gave up and returned to active duty.

Camacho's election in 1940 began an era of intensive institutional integration and economic growth. His administration was dominated by the events of World War II, the first foreign war in which a Mexican military force participated. It was a prosperous period during which there was a lull in labor and agrarian reform.

Since the 1940s, the Mexican military establishment has been a nationalized institution thoroughly under civilian control. The army's domestic activities have since included suppression of university and election-day disturbances, control of labor or agrarian demonstrations, pursuit of rural and urban terrorists, disaster relief, reforestation, road building, and public health projects. The navy has been involved in port development and promotion of fishery resources. In effect, the military establishment has been removed from elite politics and serves as the agency of internal security for all.

In 1946, PRM was renamed the Institutional Revolutionary Party (Partido Revolucionario Institucional, or PRI). PRI continues to be the dominant political party, but not without growing challenges. An overwhelming majority of seats in Congress are held by PRI representatives. In an awkward mix of single-member districts and proportional representation, the Chamber of Deputies' four hundred seats consist of three hundred that are contested and one hundred reserved for minority parties awarded on a proportional basis. As of 1989, about 85 percent of the three hundred seats in the Chamber of Deputies (where PRI had previously won nearly 100 percent of the seats) and about 93 percent of the sixty-four Senate seats were held by PRI adherents.

Although there are frequent threats of civil strife, even civil war, in Mexico because of unemployment or similar problems, major elite competition has until very recently taken place among the factions of PRI (Ronfeldt 1976, 298). Labor, dominated by the Mexican Labor Confederation (Confederación de Trabajadores de México, or CTM), has been the most potent of the PRI factions in recent decades. Some union leaders—particularly those at the head of the oil workers' union—have built fearsome political machines ready to use force and corruption in order to maintain their influence.

The principal opposition party has been the conservative National Action party (Partido de Acción National, or PAN), whose electoral strength has been concentrated in the state of Chihuahua along the

Texas border. In recent elections, PAN has been increasingly energetic in its campaigns, less willing to overlook illegal PRI election practices, and more popular with the voters. In 1983, PAN candidates won office in several major cities. If PAN were able to reach beyond its regional base and develop a national constituency, it could provide Mexico's party system with a more broadly competitive and adaptive elite structure. PRI leaders tenaciously resist this prospect. At a recent PRI national convention, nine PRI state governors denounced the concept of a two-party nation.

With unemployment hovering around 50 percent and Mexico in economic crisis throughout the 1980s, popular discontent with PRI and the pressures for political and economic change have held promise of throwing the one-party system into chaos. One observer summarized the situation as follows: "The PRI rule may simply deteriorate until law and order finally breaks down" (Sanders 1986). In the elections of 1988, however, a more typical party development occurred: the defection from PRI of a major leader and a significant faction.

The defecting leader was Cuauhtémoc Cárdenas, son of the late president. The faction was a leftwing minority in PRI, joined by socialists and other minor parties on the left in what proved to be a formidable coalition called the National Democratic Front (Frente Democrática Nacional). The PRI candidate for president, Carlos Salinas de Gortari, himself leader of a reformist faction, won by an unprecedentedly low 50 percent of the popular vote. According to the official count, Cárdenas received 31 percent and the PAN candidate 17 percent.

Factional defections from PRI and the growing appeal of PAN may eventually lead to the competitive two-party nation so abhorred by the nine PRI governors. If this were to occur, the Mexican Congress would undoubtedly become more adequately representative of the nation's diverse centers of power and thereby acquire a more influential institutional role.

Thus, after several centuries of relative stagnation, followed by a century of civil wars, Mexico's military, representative, and party institutions have made their way through the country's critical transition from civil war to party politics. The centralization of the nation's military establishment and its subordination to the civilian branches have occurred irreversibly. Representative and party institutions are firmly in place, albeit somewhat differently from the English and American experiences. What is yet in process of change at this writing is Mexico's one-party system. Major elite competition is likely to continue among PRI's factions for some time into the future, although the emergence of other strong political parties shows substantial signs of enduring and eventually offering Mexico the stability and other advantages of a competitive party system.

Chapter 6

National Comparisons and Policy Implications

This book thus far has focused on the developmental relationship among three specific political institutions—military establishments, representative assemblies, and party systems—as experienced in England, the United States, and Mexico. The case study for each country revealed a period of convergence or critical transition among the institutions. The transitions wrought changes in the order of influence among the institutions, usually manifest by the political status of their leaders. The political parties moved from third to first place in influence, the military moved from first to third place, and the representative bodies remained in second place, between the other two. The buildup of one institution and the subordination of another were, in large measure, an outcome of transactions in political currencies negotiated between adversary political elites.

The specific patterns of institutional development leading to these changes were: the nationalization of the military establishment, the construction of a comprehensive system of representation, and the emergence of a stable political party system. These long-term developments, concluding during the critical transitions, produced institutional structures in which politically accountable civilians achieved ascendancy over the military.

Progress in the strengthening of one institution or the weakening of another is accomplished by transactions involving political currencies. The three types of political currency identified here are incumbencies

(in offices), shares (of collective prerogative, or sovereignty), and commodities (money, materials, and services). Political transactions involving incumbencies and commodities are relatively familiar, but
those involving shares less so. It is the exchange of shares of prerogative
that appears to contribute most to the achievement of civilian control
over a centralized military establishment.

Critical Transitions in Nation-Building

Have other nations had party systems that became the institutional
alternative to internal warfare? The three case studies described here
are only an exploratory beginning for such an inquiry. The institutional developments of other nations, some of which will merely be
sampled below, may help test, with some variations, the research utility
of the critical transition model. There are also practical implications
of the model that should be noted.

Since the end of World War II, there has been a trebling of the
number of nations in the world. Many of the newer nations appear to
be at a developmental stage preceding a critical transition, some of
them frequently regressing into civil war. Some of the lessons learned
from the English, American, and Mexican experiences may well provide policy insights for leaders of these countries, particularly in connection with the nationalization and professionalization of their
military establishments, the construction of their representative institutions, and the design and advancement of their party systems.

For students of history as well as leaders of new nations, it is important to appreciate that the nation-state is an intermediary political
construct evolving out of centuries of human institutional development. Earlier political communities were clans, tribes, and cities.
Nation-states predominate today. The future political communities,
already well in sight, are likely to be regional, continental, and global.

Three Superstates

Of the more than 160 nation-states in the contemporary world, the
three largest—the Soviet Union, China, and the United States—ex-
emplify the different processes by which smaller political entities (re-

publics, provinces, or states) may become integrated into larger ones. Critical transitions appear to be a significant feature of these integrative processes. Each has a centralized military establishment that, although quite influential, defers to civilian authority. Each has a comprehensive, national, representative assembly of varying degrees of influence within the respective governmental systems. Recent changes in the Soviet Union notwithstanding, each has had a stable party system, albeit that two have been authoritarian and one democratic. Elite conflicts and political transactions are actively conducted within the institutional framework provided by their political parties. The point merits a brief elaboration, particularly since we shall, by analogy, compare the national cases with developments in the European region and across the globe.

The United States, as we have seen in an earlier chapter, began as a confederation of thirteen colonies, became a federal republic, endured a costly civil war, and completed its critical transition by the turn of the twentieth century. The United States of the 1990s is a country with fifty states, several territories, and a population of more than 240 million. It enjoys a competitive two-party system and lively factional competitions within each major party. The U.S. military establishment is subject to the civilian direction of Congress, which in turn is managed for the most part by the leadership of the major parties of the country. During two centuries, smaller political communities (the colonies) have formally, and at least nominally, associated themselves into a single large one. Civil war and the critical transition among its military, representative, and party institutions have been followed by an end to internal war and a "nation indivisible."

After more than three thousand years of dynastic warfare among innumerable kingdoms, the Peoples' Republic of China is today a nation with a population of more than 1 billion living in twenty-one provinces and other subordinate units. In this century, warlords with independent armies have been replaced ostensibly by a single national-defense force presumably under the civilian control of the National People's Congress, which in turn is controlled by the Chinese Communist party. Because there is evidence that all provincial armies may not be entirely incorporated into the national military establishment nor entirely under the control of the People's Congress, there is a question whether China is past its critical transition; but there can be no doubt that all the kingdoms of previous times are today fully integrated into the PRC.

The first Russian state was established in the ninth century by Scandinavian tribal chieftains. By 1721, after centuries of internal wars and invasions by Mongol and other hostile tribes, Peter the Great founded a Russian empire that today extends across the vast Eurasian landmass. The Union of Soviet Socialist Republics is a single nation made up of fifteen republics and other units, with a population of more than 275 million. The Soviet Union has a national defense force that is subordinate to the nation's Supreme Soviet, which in turn is controlled by the Communist Party of the Soviet Union. Perestroika may well reflect a nation in critical transition, with a nationalized military force fully established, but with a representative institution and party system in flux. Despite ethnic disturbances in early 1990, however, it is highly unlikely that the Soviet Union will experience civil war or disintegrate as a political community.

As Western Europe advances further toward unification over the next decades, it, too, will acquire—already has acquired, as we shall see in the next chapter—the institutions of a single country. A United Europe would then be a political entity in a class with the three communities cited above. Europe is, of course, not yet a single country. Its population of 500 million lives in twenty-eight nations (if Germany is counted as one state) that have been divided into two political camps: Eastern Europe, previously consisting of eight nations (including Yugoslavia), and Western Europe, composed of twenty-one. Both groups are currently passing through a regional critical transition.

Variations in National Transitions

Similar developmental histories appear to have occurred or are occurring in several long-established states. China and the Soviet Union have already been mentioned. Other cases might include Japan, Turkey, Italy, and Germany. In its current efforts to achieve civilian ascendancy over the military, Argentina may also be cited as a particularly interesting case. But the distinct particulars of each country indicate that the critical transition model requires flexible application.

Nations selected for study should include those that have succeeded in traversing the period of critical transition and some that have not. Where a nation remains at risk of regression to internal war, it is likely that some or all of the pretransition circumstances described in this study will be found; namely, the absence of a centralized military establishment, the inefficiency of a representative institution, or the lack of a stable party system. The pertinent elite transactions should be described in terms of political currencies. Evidence of trust and institutional sufficiency should be gathered. In short, even a modest research agenda may contribute substantially to a further test of the critical transition model and to the development of warfare-sublimating policies.

Japan. In many ways, the Japanese experience is comparable to that of the English, another island nation. Medieval Japan was a scene of recurrent internal feudal wars, with political leadership exercised by military governors, or shoguns. The shogunate system declined in the nineteenth century, and the modern Japanese nation came into existence under the Emperor Meiji.

Defeat in World War II and occupation by United States forces led to the 1946 constitution, which established a constitutional monarchy. The constitution also renounced war and the maintenance of a national armed force. Any military force was to be sufficient for internal police functions only. National security was to rely almost entirely upon a mutual security treaty with the United States.

Under the new constitution, the Japanese adopted a parliamentary system of representation in the form of a bicameral Diet. The nation has been governed during most of the postwar era by the Liberal Democratic party, in effect, a one-party system. In several respects, the applicability of the critical transition model to the Japanese case is of general interest, particularly because the transition in large measure was imposed by a foreign power. Comparison with India, another nation unified by a foreign power, would be particularly relevant.

Turkey. After centuries of fighting, the frontier between Europe and Asia stabilized along the eastern border of what is modern Turkey. This frontier remained relatively intact after the rise of Islam in the seventh century. When the Turks established themselves in Asia Minor, they became the frontiersmen of Islam. Over some eight centuries, they sought to breach the frontier eastward, thereby provoking the Crusades from the Christian east. The internal history of the Ottoman Empire, meanwhile, was one of warring sultanates, shifting alliances, autocracies of every kind, and gradual political consolidation.

Defeat in several wars at the hands of Western powers led several eighteenth-century sultans to initiate reforms in military training and to the organization of the Ottoman army. A first major effort to centralize and modernize the armed forces occurred under Sultan Selim III (1789–1807), but ended with his assassination. His successor, Sultan Mahmud II (1808–39) did, however, create a new army according to Western models. Centralization and modernization continued relatively unabated thereafter.

The Young Ottoman Movement was started in the 1860s by a group of young army officers. Its principal objective was the establishment of constitutional government, which was seen as a panacea for preventing further decline of the Ottoman Empire. The movement produced the first Ottoman constitution in 1876 and the first Ottoman parliament in 1877. Progress was interrupted by an era of despotism under Abdulhamid II, but renewed after an uprising in 1908. This second attempt at constitutionalism also failed, ending with the defeat of the Ottoman Empire in World War I and a revolution in 1920.

The revolution led to the establishment of a republic in 1923 under the leadership of Kemal Ataturk. Ataturk, himself a military leader, firmly established civilian supremacy over the army, which was a major reform advocated by the Young Ottomans and their successors, the Young Turks. Ataturk, as head of the Republican People's party, also launched the nation's first modern party system. A Turkish critical transition was apparently in progress from 1908 into the 1950s.

Italy. Following the fall of the Roman Empire in the fifth century, the territory that became modern Italy was a fragmented collection of principalities, duchies, city-republics, kingdoms, and religious states (that is, the Vatican and states under its influence). War among these political entities was frequent, "internal" wars in the sense that all had a common Roman heritage eventually manifesting itself in the Italian unification movement of the nineteenth century.

National unification was concluded in 1870. The political system adopted was a parliamentary monarchy under the House of Savoy. As in the English, Mexican, and other cases, territorial unification and a declaration of nationality did not necessarily signify an integrated nation. Italy's system of representation remained in flux, following the syndicalist model under Mussolini's fascist dictatorship. A new, republican form was established by the constitution of 1948, under which an oversized bicameral legislature was created.

The Italian armed forces have been fully nationalized within the constraints of post-World War II treaty limitations and the nation's membership in NATO. While the country is often subjected to Communist-led strikes or the operations of several terrorist groups, the probabilities of an internal war are almost nonexistent, given the centralized and professionalized military establishment.

The multiparty system is stable in an unusual way, suggesting that the nation's critical transition may not yet be complete. The three major parties are the Christian Democrats (principal party in nearly all post-World War II Italian governments), the Communists (largest Marxist party in Western Europe), and the coalitions frequently formed by the several Socialist parties. The Communists, despite their substantial popular support, have yet to be represented in the national executive branch, are modifying their organization at the grass roots, and are reconsidering their ideological direction. This anomaly raises questions about the comprehensiveness of the system of representation and the stability of the party system. The Italian case departs somewhat from the critical transition pattern described in the English, American, and Mexican cases.

Germany. The story of German unification spans several centuries. The territory of the present-day Germanies—the Federal Republic of Germany (West Germany) and the Democratic Republic of Germany (East

Germany)—was a scattering of independent tribes and states during the early and late Middle Ages and the Renaissance. Warfare was common between and within these communities. Civil war was particularly prevalent during the religious conflicts of the Reformation. In the eighteenth century, Prussia and Austria emerged as the leading competitors for leadership and control of the German Confederation. Germany was finally unified by Bismarck in the nineteenth century.

German military forces, centralized under the Kaiser, became an international threat before World War I and later the pillar of Nazi dictatorship under Hitler. Germany was disarmed and divided as a consequence of World War II. West Germany has since been allowed to revive its military establishment within the framework of NATO. East Germany took its place within the Warsaw Treaty Organization. One of the perennial issues of German and European politics has been whether the Germanies would ever be reunited as a single nation with a single military force, a prospect—rapidly becoming reality at the time of this writing—that the Soviet Union, France, and Poland view with concern.

Germany's experiment with a modern party system under the Weimar Republic was terminated by the Nazis. Today, West Germany has a vigorous multiparty system, whereas East Germany has had until 1990 a monolithic Communist party. The military and party circumstances of the two Germanies raise many questions about critical transition and the current moves toward integration of the German nation.

These, then, are a few of the nations for which the critical transition model may help explain, with variations, certain domestic institutional developments. Each case appears to lead to an end of civil wars and to civilian supremacy over the military. Other examples of probable transitions-in-progress may be found in the chronicles of current history: Spain after Franco; Portugal under Soares; the Philippines under Aquino, Chile after Pinochet; South Africa after Botha, and others. The Argentine case is of particular contemporary interest.

Argentina. A major feature of recent Argentine institutional development has been former President Raul Alfonsín's assertion of civilian supremacy over the military. Here was a case of established constitutional principle applied in a culture of traditional military paternalism.

Alfonsín's popularly elected administration pursued the prosecution of senior military leaders responsible for a period of "dirty war" in which torture, violations of human rights, murders of the *desaparecidos* (those who disappeared), and other breaches of the constitution were rampant. The trials of former presidents, junta members, police chiefs, and others affirmed, as did the Nuremberg trials after World War II, that certain moral and legal responsibilities adhere to every individual, whether a civilian or under military orders. The convictions of the Argentine military and police defendants set a precedent, not only for other nations in transition, but also in the annals of law generally.

The Alfonsín regime's attention to the powers and processes of the Argentine Congress also indicated an understanding that weak representative legislatures make for weak civilian control of the military. The president therefore led a major effort to achieve congressional reform. Inevitably this raised fundamental questions about systems of apportionment and representation, party management of legislative agendas and resources, executive-legislative relations, the role of a loyal opposition in the legislative process, and a host of other issues of institutional development.

A review of modern Argentine history reveals that civil war and alternation between civilian and military regimes have been persistent parts of that nation's development. The most recent cycles began with the election of Juan Perón as president in 1946, following an interim military regime that had assumed power in 1943. By forming a coalition between the military—an already centralized institution—and his National Justicialist party, Perón was able to maintain a harsh dictatorship until 1955. A popular uprising sent Perón into exile, although many of his supporters remained in Argentina, organized and active in partisan affairs.

For the next eighteen years, civilian and military governments rose and fell, following the dynamics that seem to be associated with critical transitions. Political parties were sometimes banned, sometimes legalized. A legalization of parties authorized in 1971 led to the reactivation of the Peronist National Justicialist Movement and the founding of the Radical Civic Union (UCR), a left-of-center party. In March 1973, UCR's presidential candidate was defeated by a Peronista. After four months in office, the Peronista president resigned so that another election would have to be conducted, for which the exiled Juan Perón could legally be a candidate. Perón was swept into office; his wife, "Isabelita," was elected as his vice-president.

Perón found deep divisions within his party and serious military threats from numerous left-wing guerrilla movements. When Perón died unexpectedly on July 1, 1974, he was succeeded in office by his wife. In the political chaos that ensued, a military junta, consisting of leaders of the army, navy, and air force, ousted Isabel Perón in March 1976 and kept her under house arrest for five years before allowing her to go into exile.

The three-man military junta, led by General Jorge Rafael Videla, dissolved the Congress in 1976, banned political activity, and launched a military campaign against several terrorist groups. The Videla junta dedicated itself to achieving "final victory" over the terrorists, inaugurating what came to be known as "the dirty war." The dirty war was a period of extreme repression during which all political activity was banned, and human rights were gravely violated. These included torture, the perpetration of "disappearances"; that is, kidnappings and killings of some nine thousand persons suspected of opposition to the regime, plus censorship, and similar outrages.

The excesses of the junta were resisted by a younger generation of trade union leaders and by civilians prominent in many of Argentina's numerous political parties and interest groups. By the end of 1979, the junta, acceding to pressures from these sources, withdrew many of the restrictions on political activity, banning only those parties with "totalitarian ideologies."

The Videla junta remained in power from 1976 to 1981. By early 1981, the regime faced an inflation rate of 100 percent, a recession, unhappy middle and business classes, and international disrepute for the official terrorism of its dirty war. In March 1981, the junta designated General Roberto Viola as president. In a gesture of conciliation, Viola appointed civilians to seven of the thirteen positions in his cabinet and initiated a more open approach to the political parties.

Hardliners in the regime, however, began to issue warnings against returning to "populism and anarchy." By December 1981, military factions led by Generals Leopoldo Galtieri and Cristino Nicolaides overthrew Viola, chose Galtieri as president, and embarked upon an unpopular and ineffectual program of economic austerity. Hoping to excite a wave of patriotism that would strengthen their troubled regime, the Galtieri junta embarked upon an invasion of the Falkland Islands on April 2, 1982. No small part of their motivation was the expectation that they could in this way acquire untapped petroleum deposits in the region of the islands.

The islands had been a subject of dispute between Great Britain and Argentina for decades. The population was nearly entirely British in origin. The British claim dated back to 1771 and the Argentine to 1820. British Prime Minister Margaret Thatcher responded to the attack immediately by dispatching a large naval task force to defend the islands. Upon arrival, some five thousand British troops quickly drove back fifteen thousand Argentine soldiers. Anticipating defeat, President Galtieri resigned. Thoroughly discredited, his military junta was dissolved. The Argentine troops surrendered to the British on July 15, 1982. General Reynaldo Bignone assumed office as interim president.

During the preceding two years, political coalitions had been coming together from among the large array of political parties. The Union of the Democratic Center gathered eight minor parties and announced its determination to end the dominance of the more populist movements. Shortly after, leaders of seven other parties, including factions drawn from the Peronist, Radical, Socialist, and Communist parties, created a Forum for the Defense of Sovereignty, Democracy, and the National Heritage, declaring their opposition to the policies of the junta. By mid-1981, leaders of five of the more important parties and factions—Christian Democrats, Peronistas, Radicals, Desarrollistas

(Movement of Integration and Development), and Intransigents—announced the Multipartidaria, a multiparty front whose principal objective was resistance to the extreme right wing among the military. Under pressure from these coalitions, the ban on parties was finally ended with the inauguration of General Reynaldo Bignone as president on July 1, 1982.

Bignone called for a general election to take place before March 1984. He eventually set the date for October 30, 1983. More than three hundred parties, movements, and other groups participated. However, 92 percent of the actual vote was divided between the Radical Civic Union, whose winning nominee was Raul Alfonsín Foulkes (51.8 percent of the popular vote), and the Justicialist Liberation Front, whose presidential candidate was Italo Argentino Luder (40.2 percent of the vote).

Equally significant was the reactivation of the National Congress. The Justicialist Liberation Front won 21 seats and Alfonsín's Radical Civic Union 18 seats in the 46-member Senate, the remaining seven going to minor parties. The party distribution in the 254-member Chamber of Deputies gave the Radical Civic Union 129 seats, the Justicialist Liberation Front 111, with fourteen going to minor parties. What emerged was a competitive two-party system and a revitalized representative legislature.

President Alfonsín thus was confronted by a potent opposition (Justicialist Liberation Front) that at times boycotted sessions of Congress to prevent a quorum. Alfonsín's careful negotiations with the Justicialists calmed the partisan turbulence. Another serious challenge came during the 1985 congressional elections. As the election campaign progressed, violent tactics by terrorist and right-wing groups threatened to disrupt the otherwise open and fair electoral process. Alfonsín managed to take a difficult posture in a democracy just emerging from decades of martial law under military juntas, declaring a national emergency for the duration of the campaign. He expressed his determination to show "that a democratic government can maintain order." His action was widely applauded by the Argentine public and the leaders of the opposition parties.

In his 1983 presidential campaign, Alfonsín had promised punishment of the military responsible for the outrages of "the dirty war." The vigor with which former military leaders were prosecuted by his administration nevertheless came as a surprise to most observers and drew international attention and encouragement. Alfonsín was determined to establish the principles of civilian supremacy and military accountability as well as to build a more strictly professional role for the military.

In Argentina, as in other Latin American countries, the intrusion of the military into domestic party politics was traditionally rationalized as essential for national unity and independence. This represented a traditional value among military leaders, who felt it their duty, not only to put down insurgencies, but also to remove civilian officials who failed to maintain public order or seemed incapable of advancing the nation's economic and social development. Regardless of whether it was paternalism or arrogance, this attitude toward civilian leaders resulted in civil-military relations that placed elected civilians into the role of junior partners to the nonelected military. The military—despite the absence of a popular mandate—felt supremely patriotic about taking over their government. That governments are organizations best managed by party leaders skilled in political brokerage and electoral accountability was an alien proposition for the military. Accustomed to managing strict hierarchies, the military leaders invariably organized political versions of military hierarchies, namely, military dictatorships (See Goodman et al. for a survey of contemporary Latin American conditions).

President Alfonsín's prosecution of junta members, senior officers, and several hundred lower-ranking officers for breaches of human rights and other crimes was initiated promptly. By December 1985, five former junta members, including two former presidents, received jail terms ranging from four-and-a-half years to life.

One notorious trial concluded in December 1986. In this case, the former chief of police of Buenos Aires province and several of his aides received sentences of four to twenty-five years for multiple counts of torture. In the latter case, the court rejected the defense argument that their conduct was in obedience to military orders. Instead, said the six-judge panel, even military orders can be illegal. "In a legal state, there is no authority that is above the law." Civilian rules, not the military, were henceforth to take precedence. The convictions were expected to discourage military takeovers and excesses. The punishment of military leaders according to due process under the law set a model for other countries having similar problems.

It did not take long for the military to start resisting the Alfonsín administration's prosecutions. Alfonsín's personal popularity, Argentina's relatively well-developed legal system, the strength of the unions and other organized interest groups, and the renewed vitality of the party system undoubtedly played a substantial part in Alfonsín's ability to carry off this challenge to the military. The president recognized, however, that the nation would be ill-served by a demoralized armed force.

Early in December 1986, Alfonsín took steps to limit the damage to military morale. He sent to Congress a draft bill that would speed up the trials of military personnel for human rights violations and fix a final date for filing additional cases. The proposed legislation caused great controversy. Military officers met in garrisons throughout the country to debate the bill. Civil rights groups condemned the new law as a "hidden amnesty."

To defend this controversial move, Alfonsín made a national television address in which he urged his countrymen to "lay aside the differences that separate us." He further declared that "There cannot be one Argentina for civilians and one for the military."

> It is not enough for a serious country to want . . . simply for the armed forces to abstain from coup d'etats. A country that faces such a period of renovation and transformation needs its armed forces totally integrated in the process and to the nation.
>
> Each Argentine knows now that political terror does not and will not again go unpunished.

On December 26, the legislation was signed into law. It established a sixty-day deadline for new indictments of military officers, police, or other suspects (including members of guerrilla groups) of abduction, torture, and disappearance of people during the 1976–83 period. Within the following month, eleven Argentine human rights groups filed more than one thousand charges against about 650 military and other personnel, including at least 98 retired generals and admirals. By the end of the sixty-day statute of limitations, about 140 military and police officers, including former President Galteiri (already serving a twelve-year prison term), were indicted.

The achievements of the Alfonsín administration in asserting civilian control of the military were diluted somewhat by the subsequent president, Carlos Menem. Shortly after assuming office in 1989, Menem pardoned thirty-nine officers and others still liable for prosecution for human rights abuses, one hundred sixty-four military personnel involved in three uprisings against the Alfonsín administration, and sixty-four leftist leaders who had been sought out during the dirty war. Menem justified the pardons as a step toward national reconciliation, although several Argentine human rights organizations vigorously disagreed.

Also high on President Alfonsín's agenda was the revision of the constitution. Alfonsín and his advisers saw a need to modernize the basic law, particularly with respect to the legislative process. Recognizing that a vigorous democracy requires a truly representative assembly, and frustrated by the opposition's frequent boycotts of legislative sessions, Alfonsín initiated meetings with opposition deputies to explore the possibility of convening a special convention to consider constitutional revisions.

Following his discussions with opposition leaders, Alfonsín appointed an advisory council for the Consolidation of Democracy. The council consisted of approximately fifty members drawn from all sectors of society, including playwrights, athletes, and scientists.

The heavy concentration of population and of political, social, and economic resources in the capital city of Buenos Aires presented several difficult issues for the council: the relevance of federalism; the redistribution of power between the weak legislative branch and an extremely strong presidency; improvement of the low level of popular participation in the political life of the country; the institutionalization of traditional Argentine values; the means for protecting human rights, to mention a few of the issues.

The Argentine case, even in this brief account, illustrates some of the factors that are likely to be involved in more contemporaneous national critical transitions. Modern critical transitions within nations are likely to be foreshortened when compared to the long periods required by the English, American, and Mexican cases. Centralization of the nation's military establishment is more likely already to have been achieved, although the military's professionalization and deference to civilian public officials may be lacking. The widespread preference for strong national chief executives tends to be accompanied by poor arrangements for making representative assemblies influential. Knowledge of party systems and their functions, although available, is not of much use to party officers severely unskilled in party management and strategy. The notion that a stable party system could be an alternative to recurrent civil war is a thought that rarely, if ever, crosses the minds of these officers.

Development Policy and the Critical Transition Model

Of the more than one hundred new nations that have been established since the end of World War II, most continue to have military dictatorships, civil wars, and autocratic one-party systems. Can the critical transition model suggest strategies and transactions that would help prevent potentially regressive cases from descending into civil war and repression? Since most of these nations have yet to experience a critical transition, those of their leaders seeking to establish internal peace may find helpful insights in the critical transition model.

Military centralization. The typical military situation in a nation's development before a critical transition consists of competing armies or army factions, recurrent civil war, military dictatorship, and repression of opposition or dissident political movements. Under the best of circumstances, the military may temporarily remove a civilian regime on the grounds that national stagnation or chaos has resulted from the failings of civilian leadership. Under the worst of circumstances, an ambitious military leader may form a coalition among military officers in an arrangement for grasping oligarchic power. In either case, centralization of the military establishment may ensue as lesser military forces or leaders are defeated or co-opted. A complicating feature of modern military nationalization is the influx of military aid from external sources, usually an ally intending to stabilize the recipient regime or to serve the prestige and national security of the ally itself. There are, of course, other modes of military centralization.

What policies does the critical transition model suggest for facilitating a successful and relatively nonviolent period of change? Some particularly relevant policies may be summarized as follows:

1. Professional training of all military officers at all ranks, concluding with an oath to uphold the constitution as interpreted by a national supreme court and a constitutionally elected chief executive regardless of party. The constitutionally elected civilian chief executive should be the only person bearing the title and powers of commander in chief of the armed forces.

2. A constitutional rule that military personnel may not be candidates for or hold legislative, executive, or other public office until two or more years after resigning or retiring from military status.

3. The inclusion of human rights provisions in military law, with infractions subject to court-martial and review by civilian courts.

4. Legislative review of military budget proposals yearly or biennially.

5. Statutes or policies that assure amnesty and employment for officers and troops of nongovernmental military forces who voluntarily surrender themselves to appropriate public officials, except in those cases in which human rights violations have been perpetrated.

Studies of civil and other wars rarely comment on the unemployment consequences of defeat or demobilization for the military personnel involved. In many developing nations, military service is an important, sometimes sole source of regular employment. Employment is often a principal motivation for insurgencies and rebellions. The Mexican case study illustrates how caudillo armies may be disbanded by "buying out" their generals and finding employment for their rank-and-file soldiers.

6. The establishment of civilian military reserve units subject to the joint authority of the chief executive and the national legislature.

7. Continuing surveillance of national military organization and programs by a specific committee or other agency of the national legislature.

Comprehensive Representation. One thousand years of experience with issues of apportionment, representation, election systems and their behavioral consequences, federalism, party and legislative organization, and other aspects of representative systems are recorded, analyzed, and readily available. What soon becomes apparent from this body of knowledge is that systems of representation acquire institutional strength and durability when

1. they widely disperse units of national power (through such arrangements as separation of powers among government branches, bicameralism, inclusive suffrage, equal legislative districts, and similar devices);

2. they defend the legitimacy of freely organized political parties on condition that party leaders abide by electoral and legislative decisions;

3. they provide offices (such as a position of leader of the Opposition, minority staffs on legislative committees, and other institutionalized patronage) and other resources to assure loyal oppositions the opportunity and capacity to perform their important function of dissent; and

4. they create opportunities and resources with which incumbent representatives may maintain constituency contact and render constituency services.

Above all, the nation's representative assembly must be the community's busiest political marketplace, available for legitimate transactions among citizens, organized interest groups, political parties, and the various agencies of government. Probably the most significant transactions will be those between party leaders within the legislature and the military leaders outside, particularly in connection with military budgets and taxation.

National party system. Party systems are no longer novel institutions. Practically every modern nation has at least one major party. Therefore, modern critical transitions need no longer wait upon the "discovery" of political parties. What contemporary policy must accomplish is the facilitation and stabilization of a competitive party system. This fundamental step is not usually an easy one. Parties may not be a sufficiently powerful counterforce to a military dictatorship. Consequently, grass-roots mobilization, campaigns for office and change, and all the associated civil liberties may be weak or at risk. Nevertheless, in the light of the present study, it is of fundamental importance that competition among the nation's elite be encouraged.

1. A comprehensively representative assembly should be the primary site for the initial development of parties.

2. The parties in the system should be entirely separated from any organizational connection with the military establishment.

3. Probably the best assurance that these conditions will be met is the development of vigorous organized interest groups; that is, labor unions, business associations, farm cooperatives, professional associations, trade associations, and the like. In order to diminish military influence and advance that of the political parties, these groups must be free to form coalitions on such issues as military budgets, military service, taxation, free elections, and civil rights.

4. The freedoms of expression and association, both essential for the emergence of a stable party system, are always at risk under totalitarian or authoritarian circumstances. The implementation and protection of these freedoms need to be an important objective for political transactions among the adversary elites. For example, in the English tradition, taxes (commodities) should be withheld until exchanged for guaranteed free elections (shares).

Once political parties are established within an elected representative assembly, they will necessarily endeavor to mobilize electoral constituencies in an enduring way. This effort is nothing less than implementation of popular sovereignty. It will be accompanied by the political "noise," competitive organizing, and leadership posturing that always accompanies pluralistic party politics.

Unfortunately, the "noise" tends to be misunderstood by and appear threatening to more traditional elites, the military, and the incumbents in governmental office. Uneasy with the essential civil liberties of free expression and freedom of association, fearful of foreign subversion and intervention, untutored in the skills of nonviolent competition, and uncertain how to give up their power in limited stages over a short period of time, these established interests are likely to resist the development of a vigorous party politics. Hence their readiness to resort to violent and repressive tactics. Elites of this type fail to appreciate that their own security is likely to be better served over the long run by a truly pluralistic party politics in which civil liberties are actively protected. The institutional arrangements for such assurances should be the subject-matter of elite negotiations and constitutional transactions.

How to promote a vital pluralistic political party system is still a question of lively concern and debate among experts. The following generalizations are not offered as well-confirmed empirical truths. They simply display some of the issues usually involved in the institutional development of parties.

1. During the earliest period in which a people embarks upon nationhood, a single dominant party; that is, a one-party system, is often defended as essential for strengthening national unity, preventing competitive chaos, and otherwise guiding a politically inexperienced populace on to stable self-government. Experience shows that a dominant party tends to attract the best among the politically ambitious, leaving little talent, resources, or opportunity for the development of a substantial opposition capable of governing if elected. One strategy for creating or strengthening a pool of loyal opposition leaders is to promote the development of organized interest groups.

2. Should the party system be two-party or multiparty in structure? There is evidence that a two-party system encourages coalitional politics at the constituency level, the emergence of moderate leaders, a proliferation of interest groups, and greater clarity of popular mandates. Multiparty systems, for their part, allow direct participation in

government of all major ideological or policy interests, promote coalitions at the leadership level, tend to discourage the recruitment of new generations of party leaders, and introduce a large degree of ideological and policy rigidity into the nation's politics.

3. What form of first-election or nomination is best? An elaborate nominating system, as in the United States, reduces the number of candidates to be assessed by the electorate and encourages coalitions of group interests to take place within each of the parties. First-elections and runoff elections, as designed in France, tend to move coalition-formation from within the parties to negotiations between the parties, again giving party elites dominant control.

4. What suffrage standards should be established for the electorate? In the older democracies, early suffrages tended to be restrictive and slowly extended to new constituencies. In contemporary democracies, standards are much more inclusive regardless of popular experience or other criteria. Should modern suffrage requirements be phased in gradually or made all-inclusive immediately, despite the frequent absence of effective voter-mobilizing parties?

The greatest need is to inculcate competitiveness and stability in the party system. Policies favoring party development ought to be at the top of any national agenda of institutional development. The underlying objective is, of course, to traverse the critical transition and leave behind internal warfare as the recurrent method of elite competition.

Chapter 7

Regional Critical Transitions:
The European Case

Contemporary studies of political development usually employ the nation as the unit of comparison; for example, comparisons between advanced industrial nations and those less developed. Comparative studies of different levels of political community—tribes, cities, nations, regions, and world—are more difficult and more rarely found. Nevertheless, political structures and processes at the different levels are often comparable. A notable example is the insights for modern national and international politics that continue to be garnered from Plato and Aristotle's observations about the Greek city-states. This case report undertakes a comparison of institutional development in three national cases with developments in a continental region—Western Europe.

Is Western Europe experiencing a critical transition, as defined in this study? The institutional components for a critical transition are indeed present.

1. The modern phase of a trend toward military centralization began when the Western European Union was formed in 1948 and continued with the North Atlantic Treaty Organization established in 1949. The direction of the trend is evident in the recurring proposals for a distinct European Defense Community.

2. A contemporary representative institution for Western Europe began with the six-nation Common Assembly that later became a

twelve-nation European Parliament. The members of this Parliament are the first representatives to a supranational political institution who have been directly elected by the voters of member nations.

3. Although European transnational political party collaborations reach back into the nineteenth century, they have become enduring organizational entities since the 1950s. They include the European branches of the Christian Democratic International, the Socialist International, the Liberal International, the Conservative International, and, in a less organized way, the Eurocommunists and the Greens.

The Long History of Intra-Regional Warfare

Europe has had a long history of warfare. Its many peoples share a common past, originating in Greek and Roman civilization. The Greeks were energetic colonizers of Asia Minor to the east and the shores of the Mediterranean Sea to the west. The earliest European military alliance systems were the various leagues of Greek city-states. These leagues failed to stop the Romans in the second century B.C. Thus began the rise of the Roman Empire and, with it, the notion that Europe could be a single political community. The empire was also the avenue through which Greek culture and Christian religion made their way into Europe.

As noted earlier, at its height in the second century A.D., the Roman Empire had a military establishment capable of managing approximately three hundred thousand men under arms. As the Roman legions conquered places remote from the center of Rome, they came in contact with growing numbers of Germanic tribes in central Europe. These tribes were migrating south and east in search of land to cultivate. What began as a symbiotic accommodation between Roman and Germanic settlers ended with the defeat of Rome and the rise of numerous Germanic kingdoms during the fifth and sixth centuries.

Christianity became the official religion of the empire during the fourth century. The papacy gained special political status and eventually became, for all practical purposes, the ruler of the city of Rome. For the next four hundred years the church served as the preeminent religious, cultural, educational, and political force in Europe, giving that continent whatever sense of community it had.

The period known as the Dark Ages in Western Europe extended from the middle of the fifth to the middle of the eighth century. It was marked by contests among petty kings and efforts to consolidate kingdoms. Of particular political as well as religious importance were the proselytizing efforts of the church. When the Frankish king, Clovis, converted to the Catholic faith at the end of the fifth century (496), this was the act that sealed a major political transaction. It was also a turning point in the development of Europe. Clovis agreed to become the sole Catholic among the Germanic kings (incumbency), for which he received the active support of the church and the populations subject to Roman and Gallic rule (shares and commodities). This paved the way for the rise of the Carolingian dynasty and the imperial exploits of Charlemagne in the years from 742 to 814.

As the Roman Empire disintegrated in the west, its Byzantine eastern half flourished. However, dissension among Greek and eastern versions of Christianity proved to be a major weakness. During the sixth century, the Islamic prophet, Mohammed, united several Arab populations under his leadership, a movement that encompassed lands from Spain to western India by the end of the seventh century. This Arab empire became a threat to the Byzantine emperors and led to another transaction that profoundly affected the political evolution of Europe.

By the middle of the eighth century, the Merovingian kings who succeeded Clovis proved to be ineffectual, causing them to become dependent for royal policies upon the mayors, or heads, of their palace in Paris. At this time, too, the pope was beset by the invasions of the Teutonic Lombards from the north. In Constantinople, the Byzantine emperor was preoccupied with the defense of his lands against the militant Muslims. When the pope could get no military help from Constantinople, he turned to Paris. There, the palace mayor, Pepin the Short, agreed to intervene against the Lombards (commodities). Pepin's price was a papal promise to help depose the Merovingian king and to consecrate Pepin as the new king of the Franks (incumbency).

Once installed as king, Pepin recovered Byzantine territory lost to the Lombards. Then, without the approval of the Byzantine emperor, he gave the territory to the pope so that the latter could establish secular papal states. The papal chancery claimed that this transfer was legal under the Donation of Constantine, a document that was later discovered to be a forgery.

Pepin, meanwhile, proceeded to bring the Gallic nobility under his command and to drive the Muslims back across the Pyrenees. His son, Charlemagne, continued the process, conquering most of the Germanic and Slavonic tribes, the Lombard kingdom in Italy, and a portion of Spain. Thus, most of continental Europe came under Charlemagne's direct control. On Christmas Day 800, Pope Leo III crowned Charlemagne emperor of the Holy Roman Empire. For the next fifty years Europe came as close to being a single political community as was administratively feasible in that era.

Imperial disintegration followed Charlemagne's death (875). The breakup was caused in part by the practice of dividing inherited kingdoms among surviving sons and in part by Viking and Magyar invasions from the north and the east. The invaders were eventually turned back by Alfred the Great in England and Otto I, "the Great," in Germany. The nobility of western Europe were now free to arrange and rearrange, usually with violent tactics, their feudal relationships of lord and vassal in countless combinations and permutations.

By the twelfth century, the Holy Roman Empire and the papacy experienced a revival in organization and authority that lasted well into the thirteenth century. During this period, another centralizing tendency was in progress in the secular realm. In communities such as England, France, and Spain, kings were building modern nations and claiming to be supreme sovereigns in all areas of national life. Although economically debilitating, even the Hundred Years' War (1337–1453) strengthened the monarchies. The French kings taxed heavily and at will to maintain a standing army. The English kings' large military expenditures were constrained only by the need to win Parliament's approval, a requirement that strengthened the latter institution even more than the monarchy. In Spain, the Inquisition as well as a large army and navy enabled the monarchs to expel the Moors and the Jews, in the process of creating a powerful absolutist state.

When Pope Boniface VIII (1294–1303) forbade royal taxation of the clergy without the consent of the pope, the power of the papacy came into direct conflict with the growing influence of the kings. As the French and English kings soon demonstrated, the papal requirement could not be enforced by any pope. The mix of secular and church politics led to a decline in papal influence, the continued growth of strong national monarchies, and the emergence of Protestant movements.

Nationalist institutionalizing tendencies were pervasive in Europe during the sixteenth and seventeenth centuries. The monarchs of western Europe embarked upon grand empire-building enterprises at the same time that domestically they were organizing powerful administrative, judicial, financial, and military systems in their drive for national unity. Kings encouraged the development of new military technologies and sustained large standing armies of professional soldiers and mercenaries.

When kings established permanent embassies in each other's capitals, all of Europe became a turbulent political marketplace in which the monarchs were the principal transactors. They were joined in the marketplace from time to time by Catholic and Protestant religious leaders as well as a new breed, the international bankers who helped finance their wars, explorations, and trade. The political currencies of the era included marriage (incumbencies), military alliances (shares and commodities), territory (commodities), religious favors (currencies of all types), subventions and loans (commodities), and so on. The complexity and ferocity of inter-nation relations led one Dutch observer, Hugo Grotius, to prepare the first text on international law, *On the Law of War and Peace* (1625), whose precepts continue to provide basic rules for international transactions.

From the emergence of nation-states to the end of World War II, Europe's national leaders have never lacked motivation for carrying on wars against each other's nations: territory, empire, ethnicity, religion, personal ambition, obligations of an alliance, economic resources, and so on. In particular, the religious turmoil of the late sixteenth century led to the Thirty Years' War of the early seventeenth century (1618–48) during which the armies of Sweden and France devastated much of Germany. The negotiations that produced the Treaty of Westphalia (1648) established for the first time a European-wide charter with rules for peaceful settlement of disputes and collective sanctions against aggressors.

The treaty marked the abandonment of the feudal structure as well as the myth of a Holy Roman Empire. Instead, the treaty substituted a system of nation-states, each sovereign within its own territory, legally equal to one another internationally, and each free of any external earthly authority (Gross 1948, 42: 20–41). Russia and Turkey, each with territory in Europe, were subsequently brought into the system, which, for all practical purposes, became a military collaboration to maintain the monarchical status quo.

Lutheranism provided the theological assumption that God-given powers resided with secular rulers, and this assumption was eventually proclaimed as the doctrine of divine right of kings. European monarchs were pleased to adopt the doctrine and used it liberally to challenge the prerogatives of their parliaments and the church. An era of absolute monarchs ensued, accompanied by royal executive cabinets, growing bureaucracies, state intervention in economic enterprises (mercantilism), particularly those in colonial empires, the growth of diplomacy in interstate relations, the emergence of the balance-of-power principle in the maintenance of peace and security, and the development of professional officer corps in the royal military establishments. England, Austria, France, and Russia became the dominant powers in Europe up to the time of the American and French revolutions.

The American Revolution, with its guerrilla tactics and novel republican form of government, was a distant worry for a continent of absolute monarchs whose empires could easily become restless and whose military forces were for the most part unreliable. A more immediate and proximate threat was the French Revolution.

Congress System and the League of Nations

Revolutionary France, with its popular army replacing the mercenary, sought not only to expand its territory, but also to export its ideology in hope of creating a new Europe in its own image. After two million had died in the French revolutionary and Napoleonic Wars, a new conception of a United States of Europe was fashioned at the Congress of Vienna. The objective of the victorious powers—England, Austria, Prussia, and Russia—was to avoid war among themselves, yet maintain a collective influence in a new era of growing nationalism in places such as France, Germany, and Italy. The complex transactions at the Congress of Vienna returned most territories to their legitimate rulers, always with balance-of-power considerations in mind.

One outcome was the Concert of Europe and the establishment of the Congress System. Under this System, any European nation could initiate a call for a conference with the others. The Congress System handled some thirty conferences during the nineteenth century, mainly to settle conflicts over distant territorial possessions of the several empires. At the time of the Hague Conferences of 1899 and 1906, the Congress System reached beyond its European members to invite the United States and the countries of Latin America to participate.

The vision of a politically as well as diplomatically united Europe was entertained by several thinkers during the nineteenth century. Victor Hugo, for example, wrote in 1849 of a day "when cannon balls and bombs will be replaced by votes, by popular universal suffrage, by the real arbitration of a sovereign parliament which will be for Europe what the Commons are for England, what the Diet is for Germany, what the Legislative Assembly is for France" (Cross 1979, 20).

World War I ended the Congress System and installed another, the League of Nations. The Covenant of the League was a deliberate effort at institution-building. Its two "houses" had the appearance of a representative body: the Council to be made up of five permanent members (the United States, Great Britain, France, Italy, and Japan) and four others elected by the Assembly, it to consist of the approximately three score nation-states of the world at that time. The League was intended to be a world organization, but when the United States and the new regime of the Soviet Union failed to become members, the League became Europe-centered, dominated by England and France.

In many respects, the Covenant recorded an incomplete transaction. The League was global in concept, but regional in reality. It had some of the elements of a regional confederation, but lacked the key institutions of a political community. The representativeness of the Council and the Assembly was questionable. Collective security was contingent upon submission of disputes for settlement rather than automatic activation of any peacekeeping force. Other than the Marxist internationals, transnational political parties consisted of little more than an occasional international conference among leaders of like-minded national parties.

World War II brought a separation of regional from world institutional development. On the global side, the United Nations Organization was principally the creation of the major allies of the war, aspiring seriously to universal membership of all nations. European regional integration became a separate developmental process, one that has manifested all the attributes of a critical transition.

Regionalization of the European Military

An initial postwar development was the creation of a military alliance among the countries that twice bore the brunt of German assaults. In 1947, Great Britain and France signed a fifty-year security pact; namely, the Dunkirk Treaty of Alliance and Mutual Assistance. In 1948, Belgium, the Netherlands, and Luxembourg joined the British and the French to establish the Brussels Treaty Organization.

The Brussels Alliance provided that if any one of the parties should be the object of an armed attack in Europe, "the other . . . parties will, in accordance with the provisions of ARTICLE 51 of the Charter of the United Nations, afford the party so attacked all military and other aid and assistance in their power." This language was adopted in the founding of the North Atlantic Treaty Organization the following year. The Brussels Alliance also arranged for a single supreme command for its military forces, with headquarters in France. This was to facilitate peacetime military cooperation and was, in effect, a major step toward regional military centralization.

In February 1948, the Soviet Union perpetrated a coup in Czechoslovakia. In June of that same year, the Soviet Union set up a blockade of West Berlin. These events spurred cooperation in the West. In 1949, the Brussels Treaty Organization was, for all practical purposes, superseded by the North Atlantic Treaty Organization.

NATO included two non-European powers—the United States and Canada—and excluded West Germany. The other members of NATO were the three Benelux countries, Denmark, France, Iceland, Italy, Norway, Portugal, and Great Britain. The only organization prescribed by the treaty was a council of all members, a defense committee, and any other subordinate bodies deemed necessary. It was not until General Dwight D. Eisenhower was appointed the first Supreme Allied Commander in Europe in 1951 that NATO's organizational life began in earnest. In 1952, Greece and Turkey joined, strengthening the southeastern rim of the alliance.

The question of West Germany's role in the defense system of Western Europe elicited much debate and several proposals. By 1951, during a period when the idea of a United Europe was popular, one proposal was to create a separate European Defense Community (EDC) with an integrated armed force of fifty divisions under a federal government. This federal entity would provide the political structure within which West Germany could rearm without becoming the threat it had been in the two world wars. The proposal was shelved because of French unwillingness to incorporate its military forces into any system that could possibly be dominated by the Germans. The European Defense Community concept persists, however, in many European quarters, in anticipation of a time when Europe will have to pursue a distinctively regional foreign and defense policy.

Following France's rejection of EDC in 1954–55, the British proposed reactivation and enlargement of the five-nation Brussels Alliance as a military framework for including the West Germans and the Italians. On May 5, 1955, NATO agreed to allow West Germany to rearm itself within certain limitations. The following day, May 6, the Brussels Treaty Organization became the Western European Union (WEU), with West Germany and Italy as its new members.

WEU dedicated itself to the progressive integration of Europe. It set standards for member military contributions to NATO, including the maintenance of British forces on the Continental mainland and West Germany's promise to refrain from manufacturing atomic, chemical, biological, and certain other types of weapons. WEU's founding was followed, within the month, by a Soviet response: the creation of the Warsaw Treaty Organization composed of the Soviet Union and its East European satellites.

Although NATO began as an alliance of sovereign nations with fifteen independent military forces, it soon developed an organizational structure that gradually advanced regional military coordination and centralization. NATO's Council consists of ministers from all member countries, and it is chaired by the Secretary-General of NATO. The Council presidency is rotated alphabetically among the members. The chiefs of staff of each country make up a Military Committee. There is a Supreme Allied Commander in Europe (SACEUR) and a Supreme Headquarters-Allied Powers in Europe (SHAPE). When General Eisenhower activated SHAPE in January 1951, NATO had twelve divisions, about four hundred planes, and some four hundred ships under his command. Over the next three decades NATO grew to be the most powerful military establishment in the world.

Whether as NATO or as a prospective European Defense Community, Western Europe's military regionalization is clearly an advanced and irreversible development. Despite occasional minor military skirmishes between some of its members; for example, the Turkish-Greek and British-Icelandic encounters, it is unlikely that major war will break out again among its fifteen members. The same forecast cannot be made with equal confidence regarding potential future wars between Western and Eastern Europe, although post-Gorbachev perestroika in several East European nations dramatically diminishes the chances of armed conflict.

Further reasons for assurances about Western Europe exist, particularly the development of the two other institutions that comprise a critical transition; namely, the European Parliament as the region's institution of representation and a European transnational party system.

Representation of Europe's Electorate

Europeans have long been familiar with various systems of representation. The early church not only constituted its College of Cardinals as a representative assembly, but also devoted attention to the formulation of principles of representation. The thousand-year evolution of the English Parliament from a body representing classes to one representing communities and voters is an important part of the European experience. Even the autocratic kings of France had their estates-general.

As an all-Europe consultative body, the Congress System of the nineteenth century was comprehensive in its representation of the most influential powers. A successor system of representation was the League of Nations, a first attempt to establish a bicameral supranational body. Although the League provided the model for the more universal United Nations, it is perhaps accurate to say that the more direct descendant of the League is the European Community.

The post-World War II development of Europe's representative institutions has proceeded concurrently with the development of its centralizing military institutions. Three principal representative bodies have emerged: the Assembly of the Western European Union, the Parliamentary Assembly of the Council of Europe, and the European Parliament of the European Community.

Western European Union. The seven-nation Western European Union consists of a Council of the foreign ministers of its members and an eighty-nine-member consultative Assembly. The Assembly meets in two sessions each year, sets its own agenda, offers recommendations to the Council, and concerns itself primarily with the security needs and resources of Western Europe. Its reports are considered highly authoritative. WEU has remained primarily a European military alliance apart from the more all-embracing NATO. The consultative Assembly is the most likely originator of future proposals for a European Defense Community.

Council of Europe. The Council of Europe and its Parliamentary Assembly have a different origin. In 1946, Winston Churchill proposed a "United States of Europe." Several international movements joined to support the proposal. The five members of the Brussels Treaty Organization provided a forum for negotiations leading to a Statute of the Council of Europe, signed on May 5, 1949, by ten European nations. The council has grown to twenty-one member states. Its principal purpose is to promote European unity and development and to uphold the principles of parliamentary democracy, the rule of law, and human rights. Military matters are deliberately outside the scope of its concerns.

The council's structure includes a Committee of Ministers from all member states and a Parliamentary Assembly of 170 delegates. The members of the assembly are also members of their national parliaments, representing both the government and the opposition. Membership is apportioned according to population, with national delegations ranging in number from two to eighteen. The council and the assembly are served by a large staff. The Council of Europe has had its most significant influence in the areas of human rights, the law of the sea, and the promotion of democracy (Secretariat, Council of Europe 1969).

European Community. The most prominent agency of West European integration is the European Community (EC). EC grew out of the merger of the European Coal and Steel Community (ECSC), the European Economic Community (EEC, or Common Market), and the European Atomic Energy Community (Euratom). The organization consists of twelve member nations. All members are represented on its Council of Ministers and in its 518-member European Parliament. The third organ of EC is a European Court of Justice.

At the end of World War II, encountering intense nationalism, the proponents of a united Europe, led by Jean Monnet, Robert Schuman, and Paul-Henri Spaak, soon abandoned hope for early political union. Instead, they directed their efforts toward the more feasible and urgent cooperation needed for Europe's economic recovery. Thus, their strategy emerged to build a European representative assembly gradually and indirectly.

This approach led to the founding of the European Coal and Steel Community (ECSC) in April 1951, with a Council of Ministers, an executive High Authority (or Commission), an Assembly, and a Court of Justice. The ECSC Assembly was made up of seventy-eight members drawn in fixed proportions from the national legislatures of the original six member countries: France, Italy, West Germany, Belgium, the Netherlands, and Luxembourg. The British demurred, still firmly attached to their Commonwealth and American connections.

ECSC was a significant step toward a more integrated regional political system. The delegates to ECSC's Assembly were at first drawn from the elected membership of their respective national parliaments. Each parliament was free to follow its own rules for selecting an ECSC delegation. The usual practice was to compose the delegation in proportion to the political party representation in the home parliament. Paul-Henri Spaak presided over the first Assembly where the outlines of future institutions were thoughtfully discussed. Transnational party collaborations were recognized by the formation of staffed party groups, or caucuses, within the assembly.

Institutionalization took a major leap forward with the signing of the Treaty of Rome in 1957. The treaty called for the establishment of two additional communities: the European Economic Community, popularly known as the Common Market, and the European Atomic Energy Community, both within the framework of the established ECSC institutions. The commission was the high authority that formulated and implemented policies approved by the council. The assembly was advisory to the executive. The Court of Justice interpreted relevant treaties. In 1958, the assembly was enlarged to 142 members and renamed the European Parliament. It was enlarged further in 1973 when Denmark, Ireland, and Great Britain joined (Scalingi 1980).

The 198 members of the European Parliament met alternately in Strasbourg, France, and Luxembourg City. Representation was apportioned as follows: thirty-six delegates each to France, West Germany, Italy, and the United Kingdom; fourteen each to Belgium and the Netherlands; ten each to Denmark and Ireland; and six to Luxembourg. Delegates were selected by each nation as they had been for the first ECSC Assembly. Interest in serving in the European Parliament increased substantially during the 1970s despite the burden of double duty required by the national and the European bodies.

Negotiators of the Treaty of Rome were aware of the weaknesses of the ECSC institutions that were to govern the three organizations: ECSC, EEC, and Euratom. The Assembly (later the European Parliament) possessed no legislative powers and was almost exclusively advisory. Participation was a part-time job for its delegates. The assembly could not name or approve a new executive commission, but it could dismiss the commission, a power it never exercised. Nevertheless, with an eye to the integrating effects of popular sovereignty, the authors of the Treaty of Rome made certain to keep a provision of the original ECSC treaty calling for proposals for elections of delegates to the assembly by direct universal suffrage pursuant to a uniform procedure in all member states.

No deadline was set for receiving the proposals. Draft proposals were first offered in 1960 but under French pressure were tabled until 1974. One problem involved reconciling the British single-member district with the multimember districts employed on the Continent. In the end, each country was permitted to arrange its own district structure. The problem of dual membership of representatives in both a national legislature and in the European Parliament was left for each country to resolve. The negotiations concluded with the signing of the European Elections Act in Brussels on September 20, 1976. At the same time, the membership of the European Parliament was increased from 198 to 410, further enlarged to 434 in 1981 with the admission of Greece.

In June 1979, the first direct elections to the European Parliament took place. The voters of France, Great Britain, Italy and West Germany elected eighty representatives each; delegations from the Netherlands, Belgium, Denmark, Ireland, and Luxembourg ranged from six to twenty-five; and, later, the Greeks sent twenty-four. The elections were historic principally as the first direct popular delegation of a supranational parliamentary body. Particularly significant was the role of transnational parties in the campaign, in the returns, and in the party groups in the Parliament.

In June 1984, a second direct election took place, with only 60 percent of the eligible voters participating, about two or three percent lower than the turnout in 1979. The European press, accustomed to high voter turnouts, viewed this as a serious reflection on the declining popularity of the European Community. Americans, accustomed to 50 percent election turnouts for members of Congress, even in high-interest presidential elections years, considered the European figure quite respectable.

In the period between the first two elections, the European Parliament began to set precedents for the long term. For the first time, a Common Market budget proposed by the Council of Ministers was rejected, compelling six months of further financial negotiations on what had been a pro forma approval process. Perhaps as important was the Parliament's new interest in the coordination of foreign policies of its member nations, with the intention of converting the community into a single, unified actor in world affairs and a match for the superpowers.

As John Fitzmaurice observed in 1975,

> In many ways the European Parliament today has the character of the eighteenth-century House of Commons: it is an emergent entity. It is not, as the Commons was then not, the unequivocal focus of political life; influence and power lay elsewhere; men making political careers did not need to choose that route any more than today a political career can be made exclusively in the European Parliament.... [However,] compared with the centuries-long evolution of national parliaments the development of the European Parliament has been rapid. Within the short span of less than twenty years a parliamentary ethos has been evolved, synthesized out of first six then nine national parliamentary traditions; party groups, albeit weak, have been formed and the powers of the Parliament have already been considerably extended beyond those laid down in the original treaties (1975, 205).

The European Parliament, according to Fitzmaurice, has been "a pressure group for [European] integration" (1975, 17).

Europe's Transnational Party System

A European party system has been gestating for well over a century. This is the third of the political institutions that participate in critical transitions. In this case, the political parties are transnational, including principally the Communist, Socialist, Christian Democratic, Liberal, and Conservative internationals (Goldman 1983).

A transnational party is an organization composed primarily of national political parties cooperating with each other across national boundaries. Transnationals are formal in that they have officers, headquarters, members, and other elements typical of all organizations. Transnational parties operate overtly and may be formally recognized by public bodies such as the United Nations or the European Parliament. Like all political parties, transnationals seek to place their leaders into governmental offices, whether national or supranational.

The Marxist internationals are the oldest of the transnational parties. When Karl Marx and Frederick Engels joined the International Working Men's Association in 1864, that association came to be known as the First International. It consisted mainly of British and French trade-union leaders promoting unionism (illegal in many countries) and working-class political action. Although successful in advancing trade unionism and partisan affiliation in several countries, the First International was disbanded in 1877 as a consequence of factional strife between the trade-union Marxists and the Bakunin anarchists.

In 1889, the Second, or Socialist, International was organized by a number of Marxist revolutionary groups, trade unions, and reformist political parties. This was an unlikely coalition, ranging from the British Labour party (with a parliamentary, unionist orientation) to the Russian Socialist-Revolutionary party (with its emphasis on violent overthrow of regimes). The Second International conducted nine international congresses, some with nearly 900 delegates from twenty-three nations. This international foundered on the issue of preventing capitalist states from starting wars and discontinued meeting at the outbreak of World War I. The occasion was an opportunity for Lenin to call for a revolutionary movement that could emphasize the "dictatorship of the proletariat" as the vanguard of change. The Bolshevik Revolution in Russia in 1917 established the first Communist-controlled government.

The first congress of the Third International was held in Moscow in March, 1919. Known as the Comintern (Communist International), it was attended by nine bona fide Communist parties from Eastern and Central Europe as well as by Swedish, Norwegian, and Italian Socialists; there were delegates from thirty countries in all. The organization of the Comintern included its Congress, Executive Committee, and Presidium, with a Political Secretariat and associated bureaucracy in Moscow. A newspaper, *Communist International,* was established, and many country and auxiliary organizations proliferated. Before his death in 1924, Lenin proclaimed England and Germany as the targets for the next revolutionary efforts.

Lenin's demise led to factional struggles, mainly among the Russian leaders, that rent the movement. Stalin's group first overcame the Trotsky-Zinoviev bloc, then Bukharin, and finally the anti-Stalinist leaders in the national parties elsewhere. When he came to power in 1928, Stalin postponed the goal of world revolution and dedicated the Soviet Union to the task of "socialism in one country." Nevertheless, the Comintern, which was almost entirely a European organization, continued its work with national parties and with its principal auxiliaries: the Communist Youth International, the Red International of Labor Unions, and the International Peasant's Council. The international movement made substantial progress in France, Italy, and several states of Eastern Europe.

When Hitler invaded the Soviet Union in 1941, the United States and its allies sent the Russians lend-lease and other aid. The Allies at the same time demanded that the subversive activities of the Comintern be discontinued. In 1943, Stalin agreed to dissolve the Comintern. In 1947, however (at the end of World War II), a Communist Information Bureau (Cominform) was established by representatives of six East European Communist parties and three from the West (France, Italy, and Czechoslovakia). The Cominform's tasks were to coordinate the activities of Europe's Marxist parties. The Cominform lasted until

1956. More recently, although lacking formal organization, European Communists, mainly the Italian and the French parties, have been described as Eurocommunists, often pursuing policies independently of those of the Soviet Union, but just as often following courses of action independent of each other. As a consequence of developments in the Soviet Union and Eastern Europe during 1989, European Communists have not only lost electoral support but have also drastically reorganized themselves, even to the point of changing party names.

Europe's other major transnational political party movements have been the Socialist International, the Christian Democratic International, and the Liberal International, and, most recently, the environmentalist Greens. The Socialist International was inaugurated in 1922, but floundered until the end of World War II. A series of conferences begun in 1945 led to the establishment of the International Socialist Conference in 1951. Some thirty-four Socialist, Social Democratic, and Labor parties from different regions of the world joined. Ardently anticommunist and antifascist at first, the Socialist International modified its attitudes toward the Communists during the mid-1970s as a feature of the European detente strategy of its president, Willy Brandt, former chancellor of West Germany. Socialists have since taken a hardline attitude toward Communists in Europe but a united-front approach in many parts of the third world. The revolutionary events in Eastern Europe during 1989 have apparently been a mixed blessing for Socialists, who have gained some electoral support from many former Communists but also bear the onus of popular rejection of former Communist regimes.

Christian Democracy has had an international reach since the early nineteenth century, particularly in Europe and Latin America. Originally tied closely to Catholic doctrine and interests, Christian Democrats became increasingly secular in the years following World War II. In 1947, European Christian Democrats organized themselves transnationally as the *Nouvelles Equipes Internationales,* changing that name to European Union of Christian Democrats in 1965. In 1950, exile organizations from Yugoslavia, Czechoslovakia, Lithuania, Latvia, Poland, and Hungary organized themselves as the Christian Democratic Union of Central Europe. The Christian Democratic World Union, that is, the worldwide transnational, was founded in 1961. During 1989, West European Christian Democrats were active in providing campaign and other support transnationally to their colleagues in Eastern Europe.

Liberals were among the principal party organizers of the nineteenth century, often referred to as the Liberal Century. By 1910, Liberal leaders from several countries began to meet regularly to explore the prospects for transnational cooperation. In 1924, Liberals formed the *Entente International des Partis Radicaux et des Partis Democratiques*; parties from eleven countries joined in a matter of months. The Liberals were among the first to feel the whip of fascism and did not resume their international efforts until the end of World War II. In 1947, Liberals from nineteen countries, mainly European, signed a manifesto creating the Liberal International. As in the case of the other transnational parties, the Liberal International was deeply involved in the East European developments of 1989.

Although their global activities expanded substantially after the 1950s, the four transnational parties remained predominantly Eurocentric for most of the next quarter century. Non-Europeans, particularly North Americans, viewed the transnationals as strictly a "European phenomenon."

In the European Parliament, the transnational collaborations were formalized as party groups; that is, official caucuses of like-minded party members from the different countries of Europe. The first evidence of a full-blown party *system* in Europe came in the elections of representatives to the European Parliament in 1979, and again in 1984 and 1989. These Europe-wide elections also meant Europe-wide party campaigns.

The Socialists founded the Confederation of Socialist Parties of the European Community in anticipation of the elections. Most European Christian Democratic parties came together as the European Peoples party (EPP), which permitted them to include parties outside the formal membership of the European Christian Democratic Union. A Liberal federation promoted the cause of Liberal candidates. Conservative parties, including some Christian Democrats, came together as the European Democrat Union (EDU). In the light of differences between the Italian and French parties, Eurocommunists failed to cooperate substantially in the campaign.

The strength in seats held by the party groups in the European Parliament was relatively stable during the twenty years before the 1979 elections: between 33 and 44 percent Christian Democrats, about 25 percent Socialists, 10 to 20 percent Liberals, 10 percent Conservatives and Gaullists, and a few unaffiliated members. The 1979, 1984, and 1989 elections resulted in the distribution of seats given in table 7.1. The three elections again confirmed the stability of the European transnational party system.

European Critical Transition in Midpassage

To repeat, a critical transition involves a shift in the relative influence of three institutions within a political community: the military establishment, the representative assembly, and the party system. The transition occurs as trends in the development of the three institutions reach a certain point of convergence. There must also be a concurrent willingness—voluntary or otherwise—on the part of competing elites to transact the necessary exchanges. Has a critical transition occurred

Table 7.1. *Transnational Party Alignment, European Parliament 1979–1989*

Party	1979	1984	1989*
Social Democrats	113	130	180
Christian Democrats	107	110	121
Conservatives	63	50	51
Communists	44	41	42
Liberals	40	31	50
Greens	0	20	30
Other	43	28	44
Total	410	410	518

*Unofficial returns

in the supranational region of Western Europe? The developments surveyed suggest that such a transition is in progress.

With respect to the centralization of Western Europe's military institutions, this has been achieved mainly through the agency of the North Atlantic Treaty Organization. NATO may not be as unified a military force as one finds in the national cases, but there is no question that the defense forces of NATO's sixteen members operate under a unified command, use standardized weaponry and equipment, and conduct training as for a single force. These conditions will be even more prevalent when Western Europe puts together its own European defense community.

NATO's members maintain their national military forces intact, comparable in some degree to the state militia in United States history or the provincial caudillos in the Mexican case. While NATO is not subject to the control of a single civilian European institution, it is under the supervision of the North Atlantic Council: nonelected civilian ministers from the member states. As a centralizing military institution in the West European region, NATO, however, does differ somewhat from similar military establishments in the three national cases. For example, NATO membership extends beyond Western Europe to North America; that is, "outsiders" belong to a predominantly regional organization.

It would not require much organizational change to achieve a single, centralized European military establishment, whether or not national military forces are merged. The Allied Command Europe, headed by a Supreme Allied Commander Europe (SACEUR), within the NATO military structure, could theoretically be transformed into the military command of a European Defense Community. The Assembly of the Western European Union and its knowledgeable military affairs committees are available to assume civilian authority within a European Defense Community. Finally, there is the European Parliament, a representative assembly, popularly chosen, with budgetary powers that are likely to grow with the years, as will the inevitable interest in the costs of maintaining defense forces for Western Europe. Its budgetary prerogatives are likely to provide a major motivation for the further involvement of the European Parliament in the regionalization of Europe's military establishment. In this connection, the Treaty of Rome assigns to the Council of Ministers the responsibility for coordinating the general fiscal and economic policies of the member states. The council and the executive commission together draft the Community's budget, which has been largely concerned with the costs of community administration, the European agricultural program, and income from the value-added tax. Final approval of the budget is the prerogative of the European Parliament.

In the history of most parliaments, this "purse strings" prerogative has been a principal instrument in the expansion of parliamentary powers. History also suggests that budget negotiations about the military needs of the community offer the best opportunity for exercising this power. The European Parliament has already, as we have noted, tried out its budgetary veto in a relatively mild way by rejecting the council's 1980 budget. The role of the Parliament in the budgetary process has since been greatly enhanced.

It is noteworthy that Western Europe has created not one but three regional representative institutions. Although there is little question that the popularly elected European Parliament is the principal of these, the Assembly of the Western European Union and the consultative Assembly of the Council of Europe cover different constituencies and different areas of European policy making. It may be a matter of time and political circumstance before these three representative institutions merge into one. Meanwhile, there can be no doubt that Western Europe's regional representative institutions have developed sufficiently to be part of a critical transition.

Nor can there be any doubt about the existence of a European party system. Although the parties are transnational in structure today, if a United States of Europe were founded tomorrow, very little change would be necessary to convert these transnationals into components of a "domestic" party system. The transnationals have campaigned not only for offices in a supranational body, the Parliament, but have also helped each other in their campaigns for their respective national offices. Most of the transnational parties have European headquarters

and party bureaucracies, and their interparty and intraparty programmatic debates are as complex and continuous as any in the world. All
that is lacking is the formality of a United States of Europe to provide
the familiar governmental structural context for a "normal national"
party system.

By juxtaposing the development of Europe's military, representative,
and party institutions, it seems reasonable to conclude that the European political community is far along the way to a regional critical
transition. In the foreseeable future, the European transnational parties
will continue to link popular sovereignty to the management of the
European Parliament. The Parliament is bound to exercise increasing
civilian authority over a European Defense Community, as soon as
one comes into being. This is a prospect that has been urged upon
the European Parliament by the Assembly of the Western European
Union since 1980 (Wood 1981, 36). When it happens, wars among
the members of the European Community will undoubtedly and per-
manently be matters of the historical past. This prospect may be complicated and delayed, but not prevented, by German reunification and
current efforts to bring some of the new democracies of Eastern Europe
into the European Community and NATO.

Europe as a Model for Other Regions

Assuming that the evidence for such forecasts is substantial, can the
European experience serve as a developmental model for other regions
of the world? Several regions have established organizations that seem
to have prima facie similarities to the European Community: the Or-
ganization of American States (OAS), the Organization of African
Unity (OAU), the defunct Association of Southeast Asian Nations
(ASEAN), the Arab League, and the Central American Democratic
Community. Without exception, each has a collective security problem
(Zacher 1979; Feld and Boyd 1980).

What is there about the development of the European Community
that could suggest strategies and policies by which these regional organizations may advance through a critical transition into an era of
peace, civilian supremacy over the military, regional political integra-

tion, and democracy? Could their critical transitions be traversed in something less than the millennia Europe required? Would strategies for regional critical transition be different from those employed for nations?

Military Centralization

Although members in each regional organization continue to engage each other in limited wars or are themselves experiencing civil war, certain security needs of entire regions require a measure of military collaboration and centralization. Regional security and peacekeeping are invariably significant international issues in the regions.

Every region seems to have had at least one disruptive member, a common enemy, or an unstable regime; for example, Nicaragua in Central America, South Africa in Africa, Libya in the Middle East, Cuba in Latin America. A NATO-type alliance system would permit cooperating nations in a region to develop a mutual security and peacekeeping force sufficient to constrain a disruptive member or discourage the aggressiveness of a common external enemy. Thus, in 1979, at the meeting of the Organization of African Unity, several countries expressed for the first time a need for a Pan-Africa security force to be supervised by an OAU Political Security Council.

Conceivably, if such regional security measures were endorsed by a major-power weapons supplier such as the United States or France, might this not help inaugurate regional military cooperation, particularly with respect to the development of sound rules for the use of the weapons supplied. Even if each nation kept its own military establishment intact, a distinct regional military force would require consultation, coordination, standardization, and shared costs; that is, a degree of cooperative effort that would ameliorate relationships and reduce the incidence of warfare. Assurances of mutual security are likely, in the long term, to overcome ideological and other sources of resistance to regional cooperation.

This type of military centralization would undoubtedly need a civilian representative assembly to organize and manage it.

Representative Institution

Proposals for the formation of regional parliaments will undoubtedly encounter diverse political circumstances. What could be relatively easy to arrange in, say, the Central American Democratic Community could be difficult in the Organization of African Unity. Whatever the regional problems, the experience in Europe and elsewhere suggests that regional parliamentary institutions are most likely to be developed initially along functional lines (Huntley 1980). Political development may then proceed in fairly identifiable phases: first, as a confederational parliament of sovereign nations; then, a federal parliament of mutually dependent states; and finally, a unitary and popularly elected representative assembly for the entire region.

At each phase, the architects of a regional system of representation will undoubtedly find their efforts accompanied by the development of transnational political parties in the region. In time, the parties will be the agencies for building and mobilizing a regional electorate able to choose its representatives (Goldman 1989). For some regions the process may require decades, for others generations.

As in the case of the European Parliament, a feature of growth common to most representative institutions is likely to emerge; namely, institutional chauvinism. Regional parliaments will want to assume prerogatives greater than those originally given them. This process we have already noted in the European Parliament's implementation of its new budgetary prerogatives. Representative assemblies that control purse strings eventually control the sword.

Party System

The major transnational parties have already made their presence felt in several regions. They are well established in Europe. Christian Democrats are influential transnationally in South America. The Socialists have a strong presence in Africa. The Communists have been everywhere. The development of regional transnational parties would undoubtedly be further stimulated by the creation of regional military establishments and regional representative assemblies.

Again, the European Community is a useful model (Huntley 1980). The transnational ties of national parties in Europe have been recognized by the establishment of party groups in the European Parliament, complete with legislative staffs and similar resources. The transnational parties themselves have organized regional bodies and headquarters. Party leaders in other regions can do no better than to examine the European experience and adopt what is most relevant to their own situations.

Chapter 8

Critical Transition at the Global Level

Are supranational institutional trends at the global level proceeding along the patterns found in the three national and the West European case studies? If the critical transition model applies, the world should presumably have transnational parties sharing control over a supranational civilian representative institution to which a world military institution would be accountable.

The Global Military Establishment

The planet sometimes seems to be a battlefield for more than 160 national defense and police forces, a few dozen insurgent armies engaged in civil wars, and scores of independent or state-supported terrorist groups. This impression comes from images conveyed by the media as well as from hard facts. Estimated total world expenditures for military programs reached $1 trillion a year in 1988. Sixty-four nations and more than 1 billion people were ruled by military governments in the same year. There was one soldier for every 240 inhabitants in the developing world. Developed nations were spending at the rate of 5 to 6 percent of their Gross National Product for military purposes (Sivard 1989). These and other data support the portrayal of the world as an overwhelmingly militarized place.

Two-Tier Military Centralization

The globalization of the world's military establishments has proceeded at two levels, or tiers: the nuclear and the nonnuclear or conventional.

The "upper" tier encompasses the nuclear superpowers and their associated military alliance systems: the North Atlantic Treaty Organization and the Warsaw Treaty Organization. The "lower" tier consists of a less clearly delineated profile that includes the relatively unarmed United Nations peacekeeping missions and the nonnuclear or conventional military establishments of middle-sized powers and less developed countries.

There has been great stability and predictability at the nuclear tier despite its balance-of-terror image. The two major military alliances, both under relatively coordinated commands, have been responsible for more than 82 percent of the world's military expenditures from 1960 to 1988, each side spending approximately equal amounts. In distant third rank is the People's Republic of China, which belongs to no alliance system and accounts for only about 4 percent of the world's military expenditures. The NATO and Warsaw Pact alliances employ about 20 percent each of the world's total military manpower; again, China ranks third. Ninety-nine percent of the world's 57,000 nuclear weapons are possessed by the two alliances; the remaining nuclear weapons are in the hands of Great Britain (600), China (350), and France (450). To the extent that military intelligence permits, each side maintains a precise tally of the other's weapons and their disposition.

Although each of the sixteen nations of NATO and the seven nations of the Warsaw Pact has its own military force and may use it independently of the others, superpower influence and alliance constraints make such action unlikely. Further, the massive balance of military power and weaponry, both nuclear and conventional, between the two superpowers and their alliance systems has been and is likely to continue to be a deterrent to large-scale military actions by either side. In fact, there is a growing body of expert opinion that believes the two armed camps are, for the most part, so equal and stable that major wars have become obsolete and strategic nuclear weapons useless for realistic military purposes (McNamara 1986; Mueller 1989).

Taken separately or together, NATO and the Warsaw Pact are manifestations of a trend toward the global centralization of the world's military institutions. The United States and the Soviet Union have in effect become a global military duopoly providing, as undisputed major transactors in world military affairs, substantial leadership, predictability, and stability in the military marketplace. Significantly, these military duopolists have transacted the greatest number of far-reaching arms control agreements in human history. Even a short list of these agreements is impressive.

1. The preventive treaties: Antarctic Treaty, Outer Space Treaty, Latin American Nuclear-Free Zone Treaty, Seabed Arms Control Treaty, and South Pacific Nuclear-Free Zone Treaty. These treaties agree to foreclose the militarization of specific regions of the planet.

2. The duopoly-maintaining treaties: SALT I, Limited Test Ban Treaty, Nuclear Nonproliferation Treaty, Threshold Test-Ban Treaty, Peaceful Nuclear-Explosions Treaty, SALT II, and INF Treaty. These treaties were intended to restrain vertical and horizontal proliferation of nuclear weapons and nuclear possessors.

3. The emergency communication treaties: "Hot Line" Agreement of 1963, "Hot Line" Modernization Agreement of 1971, 1971 Agreement on the Prevention of Accidental Nuclear War, 1973 Agreement on the Prevention of Nuclear War, and Nuclear Risk Reduction Centers Treaty. In these, the duopolists demonstrated a shared concern for preventing accidents and controlling emergencies.

4. Treaties and conferences on conventional arms: the Conference on Mutual and Balanced Force Reductions in Central Europe, the Conference on Security and Cooperation in Europe, and the Negotiation on Conventional Armed Forces in Europe. These have largely been efforts to disengage from some of the costly military aftermaths of World War II.

These treaties have involved an unprecedented number of transactions during a long series of negotiations about extremely complex military issues. They represent powerful but not complete dual control of the world's nuclear arsenal and they are a formidable achievement, too often discounted in a world mesmerized by the threat of nuclear holocaust.

A concomitant but less visible outcome has been institutionalization of the arms-control negotiation process—bilaterally between the duo-polists, multilaterally at the United Nations and in other forums. The nuclear tier had been internationalizing the security functions of national governments and supranational organizations, hostile rhetoric from the superpowers notwithstanding. Whether the nuclear duopoly continues or, as conceptualized by the Baruch Plan, becomes an internationalized monopoly, the nuclear tier is likely to remain the dominant and recurrent issue in transactions leading to arms-control agreements.

The duopolists, jointly or spurred on by others, will undoubtedly continue to spawn treaty organizations or regimes such as the International Atomic Energy Agency and, possibly, the United Nations Military Staff Committee (Goldman 1990). These international bureaucracies will increase both the interdependence of the duopolists' military establishments and the potential for being the nuclear tier's organizational core, thus furthering institutionalization or symbolic integration of the world's principal military systems. One sign of this trend is the practice inaugurated in 1988 of private conferences between senior U.S. and Soviet defense officials: at the civilian level, U.S. Secretary of Defense Frank C. Carlucci and Soviet Defense Minister Dmitri Yazov and, at the military level, Admiral William J. Crowe, Jr., chairman of the Joint Chiefs of Staff, and Soviet Marshal Sergei Akhromeyev.

At the lower, or conventional, tier other tendencies are observable elsewhere in the world's military establishment. Approximately 113 developing nations in the Middle East, Asia, and Africa are responsible for about 27 percent of global total military expenditures and employ about 62 percent of the world's military manpower. Among these are the countries whose weapons are most likely to be purchased from the superpowers, who are most likely to use arms for external aggression or internal repression, and who may be most inclined to train and employ terrorist groups as agents of sublimated warfare. Taken together, these countries are major sources of instability in world security affairs. Nevertheless, this conventional tier is also experiencing military globalization.

Whether for aggression, repression, rebellion, or the maintenance of domestic order, governmental and other political leaders of developing countries are arming themselves, often as clients of one or the other superpower. This militarization of third-world countries is usually one aspect of ongoing elite conflicts in civil wars, in international vendettas between neighboring countries, or in struggles for national independence from what is left of nineteenth century empires. As weapons and personnel are poured into these wars, arms races, and military buildups, the pace of global militarization appears to quicken.

The latter trend is most evident in connection with United Nations peacekeeping missions. According to one study, between 1945 when the United Nations was founded and 1974, there were approximately 400 cases of internation military conflict. The United Nations, as the world's principal third party in such conflicts, interceded in 120 cases. Despite its own fragility and lack of military resources, the United Nations succeeded in moving the parties toward resolution in a large number of cases (Butterworth 1978). Many of these instances required the use of lightly armed peacekeeping missions.

Written before the dropping of the first atom bomb on Hiroshima, the U.N. Charter contains impressive but yet-to-be-implemented provisions for an integrated world military institution (see chap. 7). These provisions assumed a nonnuclear world of conventional weapons and military forces (Fabian 1971; Goldman 1982).

Chapter 7 was written after more than two decades of diplomatic and academic discussion between world wars. It reflected the concept of international collective security. The authors of the Charter assigned responsibility to the U.N. Security Council to "determine the existence of any threat to the peace, breach of the pace, or act of aggression" and to decide what measures should be taken to maintain or restore peace and security (ARTICLE 39). It was a mandate for a world police force.

In view of the fact that the five Permanent Members of the Security Council—the United States, the Soviet Union, Great Britain, France, and, at that time, Nationalist China—were also the victors in World War II and, together, the most powerful military aggregation in the world, it was assumed that "outlaw" nations, when designated as such, would be dealt with militarily by the Big Five. In addition to this expectation, all member states were expected to hold national military units immediately available for combined international enforcement actions. What the authors of the Charter could not have anticipated was the arrival of the atomic age and an era of cold war, both within months of the founding of the United Nations. These developments made many of the Charter's security provisions obsolete even before the world organization met in its first session. There could be no collective security against possessors of the atomic bomb, nor could there be Big Five consensus during a cold war between two of its members.

In ARTICLES 46 and 47, the Charter established a Military Staff Committee (MSC) to assist the Security Council in making "plans for the application of armed forces." More specifically, MSC was to "advise and assist the Security Council on all questions relating to the Security Council's military requirements for maintenance of international peace and security, the employment and command of forces placed at its disposal, the regulation of armaments, and possible disarmament." MSC was to be composed of the chiefs of staff, or their representatives, of the armed forces of the five Permanent Members. MSC was no visionary proposal, but rather, part of an international treaty design for a comprehensive and operational world military organization, devoted not only to the management of military forces for keeping the peace, but also to control of world armaments. The charter's mandate, in large measure, continues to be unfulfilled.

MSC held its first meeting in London on February 4, 1946, to begin a study of the organizational implications of ARTICLE 43. In this article, member states were to make armed forces available to the Security Council "on its call and in accordance with a special agreement or agreements" prescribing numbers and types of forces, degrees of readiness, and general location. Representatives of the Big Five agreed that they would undoubtedly supply most of the national peacekeeping contingents called for under ARTICLE 43, in keeping with the concept of collective security. They completely disagreed, however, about the structure and composition of such forces. After fifteen months of wrangling, MSC presented a divided report consisting of forty-one articles to the Security Council on April 30, 1947 (Security Council 1947; Bowett 1964; Boyd 1971; Wainhouse 1973).

In August 1948, MCS held its last substantive meeting. Disagreement led to abandonment of further effort. Since 1948, MSC has conducted brief perfunctory meetings fortnightly as required by the rules of the Security Council. On a hopeful note, Secretary-General Trygve Lie described the Military Staff Committee "as a symbol of disappointed hopes which are not dead, but have been put aside for a better day" (Lie 1954).

The need for a United Nations military component never disappeared and has been met in a variety of ways, principally as U.N. peacekeeping missions. The first major missions included the U.N. Special Committee on the Balkans (UNSCOB), the Truce Supervision Organization in Palestine (UNTSO), the Commission for Indonesia (UNCI), and the Military Observer Group in India and Pakistan (UNMOGIP). These were primarily investigative and truce-monitoring missions rather than enforcement groups.

When the U.N.'s negotiator, Count Bernadotte, was assassinated in September 1948, Secretary-General Lie called upon the General Assembly to create a United Nations Guard to protect U.N. missions in the field. He proposed a permanent corps of three hundred men and a five-hundred-man reserve. The Guard would also supervise plebiscites and monitor neutral territory under truce agreements consummated by the parties.

Opposition to the proposed U.N. Guard was immediate and intense, particularly from the Soviet Union and its allies. The Soviet bloc viewed a permanent U.N. force as a threat to national sovereignty and a Western attempt to establish an international military coalition. In a minority statement issued on November 22, 1949, the Soviet Union, Poland, and Czechoslovakia agreed only to that part of the Lie proposal that would place on call a Panel of Field Observers. The United States, too, was skeptical about the precedents to be set by a permanent force, and the proposal was tabled.

In June 1950, seven months later, North Korean forces invaded the Republic of Korea, which had been recognized the previous December by the General Assembly as the lawful government of Korea. The Korean War that followed was the first and only serious attempt to practice collective security as conceptualized by the authors of the U.N. Charter; that is, as a policing function. With this in mind, President Truman referred to the war as a "police action" in which the forces of the United Nations (but mainly the United States) were engaged in enforcing the Charter provisions by bringing an outlaw nation (North Korea) to justice.

The fortuitous Soviet boycott of the Security Council just prior to the outbreak of hostilities enabled the Council to circumvent the Soviet Union's veto and invite all U.N. members to contribute military forces to a U.N. command in Korea, led by the United States. To avoid future Soviet vetoes in this and later cases, the General Assembly shortly thereafter adopted a Uniting for Peace Resolution in which the Assembly assumed responsibility for collective security in the event that the Security Council failed to act.

The Assembly proceeded as though it were a house in a bicameral legislature. Under the Uniting for Peace Resolution, the Assembly established a Collective Measures Committee (CMC) to study methods for maintaining and strengthening international peace and security. The Collective Measures Committee submitted three reports in which it set future guidelines for political, economic, financial, and military measures (General Assembly 1951–54).

Although the CMC did not intend to preempt the responsibilities of the Council's Military Staff Committee, it did review proposals that appropriately should have gone to the MSC. One proposal from the Secretary-General recommended creation of a United Nations Volunteer Reserve of fifty to sixty thousand troops, to be recruited and trained by national military commands, but available to serve on call under U.N. command.

Departing from the Charter's assumption that the Permanent Members would provide collective security forces, CMC recommended that as many states as possible, including the smaller ones, participate in chapter 7 collective military actions. This recommendation paved the way for the subsequent development of a "peacekeeping constituency" made up of middle-sized and small powers, such as Sweden, Norway, Denmark, and Austria, willing to provide special national contingents.

The Korean War's great cost in lives and wealth laid to rest the feasibility of collective enforcement in a world dominated by superpower rivalry. A different conception of international peacekeeping had to be developed. There could be no "aggressors" among equally sovereign nations. The United Nations could not be an enforcer. What it could do is serve as a third party in negotiation of agreements between adversary parties.

From this new concept followed notable military peacekeeping missions in the Middle East, Africa, the Mediterranean, and the Asian subcontinent. The United Nations Emergency Force (UNEF) supervised the cease-fire following the Anglo-French-Israeli invasion of Egypt in the 1956 Suez crisis. The U.N. Observation Group in Lebanon (UNOGIL) investigated Lebanese charges that Egypt, Syria, and Yemen were encouraging a rebellion in Lebanon. The U.N. Operation in the Congo (UNOC), militarily the largest and most difficult since the Korean War, tried to beak up a civil war that came in the wake of Belgium's withdrawal from a mandated territory. The U.N. Force in Cyprus (UNFICYP) maintained order between Greek and Turkish Cypriots, thereby preventing an outbreak of war between Greece and Turkey. A second U.N. Emergency Force in the Middle East monitored the truce that ended the 1967 Arab-Israeli war. There have been other military missions. Recent figures report that more than 10,000 soldiers from twenty-three countries have served in U.N. missions (Department of Public Information, United Nations 1985; Rikhye 1974).

Each mission further institutionalized in one way or another the U.N.'s peacekeeping and security functions. For example, the Uniting for Peace Resolution ended the Security Council's presumed monopoly of peacekeeping responsibilities, which was thereafter shared between the two bodies. In lieu of troops from the Permanent Members, a group of middle powers—Sweden, Norway, Denmark, Finland, Nigeria, and others—became the principal providers of peacekeeping personnel, creating special regiments and battalions for the purpose. The United States and Great Britain assumed responsibility as principal suppliers of equipment for peacemaking missions. The duties, tactics, and technology of peacekeeping grew appreciably. An associated International Peace Academy was created as a training center for the nonmilitary duties of officers of peacekeeping missions. In its third-party role, the United Nations learned how to offer good offices, conciliation, and mediation as well as military contingents.

The financing of peacekeeping missions has varied in procedure, resources, success, and controversiality. Funds have come in part from the states supplying the military contingents, although national costs are usually reimbursed by the United Nations; shortage of funds has led to U.N. delinquency in such payments. Some nations have made voluntary contributions. Some funds are derived from levies apportioned among the entire membership of the United Nations.

Since the mid-1960s, difficult financial issues have arisen in connection with peacekeeping missions. Some members, notably the Soviet Union and France, refused until recently to pay their shares on grounds that certain peacekeeping missions were not properly authorized. Although such nonpayers are supposed to be denied their assembly vote under ARTICLE 19, this rule has not been enforced. In February 1965, a Special Committee on Peacekeeping Operations— the Committee of Thirty-three—was appointed by the assembly to discuss the problem and has been doing so for more than two decades.

During the twenty-second session of the General Assembly in 1967, the discussions of the Committee of Thirty-three came close to the heart of the matter. Peacekeeping was a Security Council responsibility under the Charter. Therefore, at the committee's recommendation, Resolution 2308 was adopted by the Assembly. The resolution called upon the Military Staff Committee to reopen its consideration of substantive military issues. By 1969, U.S. negotiator S. M. Finger and Soviet representative L. I. Mendelevich were approaching agreement regarding the role of MSC in peacekeeping when talks collapsed because of superpower tensions in the Middle East. In March 1972, the superpowers submitted their next communications to the Secretary-

General regarding the future of the Military Staff Committee (Security Council 1972). There has been little movement since that time, although the Soviet Union has from time to time attempted to initiate reconsideration of MSC's status (Goldman 1990; Hiscocks 1973).

The only use of the Charter's provision for a military enforcement mechanism has therefore been the disastrous Korean War. The subsequent peacekeeping missions were based upon a different interpretation of the Charter. The Military Staff Committee has had no significant part in either of these approaches.

ARTICLE 47 assigns another function to the MSC; namely, regulation of armaments and, if possible, the achievement of disarmament. MSC has been completely circumvented in these matters. Other forums have been employed: a U.N. Atomic Energy Commission in 1946; a Security Council Commission on Conventional Armaments in 1947; a U.N. Disarmament Commission in 1952; a Ten-Nation Disarmament Committee in 1959–60; an Eighteen-Nation Disarmament Committee in 1962; the Conference of the Committee on Disarmament in 1969; the Conference on Security and Cooperation in Europe in 1973; the Conference on Mutual and Balanced Force Reductions in 1973; in 1978 and 1982, Special General Assembly Sessions on Disarmament, and other forums. This list does not include the almost continuous bilateral negotiations between the superpowers.

What have been the apparent reasons for avoiding activation of the Military Staff Committee? Among the reasons: to circumvent the veto power of permanent members; to avoid interfering with the direct negotiations between the superpowers; to allow regional arms-control issues, particularly those of Europe, to be handled by the nations in the affected region; to provide the entire U.N. membership several forums in which to articulate their views, and others.

Decisions regarding security and war are generally perceived as the ultimate manifestations of a nation's sovereignty. To share such decisions multinationally in bodies such as the United Nations Security Council or the Military Staff Committee is presumed to diminish sovereignty. It is difficult enough for allies to coordinate military-security policies. Cooperation on military issues is even more difficult between adversaries. Despite these prevailing views, during the 1960s, as noted earlier, both the United States and the Soviet Union proffered official disarmament proposals that envisioned the creation of a world military force with international policing functions; namely, the Soviet Union's "Draft Treaty on General and Complete Disarmament under Strict International Control" and the United States' "Outline of Basic Provisions of a Treaty on General and Complete Disarmament in a Peaceful World" (Department of Political and Security Affairs, United Nations 1970, apps. 2 and 3).

In addition to the reluctance to give up national sovereignty on matters of security, there are other considerations, some previously mentioned. The two-tier—nuclear and conventional—evolution of world military centralization proceeds along separate lines that are difficult to bring together. Collective enforcement has been tabled as an approach to collective security and replaced by the peacekeeping concept. Peacekeeping missions have been treated as ad hoc third-party interventions, rather than as an enforcement function of the Permanent Members. International arms-control policies have been made outside the United Nations. Whereas collective security was the prevailing concept at the founding of the United Nations, no other comprehensive concept has taken its place.

It is not unreasonable to consider these resistances, changes, and other difficulties as short-term impediments in a long-term trend toward globalization of military institutions. As the infant United Nations develops, the mandate for a single global-security establishment is likely to continue to be often reiterated and implemented in small increments.

A Supranational Representative Institution?

The United Nations has the structural framework of a supranational confederation with a bicameral legislature. As a kind of upper house, the Security Council has five permanent members and ten other nations elected by the General Assembly for two-year terms. The 159 nations in the General Assembly constitute a "lower house" with a near-universal membership. Sovereign nations are the voting members in these bodies. What the two chambers lack are the legislative legitimacy that could be provided by a popular electorate and an enforcement agency capable of giving its resolutions the weight of parliamentary law. In many respects, these circumstances are identical with those of the supranational European Parliament in its earlier years.

Confederation is a familiar organizing principle for bringing together independent states or other established political entities; for example, the American colonies under the Articles of Confederation and the European Community under the Treaty of Rome. In both examples, direct election of representatives by the eligible citizenry came in later reforms. Direct election of representatives to the U.N. General Assembly may seem improbable today, and in the short term undoubtedly is. The seeds of such an institutional evolution are already planted, however, and reforms similar to those just cited may be expected over the long term, specifically, the next three or four generations. This would follow the familiar pattern of political development in which independent states are carried into confederations, confederations are transformed into federal systems, and popular electorates become the ultimate integrating sovereigns of unitary political systems. The political parties that emerge in the representative assemblies at the confederal stage tend to be the principal force for mobilizing support for these integrative changes.

Transitions in the rules of representation, however, are not easily arranged. For example, the apportionment of voting power and the political functions assigned to representatives are always matters of fundamental contention. Determining which constituencies should be represented raises questions about the locus of effective power and the kinds of political conduct that may be demanded by the different constituencies. Comprehensive and effective systems of representation are necessarily the product of difficult negotiations and transactions.

Such issues of representation have already been proposed and debated at the United Nations. The nations that make the major financial contributions have complained about having the same single vote in the General Assembly as those that make none. The nations with populations in the hundreds of millions have argued the unfairness of having the same vote as those with tens of thousands. Weighting votes according to financial contribution or population has been considered. The military criterion that applied for permanent-member status in the Security Council has been called archaic for all practical purposes, particularly since most of the actions promotive of U.N. institutional development are supported by the small states rather than the permanent members. Proposals for a popularly elected third house have been made.

For the present, the General Assembly is admittedly little more than a resolution-passing body of national delegates, essentially advisory in character and consequence. So, too, were the English Parliament, the Mexican cabinet, the Continental Congress of the United States, and the European Parliament. On the evidence of these few but important cases, it becomes entirely conceivable that a representative organ of the United Nations with real legislative powers may some day be composed of popularly elected representatives. Such a prospect becomes even more conceivable and politically feasible if transnational political parties gain influence enough to promote, as parties usually do, the process of legislative institutionalization. Already the General Assembly has arrogated functions to itself, such as peacekeeping, which were not assigned to it in the Charter. Furthermore, its near-universal membership will be comprehensive enough to represent all major constituencies in the world, as all effective representative institutions must.

A Transnational Party System?

The origins of European transnational political parties were examined in the previous chapter in connection with the development of a supranational, regional, party system. By the 1960s and 1970s, transnational party development reached well beyond Europe into all regions of the world. It is a semantic issue whether the present array of transnational parties constitutes a "world party system." From the perspective of the critical transition model, the current state of global transnational party development is comparable to the stage of party development of seventeenth- and eighteenth-century England; that is, parties that are modestly organized, lacking a substantial electorate, but capable of influencing the processes of governance, particularly in its legislative aspects. Since transnational party development had much of its beginning in Europe, some review of the European story may be necessary in describing global developments.

As noted in the previous chapter, political parties become transnational when they develop supranational organizations that cooperate in a variety of ways across national boundaries. Transnationals meet several of the definitional requirements for being classified as political parties: formality (officers, central headquarters, etc.), overtness, program, and the like. A major difference is that the membership of most transnational parties consists not of individuals but principally of national parties and national and international observer groups. Only occasionally will individual persons hold membership in the major transnationals.

Marxists. The oldest and best known of the transnational parties have been the Communist and Socialist internationals, as noted earlier. The First International existed from 1864 to 1877. In 1889, the Socialist Worker's (Second) International was formed. In connection with the Bolshevik Revolution of 1917 in Russia, Lenin founded the Third International, that is, the Communist International, or the Comintern.

The founding congress of the Comintern convened in Moscow in March 1919, where the Communist Party of the Soviet Union became the world organizing center for the new transnational party. The Bolsheviks declared themselves the vanguard of a movement that would overthrow capitalist regimes and eventually establish a Communist world order. The Comintern program declared its readiness to use subversion, espionage, united fronts, and other Marxist-Leninist tactics in the pursuit of these objectives.

Shortly after World War I, and again in the United States during the McCarthy era of the early 1950s, the worldwide campaign of the Comintern generated "Red scares" that made anticommunism and anti-Soviet policy significant issues in the domestic politics in many countries. Meanwhile, the Soviet leadership under Joseph Stalin ostensibly set aside the goal of world revolution in order to establish Communist control more firmly in the Soviet Union; that is, pursue the goal of "socialism in one country." The Comintern was officially disbanded in 1943 at the request of the World War II Allies. However, for some years, beginning in 1947, a Communist Information Bureau (Cominform) functioned as a coordinating body for Communist parties in nine countries of Europe.

Subsequent to the 1940s, there has been no formally organized Communist international. In its stead there has been the International Department of the Communist Party of the Soviet Union (CPSU). To promote the growth of the international Communist movement and to monitor its polycentrism, the CPSU maintained a large International Department, with country and regional desks for most of the countries in the world. Moscow has also given particular support to the World Peace Council, its principal front organization. Both of these organizations have served as the vehicles for Communist transnational operations.

Since the late 1940s, the world Communist movement has experienced fluctuating fortunes. Tito of Yugoslavia was expelled from the Cominform in 1948 for advocating "separate roads" to socialism. A decade later a breach between the Soviet and Chinese parties initiated an era of Sino-Soviet hostility whose repair was undertaken at the beginning of the Gorbachev era. In 1956, the Cominform was disbanded. Popular uprisings occurred in Poland and Hungary, but failed to dislodge the Marxist rulers. In 1957, the Soviet Union made an unsuccessful attempt to reestablish the Comintern or some equivalent. By 1960, Maoism became a major force in the third world. During the mid-1970s, Eurocommunists in Italy and France began distancing themselves from Moscow-centered policies. In 1990, Communist parties in both Eastern and Western Europe were changing their names in an effort to symbolize a departure from their Communist past.

Despite the absence of an explicit supranational secretariat, the transnational character of the Communist movement continues, supplemented by various forms of direct Soviet military, economic, and political aid. A network of Soviet-recognized Communist parties conduct periodic international conferences; more than seventy-one full-member national parties are in this group. There are, as of this writing, some twenty to thirty national parties in the category of "revolutionary democratic parties," of which six or seven are, in the Soviet classification system, "vanguard revolutionary democratic parties." The Nicaraguan Sandinistas, for example, have been one of the latter group.

By recent count, there were Communist parties in ninety-six countries, with a claimed party membership of ninety million. The largest memberships, as of 1987, were in the People's Republic of China (44,000,000), the Soviet Union (18,500,000), and Romania (3,557,000), followed by North Korea, East Germany, Yugoslavia, Poland, Czechoslovakia, Italy, and Bulgaria. Their variety—Titoists, Maoists, Trotskyites, Eurocommunists, and so on—is testimony to the factionalism that exists in the world Communist movement.

Socialists. Although the current Socialist International regards itself as the direct successor of the Second International, a wholly new organization was inaugurated after the Second World War. Specifically, on March 5, 1945, at the invitation of the British Labor Party, the First Conference of Social Democratic Parties, with thirteen parties represented, gathered in London for the purpose of planning a new international. By 1951, the new Socialist International came into being.

As of 1988, the Socialist International claimed a membership of forty-nine national parties, eighteen consultative parties, three fraternal organizations (for example, the International Union of Socialist Youth), and eight associated organizations. There are fourteen full-member Socialist parties in Western Europe, another eleven in Latin America, five in Asia, three in the Middle East, eleven in Africa, and three in North America. There are regional associations of Socialist parties in Europe, Asia, and Africa. World headquarters are in London.

In the early years of this revival (1951–76), a major goal of Socialist parties was containment of the spread of communism. Historically, most social democrats and laborites have advocated nonviolent change within the context of parliamentary systems. They have been staunch in their opposition to totalitarian political methods. Some Socialists have from time to time engaged in collaborations and "united fronts" with all fellow-Marxists, on the dubious assumption that governmental power could be shared and that shared power might even serve as a moderating force among the more revolutionary factions. This expectation is poorly supported by historical evidence and continues to be a matter of debate among Socialists.

In 1969, under the leadership of Chancellor Willy Brandt, West Germany adopted an *Ostpolitik* strategy of rapprochement with the Soviet Union and Eastern Europe. This softened the anticommunist stance in the international arena of West German Socialists, perhaps the most influential on the Continent, although the party's anticommunist line in West German domestic affairs remained undiminished. The strategy was carried over by Brandt into his presidency of the Socialist International in the 1970s. During that decade and more recently, there has prevailed a kind of detente between Socialists and Communists. While the Socialist International has favored firmness in dealings with Eurocommunists, it has been willing to engage in united fronts with Communists in the third world.

Christian Democrats. Christian democracy emerged in the nineteenth century as an antagonist of the dominant ideology of liberalism. Christian Democrats also opposed the centralizing tendencies of nineteenth-century nation-states. The movement was devoted to its Catholic theological origins and was active mainly in local politics. During the early years of the twentieth century, as Christian Democrats gained stature and national office in several European countries, significant changes began to appear in the orientation of their programs. This was particularly true after the Second World War when these parties began to be elected to office throughout Europe, gained influence in Latin America, and turned their attention to transnational organization.

First efforts at international Christian Democratic cooperation were initiated by Don Luigi Sturzo in 1919 shortly after the founding of the Italian People's party. The First International Congress of Peoples' Parties was held in Paris in December 1925. Successive congresses were held during the 1920s and 1930s, but without the benefit of effective transnational organization.

In 1936, Don Sturzo once again took up his campaign to create a transnational Christian Democratic party. By 1940, an International Democratic Union was organized, including many European governments-in-exile. In July 1947 was established the International Union of Christian Democrats. Principal headquarters have been in Rome and Brussels.

Today, Christian Democrats have a World Union and three regional organizations, the latter in Western Europe, Central Europe, and the Americas. Of the fifty-six member parties, twenty-two belong also to the Christian Democratic Organization of America, which was founded in July 1949. Some Christian Democratic parties are much more conservative than others; these are often informally associated with the later founded conservative International Democrat Union.

Liberals. Liberals were the major ideological force in Europe during the nineteenth century. Their parties were particularly representative of commercial and industrial interests. International conferences of Liberals made their first appearance in 1910. Not until 1947 did Liberals take serious steps toward transnational organization. On April 14, 1947, representatives of nineteen liberal parties and groups, mainly European, signed the Liberal Manifesto in Oxford, England, which became the basic document of the World Liberal Union, or Liberal International. Headquarters were established in London.

The International remained principally European in membership and policy concerns until the Canadian Liberal party joined in the early 1970s. Thereafter, the leadership of the Liberal International began to focus on issues with global rather than Eurocentric scope and to reach out to organized liberals on other continents.

Nineteenth-century ideological doctrines were modernized by the Declaration of Oxford in 1967 and the Liberal Appeal of 1981. Growth in the number of member parties has been slow, often handicapped by the minority status of Liberal parties in many countries. The National Democratic Institute for International Affairs, an auxiliary of the Democratic party of the United States, recently joined in Observer Membership status; this was seen as a triumph for the Liberal International's outreach program.

Conservatives. The International Democrat Union is a recent outgrowth of the European Democrat Union. Leading members of the latter are the British Conservative and the West German Christian Democratic parties.

In 1982, the officers of the West German Konrad Adenauer Foundation invited United States Vice-President George Bush to attend the annual congress of the European Democrat Union in Munich. Vice-President Bush agreed to head a Republican party delegation. During Bush's time in Munich, West German Chancellor Helmut Kohl cited the advantages that could be gained if Republicans and Conservatives were to unite forces worldwide.

In June 1982, the vice-president took the initiative in bringing Japanese, Australian, Canadian, and U.S. conservatives together to establish the Pacific Democrat Union (PDU). In 1983, delegates from the EDU and the PDU met in London to found the International Democrat Union (IDU). Vice-President Bush then arranged to host the first annual congress of the newly formed Conservative International at the 1984 Republican National Convention in Dallas. A second conference was held in Washington in July 1985.

By 1988, IDU's membership included twenty-seven national parties, mainly in Europe and the Pacific. The IDU claimed to represent more than 170,000,000 voters. A Caribbean Democrat Union was formed in January 1986, consisting mainly of the parties in English-speaking countries of that region. In process of implementation are plans for creation of a Democrat Union of the Americas.

Transnational Party Activities. The range and intensity of transnational party activity has increased in recent decades. Assistance has been channeled to party colleagues running for national as well as supranational offices. Closer coordination of transnational party programs is evident in the manifestos and other programmatic declarations of transnational party congresses and, in Europe, by the party groups in the European Parliament.

Promotion of party organization has been another important activity. In this, historically, the Communists have been the most systematic, assiduous, and experienced, providing training and other resources to party cadres in countries throughout the world. Running a close second in organizational experience and success are the Socialists. Christian Democrats stepped up attention to transnational organizing over the past quarter century, scoring significant successes in Europe and Latin America. Liberals, burdened by the minority status mentioned above, have been the slowest in mobilizing their transnational membership. The Conservatives, new to the arena, have been aggressive and, to a large extent, organizationally successful.

Transnational parties, like other organizations, acquire formality and vitality as a consequence of regular activity. For political parties, such activity usually relates to operations within legislative assemblies, the management of executive bureaucracies, civic education, constituency service, and the conduct of electoral and propaganda campaigns. In the case of transnational parties, this formality and vitality will undoubtedly increase with the growth of supranational political organizations generally.

A Global Critical Transition?

It is apparent that the centralization of the world's military establishments, the construction of a comprehensive institution of global representation, and the development of a world political-party system are emergent, real, and substantial prospects. Whether their maturation will require the millennia that it has taken to progress from nomadic tribes to the United Nations is a question that skeptics and visionaries will debate until the reality occurs. What is already demonstrated, hence beyond debate, is the tendency toward globalization sustained over the many centuries. Will, then, the three developing global institutions of interest here—military, representative, and partisan—continue to evolve and eventually converge as a critical transition?

Analytically, a political system is presumed to exist whenever "a group of actors are caught up in a nexus of relationships, both conflictual and cooperative, generated by common problems and the need to deal with them" (Gross and Barkun 1968, 4). Thus, for example, in 1945, nation-states, as the world's main actors, created the United Nations Organization in response to common problems. These actors held varying expectations about the United Nations, and the differences became the nexus of their conflictual and cooperative relationships. This experience is typical of every process of political integration.

Political integration occurs whenever two or more actors, such as the nations of 1945, respond to a need (for example, the elimination of war) by forming a new actor, in this case, the United Nations (Galtung 1968, 377). Given the recent patterns of global military, representative, and partisan institutional development, continuing (as they do) earlier centuries of internationalization, it seems reasonable to anticipate that these trends will go on to a global critical transition. Consequently, statesmen aware of the critical-transition phenomenon may ponder rational strategies for speeding the transition toward greater global integration in the interest of a world without war.

Patterns of institutional development in larger political communities may be the same or similar to those observed in smaller communities. Patterns of institutional development within nations may provide guidance to those wishing to promote comparable change among nations.

This study suggests that institutional development may be advanced deliberately a transaction at a time. A well-designed strategy of political transactions may speed the developmental process. For example, transactions about military hardware that are normally the concern of arms-control negotiators have also served as opportunities for military institution-building. Planning such strategies may be facilitated by viewing the things exchanged as political currencies—incumbencies, shares, and commodities. This typology will permit transactors more deliberately to broaden the range and variety of negotiables.

This study also points up the fact that the institutions most often and most specifically concerned with warfare are not only the military, but also the representative and the partisan. Recognizing this opens the way for including all three institutions in future transactions. For example, civilians may, as they often have, provide funds for the military in exchange for greater shares of legislative control over that institution. The hierarchy of influence among these institutions must be taken into account in the exchange of particular values if political transactions are to accomplish the desired passage through and beyond the critical transition.

In this conceptual and historical context, farfetched as it may seem to some, competing transnational parties may provide an institutional alternative to warfare as the principal method of global elite conflict.

In what ways may the development of global military, representative, and party institutions be advanced toward an international critical transition? The comments that follow may help to bring focus to an agenda of further inquiry and discussion.

Global Military Institution

Proposals to create a world security force capable of providing collective security, halting aggression, and enforcing international laws tend to run up against resistance in many quarters. Sovereign nations resist on grounds that such a force would diminish their capacity to make their own decisions regarding war and peace. Freedom-loving people, inclined to associate the military with dictatorships, resist out of fear that a global military force could lead to a world dictatorship. Pacifists resist in the belief that weapons and military forces "cause" war and should be eliminated entirely. Military leaders of every nation fear losses of power, employment, and safety if national security were to become dependent upon nonprofessionals.

Yet, the idea of a centralized and unified world military force persists, even among those who see themselves as realists and pragmatists. Between 1957 and 1962, as noted earlier, the United States and the Soviet Union submitted to the Eighteen-Nation Disarmament Committee elaborate proposals for general and complete disarmament. Both sets of documents presumably were carefully drawn and derived from the best thinking on how the superpowers might lead the world toward disarmament and international peacekeeping in a three-stage process. Each side made clear that any reduction in armaments would have to be accompanied by a proportionate increase in United Nations peacekeeping forces. This was, in effect, an acknowledgment that shared and controlled centralization of the world's military forces would be a necessary part of any disarmament program.

The creation of a world military force is not likely to be arranged in a single negotiation. What seems more probable is the continuation of current trends at the two tiers of globalization. At the nuclear tier, the superpower duopolists will undoubtedly continue their almost continuous arms-control negotiations. Pressure to do so comes not only from the respective domestic budget needs, but also from provisions in the Nuclear Nonproliferation Treaty calling for superpower reductions in nuclear stockpiles, from the demands of world public opinion, and from the rapid and difficult-to-control changes being brought in by new military technologies.

As superpower arms-control negotiations become increasingly institutionalized, they may foster mutual security as well as arms-control agreements. There is clearly a mutual-security dimension in preventing nuclear theft, creating nuclear-free zones, coping with nuclear terrorism, sharing certain U.N. peacekeeping arrangements, and so on.

Arms-control negotiations may also become occasions for institution-building transactions in other areas; for example, the system of representation at the United Nations, the conduct of transnational party competition, and even proposals for mutual security treaties among all five major nuclear powers, as a collective response to the possibility of nuclear contamination, theft, or terrorism.

Under favorable political circumstances, these negotiations could also consider proposals to reactivate the neglected Military Staff Committee (Goldman 1990). This committee could serve as the administrative bureaucracy for carrying out a number of military tasks of common interest to the superpowers as well as to the U.N. membership in general, at both the nuclear and the conventional tiers.

Several activities would be compatible with MSC's prescribed mission. MSC could compile public reports of national weapons' arsenals and international arms transfers. (Several commercial publications already provide unofficial reports.) MSC could administer a U.N. licensing system for all weapons transfers, perhaps in a fashion consistent with the provisions of the Nuclear Nonproliferation Treaty. An MSC-administered licensing system might afford universally shared control of the technological or qualitative arms race. In particular, MSC could monitor the nuclear weapons activities of nonnuclear states, thereby adding neutral confirmation to the findings of superpower satellite observations.

In addition to these intelligence activities, the Military Staff Committee could, in stages, be assigned several other much-needed tasks. It could monitor nuclear-weapon reduction agreements between the superpowers. It could reexamine the Baruch Plan for internationalizing nuclear energy in all its aspects, at the same time dealing with the proliferation problem.

The suggestions given above address primarily military globalization at the nuclear tier. Duties for MSC at the conventional tier may be even more feasible. The MSC could

1. continue to encourage U.N. members to make the special agreements necessary for providing national contingents for U.N. peacekeeping missions;

2. establish a professional military staff academy to augment the conflict-management training programs of the International Peace Academy;

3. supervise on-site conventional military inspection arrangements set forth in treaties between the superpowers;

4. serve as staff for arms-control negotiations, particularly those that deal with the extremely complex problem of setting limits to the qualitative arms race;

5. coordinate transnational antiterrorist services, particularly those involving nuclear threats;

6. design and promote regional security and peacekeeping arrangements among member states, including systems of cooperation between regional forces and those of the United Nations when the occasion arises, as provided in chapter 7 of the Charter.

None of these functions is performed by the current Military Staff Committee. All are possible if the superpowers accept MSC as a useful instrument of mutual security. If superpower and permanent member transactions are carefully negotiated, it may be feasible to proceed beyond cold war inhibitions toward the original collective security objectives of the Charter.

Military globalization at the conventional tier may proceed in other acceptable ways. Of three general scenarios that seem likely to lead to contemporary international wars, at least one holds reasonable promise of motivating further military centralization at the conventional tier.

The first and most frightening scenario places the nuclear superpowers in an all-out war. Given the overwhelming military resources of the superpowers, it is difficult to conceive of a military role for the United Nations. Even if it had its own stockpile of nuclear weapons, the United Nations could hardly step in to threaten or punish a superpower "aggressor." Nor is the day in sight when all nuclear powers would be willing to turn over their nuclear arsenals to the U.N., giving that body a monopoly of the world's most formidable instrument of violence. This scenario may suggest the difficulty of globalizing the nuclear tier; it does not preclude centralizing at the conventional tier.

A second scenario also illustrates the difficulties in creating a world collective security system. In this scenario, warfare occurs between middle-sized nonnuclear powers. The Iran-Iraq and other Middle East wars are cases in point. The armies of North Korea, Vietnam, and South Africa are among the largest in the world, are nonnuclear, and continue to be perceived as active threats to nearby states. A force capable of breaking up a fight between middle-sized powers would have to be of a size well beyond the entire present or near-term budget of the United Nations. Globalization at either nuclear or conventional tiers is likely to be irrelevant in this scenario. Nuclear weapons would not be involved, and U.N. budgets would not be adequate at this time.

The third hypothetical scenario has a world security force playing a significant role in coping with conflicts among the one hundred smaller nations. This is the kind of peacekeeping responsibility currently practiced on an ad hoc basis by U.N. missions; namely, a third-party mediatory role, a cease-fire and truce supervision role, or, with more troops and equipment than at present, a maintenance-of-domestic-order role.

This third conventional tier scenario is the one that appears most likely to undergo further global centralization. If the political and economic convenience of the superpowers is served by a strong, neutral, permanent U.N. force, it would not require much change for the United States and the Soviet Union to revive the peacekeeping intentions of the Charter. One issue that would have to be addressed is how to modify the permanent member veto in the Security Council. Another issue would concern the use of nonsuperpower or superpower troops in a permanent U.N. force. A third issue would relate to the role of an active Military Staff Committee. These issues seem to be within the realm of the negotiable.

Thus, in the near-term, both tiers—nuclear and conventional—are likely to continue their globalizing tendencies, albeit on separate tracks. The major actors will undoubtedly continue to be the superpower duopolists. The mechanism could be their transactions regarding strategic weapons systems, a permanent U.N. peacekeeping force, and a role for the Security Council's Military Staff Committee.

Global Representative Institution

The principles of representation at the United Nations continue to be debated, particularly in connection with proposals for financial and population criteria of apportionment. The smaller nations are overrepresented in relation to their financial contribution or population, giving the major powers cause to complain about fairness. This is a familiar domestic debate in Western democracies, usually resolved in the pragmatic negotiations of legislative parties. At the United Nations, the issues of apportionment and representativeness are likely to remain low on the institutional agenda until such time as transnational parties become more influential.

The General Assembly will probably be the forum for pursuing new principles of representation. Transnational parties, nongovernmental organizations (NGOs), and other political groups seeking improved access to the policy-making organs of the Assembly and the Secretariat are likely to be the most enthusiastic sponsors of reform proposals. Among the many suggestions are proposals that delegates to the General Assembly be chosen by direct popular election, as in the European Parliament, or that a popularly elected third house be added alongside the Security Council and the General Assembly.

A major factor in the development of the United Nations as a representative institution will undoubtedly be the extent to which the world's competing elites—political, economic, military, and social—turn to it as the political marketplace in which to negotiate their demands and differences. Military transactions at both tiers already involve U.N. agencies. The United Nations is increasingly concerned with questions of international finance and the conduct of multinational corporate enterprises. This attention to military, business, and commercial policies will undoubtedly draw the world's most competitive and influential elites into U.N. affairs. The United Nation's preparation of a code of conduct for multinational corporations has already had this effect (Feld 1980). The several functional organizations of the United Nations System—UNESCO, ILO, WHO, and so on—represent concerns of other important specialized elites.

Most of these elites favor international political and security conditions that minimize uncertainty; they promote also "rules of the game" that maximize stability. Eventually, international conditions and the gradual augmentation of rules for the global "game" will accelerate and legitimize the transactions in political currencies consummated in representative supranational marketplaces. The General Assembly and the Security Council are at this time most appropriately structured to serve as the global political marketplaces.

Transnational Party Development

This and other studies recommend policies that promote the development of transnational political parties (Goldman 1967; Goldman 1978, chap. 3). Because serious conflict among political elites has been and will always be a feature of human community, the problem has been to find nonviolent means for carrying on those conflicts. One solution calls for stabilizing competitive party systems.

A transnational party system that enables competing world elites to carry on their contests is undeniably in process. As noted earlier, Communists have claimed more than ninety-six affiliated parties and a world party membership of more than ninety million. Socialists have counted nearly sixty affiliated parties in more than fifty countries.

Christian Democrats have operated in nearly sixty countries. The Liberal International has included significant parties in countries on at least three continents. The two major parties of the United States have become affiliated with transnational parties. These parties, to a large extent, already function as members of a party system in such settings as the third world, the European Parliament, and the agencies of the United Nations.

Important sources of support for transnational party development have been the political foundations of West Germany. There are four major foundations, each of which is affiliated with one of that nation's four major parties: the Friedrich-Ebert-Stiftung (Social Democrats, or SPD); the Konrad-Adenauer-Stiftung (Christian Democratic Union, or CDU); the Friedrich-Naumann-Stiftung (the liberal Free Democratic party, or FDP); and the Hanns-Seidel-Stiftung (Christian Social Union, or CSU). A fifth foundation, that of the Greens party, has recently been established. Funds are indirectly appropriated to these foundations by the West German Parliament (*Bundestag*).

Approximately half of the attention and resources of the *Stiftungen* is devoted to foreign operations. The partisan dimension of these overseas projects is often in association with the transnational party affiliations of the German parties: Naumann, through the Liberal International; Ebert, through the Socialist International; and Adenaeur, through the Christian Democratic International. The foundations have helped finance international conferences of their associated transnational parties, have jointly coordinated third-world projects, and have otherwise supported multilateral ideological and civic educational programs conducted by the transnationals.

In the United States, the West German foundations have been emulated by the establishment of the National Endowment for Democracy (NED). Congress enacted the authorizing legislation on November 18, 1983. The purpose of the Endowment is to encourage the development of free and democratic institutions throughout the world, facilitate exchanges between United States private-sector groups and democratic groups abroad, promote private sector (particularly national party) training programs for democratic institution-building; and, in effect, serve as an open and responsible technical-aid program to all parties and groups devoted to democratic pluralism.

National Endowment for Democracy funds are disbursed chiefly to the National Democratic Institute for International Affairs, the National Republican Institute for International Affairs, the Free Trade Union Institute, and the Center for International Private Enterprise. These institutes are, respectively, adjuncts of the Democratic National Committee, the Republican National Committee, the AFL–CIO, and the United States Chamber of Commerce. One consequence of the NED program has been the relationship each of the party institutes has established with a transnational party: Republicans with the International Democrat Union and Democrats with the Liberal International.

Transnational party development may be promoted elsewhere. At the United Nations, for example, transnational party caucuses, similar to the party groups in the European Parliament, would enhance the activities and status of the transnationals. A U.N. clearinghouse for transnational party development, similar perhaps to the U.N.'s center for multinational corporations, could be another source of encouraging transnational parties.

The future of the global transnational parties would, of course, be affected by the creation of transnational electorates and supranational governmental offices to which their leaders may be elected. Long before such developments, transnational parties will undoubtedly continue to air ideological differences, encourage nonviolent elite competition nationally and supranationally, and recruit and organize their affiliates throughout the world. Given the findings of this study, the sooner a transnational party system acquires shape and stability, the sooner will a global critical transition be facilitated.

Transacting Critical Transitions

The consequences of a successful critical transition are several. Ballots take the place of bullets, that is, elite conflict is conducted through electoral (numerical) rather than military (violent) tactics. Civilian supremacy is established in civil-military relations; that is, elected party leaders manage the affairs of the representative legislature, and the legislature governs the military establishment. Democracy and popular sovereignty are reinforced as party leaders reach out to new constituencies and form new coalitions in order to pursue their competition for governmental power. This circle of relationships intensifies over time, resulting in the growth of political trust and the obsolescence of military approaches to political competition.

Critical transitions are negotiated by political adversaries, as indicated in the case studies of this inquiry. Great documents, such as Magna Carta, the Settlement of the Glorious Revolution, and the constitutions of the United States and Mexico, record the conclusions of some of these negotiations. Successful transactions require entrepreneurial leadership and an awareness of the nature and range of political currencies that may be traded.

Political currencies, as conceptualized in this study, include such phenomena as incumbencies in offices, shares of political prerogative, and political commodities of various types. A negotiation, for example, may involve one party that wishes a greater voice in that government. The tradeoff could be shares for incumbency, that is, more seats in the representative body for the first party in exchange for supporting votes to elect the second party to office.

Skilful negotiators will try to expand the range of political currencies to be traded, thereby maximizing prospects for an agreement. The positive side effects of astutely drawn agreements are likely to include procedures of nonviolent conflict resolution, incremental strengthening of one or more of the three institutions, and greater trust; in brief, social and political order. Successful negotiation and transaction are at the heart of the process of attaining political order and integration (Strauss 1978).

Because a successful critical transition leads to civilian control of the military and to stable competitive party systems, carrying forward the political transactions required for the transition should be a central

concern of politicians and policy makers. If a stable party system provides the institutional alternative to warfare, then strengthening the
party system should be an urgent goal of elites as the most promising
and most economical of all collective-security strategies.

References
Index

References

Agar, Herbert. *The Price of Union*. Boston: Houghton, Mifflin, 1950.

Barker, Ernest. *The Politics of Aristotle*. London: Oxford Univ. Press, 1946.

Blase, Melvin G. *Institution Building: A Source Book*. Beverly Hills: Sage Publications, 1973.

Blau, Peter M. *Exchange and Power in Social Life*. New York: John Wiley and Son, 1964.

Bowett, D. W. *United Nations Forces: A Legal Study of United Nations Practice*. London: Stevens and Sons, 1964.

Boyd, James M. *United Nations Peace-Keeping Operations: A Military and Political Appraisal*. New York: Praeger, 1971.

Buchanan, James M., and Gordon Tulloch. *The Calculus of Consent*. Ann Arbor: Univ. of Michigan Press, 1962.

Butterworth, Robert L. *Moderation from Management: International Organizations and Peace*. Pittsburgh: University Center for International Studies, Univ. of Pittsburgh, 1978.

Carter, Hodding. *The Angry Scar*. Garden City, N.Y.: Doubleday, 1959.

Clark, M. R. *Organized Labor in Mexico*. Chapel Hill: Univ. of North Carolina Press, 1934.

Code, Charles M. *The Military Forces of the Crown: Their Administration and Government*. London: John Murray, 1869.

Cohen, Morris R., and Ernest Nagel. *An Introduction to Logic and Scientific Method*. New York: Harcourt, Brace and Company, 1934.

Coser, Lewis A. *Continuities in the Study of Social Conflict*. New York: Free Press, 1967.

Cross, David. "Europe United; Could the Dream Come True?," *Saturday Review* (Oct. 13, 1979): 20–24.

Cruickshank, C. G. *Elizabeth's Army*. London: Oxford Univ. Press, 1966.

Curtis, Stanley J. *The Story of the British Army*. Leeds: E. J. Arnold, 1943.

Davis, Carl L. *Arming the Union: Small Arms in the Civil War*. Port Washington, N.Y.: Kennikat Press, 1973.

deGrazia, Alfred. *Public and Republic: Political Representation in America*. New York: Knopf, 1951.

———. *Apportionment and Representative Government*. New York: Praeger, 1963.

Department of Political and Security Affairs, United Nations. *The United Nations and Disarmament, 1945–1970.* New York: United Nations, 1970.

Department of Public Information, United Nations. *The Blue Helmets: A Review of United Nations Peacekeeping.* New York: United Nations Publication, 1985.

Derthick, Martha. "Military Lobby in the Missile Age: The Politics of the National Guard," in *Changing Patterns of Military Politics,* edited by Samuel P. Huntington. Glencoe, Ill.: Free Press, 1962.

Deutsch, Karl. *Politics and Government.* 3d ed., Boston: Houghton Mifflin, 1980.

Deutsch, Morton. *The Resolution of Conflict: Constructive and Destructive Processes.* New Haven: Yale Univ. Press, 1973.

Ellis, John. *Armies in Revolution.* New York: Oxford Univ. Press, 1974.

Fabian, Larry L. *Soldiers Without Enemies: Preparing the United Nations for Peacekeeping.* Washington, D.C.: Brookings Institution, 1971.

Feld, Werner J., and Gavin Boyd, eds. *Comparative Regional Systems: West and East Europe, North America, the Middle East, and Developing Countries.* New York: Pergamon Press, 1980.

———. *Multinational Corporations and U.N. Politics: The Quest for Codes of Conduct.* New York: Pergamon Press, 1980.

Firth, C. H. *Cromwell's Army.* London: Methuen, 1962.

Fitzmaurice, John. *The Party Groups in the European Parliament.* Lexington, Mass.: D. C. Heath, 1975.

Foa, Edna, and Uriel Foa. "Resource Theory of Social Exchange," in *Contemporary Topics in Social Psychology,* edited by J. W. Thibaut et al. Morristown, N.J.: General Learning Press, 1976, 99–131.

Foa, Uriel. "Interpersonal and Economic Resources," *Science* 171 (1971): 345–51.

Fortescue, John W. *A History of the British Army.* 13 vols. London: Macmillan, 1899–1930.

Galtung, Johan. "A Structural Theory of Integration," *Journal of Peace Research* (1968): 377.

General Assembly, United Nations. *Official Records.* First Report, 6th sess. (1951), supp. no. 13 (A/1891); Second Report, 7th sess. (1952), supp. no. 17 (A/2215); Third Report, 9th sess. (1954), Annexes, Agenda Item 19 (A/2713–S/3283).

Goldman, Ralph M. "The International Political Party," *Vista* (Nov.–Dec. 1967): 35–42.

———. "A Transactional Theory of Political Integration and Arms Control," *American Political Science Review* 62 (Sept. 1969): 719–33.

———. *Contemporary Perspectives on Politics.* New Brunswick, N.J.: Transaction Books, 1976.

———. "The Emerging Transnational Party System and the Future of American Parties," in *Political Parties: Development and Decay,* edited by Louis Maisel and Joseph Cooper. Beverly Hills: Sage Publications, 1978.

———. *Arms Control and Peacekeeping: Feeling Safe in This World.* New York: Random House, 1982.

———. *Transnational Parties: Organizing the World's Precincts.* Lanham, Md.: Univ. Press of America, 1983.

———. "Transnational Parties and Central American Democratization." Paper presented at the Conference on Political Parties in Central America, American University, Washington, D.C., Apr. 10–14, 1989.

———. *Is It Time to Revive the UN Military Staff Committee?* Los Angeles: Regina Books, 1990.

Goodman, Louis, Johanna S. R. Mendelson, and Juan Rial Peitho. *The Military and Democracy: The Future of Civil-Military Relations in Latin America.* Lexington, Mass.: Lexington Books, 1990.

Gosnell, Harold F. *Democracy: The Threshold of Freedom.* New York: Ronald Press, 1948.

Gross, Leo. "The Peace of Westphalia, 1648–1649," *American Journal of International Law* 42 (1948): 20–41.

Gross, Robert W., and Michael Barkun, eds. *The United Nations System and Its Functions.* Princeton: Van Nostrand, 1968.

Haswell, Jock. *The British Army.* London: Thames and Hudson, 1975.

Henning, Basil Duke, et al., *Crises in English History, 1066–1945.* New York: Henry Holt, 1949.

Hiscocks, Richard. *The Security Council: A Study in Adolescence.* London: Longman, 1973.

Hollister, C. Warren. *The Military Organization of Norman England.* Oxford: Oxford Univ. Press, 1965.

Homans, George C. *Social Behavior: Its Elementary Forms.* Boston: Harcourt, Brace and World, 1961.

Huntington, Samuel P. *Political Order in Changing Societies.* New Haven: Yale Univ. Press, 1968.

Huntley, James R. *Uniting the Democracies: Institutions of the Emerging Atlantic-Pacific System.* New York: New York Univ. Press, 1980.

International Encyclopedia of the Social Sciences. "Conflict," vol. 3. New York: Macmillan, 1968.

International Encyclopedia of the Social Sciences. "Political Parties," vol. 11. New York: Macmillan, 1968.

Jameson, J. F. *The American Revolution Considered as a Social Movement.* Princeton: Princeton Univ. Press, 1926.

James, Daniel. *Mexico and the Americans.* New York: Praeger, 1963.

Kerlinger, Fred N. *Foundations of Behavioral Research.* New York: Holt, Rinehart and Winston, 1966.

King, C. Cooper. *The Story of the British Army.* London: Methuen, 1897.

Kriedberg, Marvin A., and Merton G. Henry. *History of Military Mobilization in the United States Army, 1775–1945.* Department of the Army, Pamphlet 20–212, June 1955.

Lie, Trygvie. *In the Cause of Peace.* New York: Macmillan, 1954.

Lieuwen, Edwin. *Mexican Militarism: The Political Rise and Fall of the Revolutionary Army, 1910–1940.* Albuquerque: Univ. of New Mexico Press, 1968.

Lozoya, Jorge Alberto. *El Ejército Méxicano, 1911–1965.* Distrito Federal, México: Colegio de México, 1970.

Lunt, W. E. *History of England.* 3d ed., New York: Harper, 1947.

McNamara, Robert S. *Blundering into Disaster: Surviving the First Century of the Nuclear Age.* New York: Pantheon Books, 1986.

Mansfield, Harvey. "Party Government and the Settlement of 1688," *American Political Science Review* (Dec. 1964): 933–46.

March, James G., and Johan P. Olsen. "The New Institutionalism: Organizational Factors in Political Life," *American Political Science Review* 78 (Sept. 1984) 3: 734–749.

Mueller, John. *Retreat from Doomsday: The Obsolescence of Major War.* New York: Basic Books, 1989.

Parkes, Henry B. *A History of Mexico.* 3d ed., Boston: Houghton Mifflin, 1960.

Pennock, Roland, and John W. Chapman. *Representation.* New York: Atherton Press, 1968.

Pilisuk, Marc, Paul Skolnick, Kenneth Thomas, and Reuben Chapman. "Boredom vs. Cognitive Reappraisal in the Development of Cooperative Strategy," *Journal of Conflict Resolution* 11 (March 1967), No. 1: 116.

Pitkin, Hanna Fenichel. *The Concept of Representation.* Berkeley: Univ. of California Press, 1967.

Pitkin, Hanna Fenichel, ed. *Representation.* New York: Atherton Press, 1969.

Plato. *Republic.* Book Two.

Porter, Jack N. *Conflict and Conflict Resolution: An Historical Bibliography.* New York: Garland, 1982.

Randle, Robert F. *The Origins of Peace.* Riverside, N.J.: Free Press, 1973.

Rapoport, Anatol. *Fights, Games and Debates.* Ann Arbor: Univ. of Michigan Press, 1960.

Riker, William H. *Soldiers of the States: The Role of the National Guard in American Democracy.* Washington, D.C.: Public Affairs Press, 1957.

Rikhye, Indar Jit. *The Thin Blue Line.* New Haven: Yale Univ. Press, 1974.

Robins, Robert S. *Political Institutionalization and the Integration of Elites.* Quote is from Ralph Braibanti. Beverly Hills: Sage Publications, 1976.

Ronfeldt, David F. "The Mexican Army and Political Order Since 1940," in *Armies and Politics in Latin America,* edited by Abraham F. Lowenthal. New York: Holmes & Meier, 1976.

Russett, Bruce M. "International Behavior Research: Case Studies and Cumulation," in *Approaches to the Study of Political Science,* edited by Michael Haas and Henry S. Kariel. Scranton, Penna.: Chandler, 1970.

Sanders, Sol. *Mexico: Chaos on Our Doorstep.* Lanham, Md.: Madison Books, 1986.

Sartori, Giovanni. *Parties and Party Systems.* Cambridge: Cambridge Univ. Press, 1976.

Scalingi, Paula. *The European Parliament: The Three Decade Search for a United Europe.* Westport, Conn.: Greenwood Press, 1980.

Schattschneider, E. E. "Intensity, Visibility, Direction and Scope," *American Political Science Review* 51 (Dec. 1957): 933.

Schwoerer, Lois G. *"No Standing Armies": The Antiarmy Ideology in Seventeenth-Century England.* Baltimore: Johns Hopkins Univ. Press, 1974.

Secretariat, Council of Europe. *Manual of the Council of Europe: Its Structure, Functions and Achievements.* London: Sweet and Maxwell, 1969.

Sierra, Justo. *The Political Evolution of the Mexican People.* Translated by Charles Ramsdell. Austin: Univ. of Texas Press, 1969.

Sivard, Ruth Leger. *World Military and Social Expenditures, 1985.* Washington, D.C.: World Priorities, 1989.

Strauss, Anselm. *Negotiations: Varieties, Contexts, Processes, and Social Order.* San Francisco: Jossey-Bass, 1978.

Turner, Frederick C. *The Dynamic of Mexican Nationalism.* Chapel Hill: Univ. of North Carolina Press, 1968.

United Nations. Security Council. *Official Records, 2d Year, 1947.* Special supp. no. 1, S/336.

———. *Official Records, 1972.* Docs. A/8669 and A/8676.

Wainhouse, David W. *International Peacekeeping at the Crossroads.* Baltimore: Johns Hopkins Univ. Press, 1973.

Wilkie, James W. *The Mexican Revolution: Federal Expenditure and Social Change Since 1910.* Berkeley: Univ. of California Press, 1967.

Wood, David. "The European Parliament: A Future Forum for Defense Debates?," *Europe* (Jan.–Feb. 1981): 36.

Woodward, C. Vann. *Reunion and Reaction.* Garden City, N.Y.: Doubleday, 1956.

Wright, Quincy. *A Study of War.* Chicago: Univ. of Chicago Press, 1942. App. 28, p. 1385 and passim.

Yin, Robert K. *Case Study Research: Design and Methods.* Beverly Hills: Sage Publications, 1984.

Zacher, Mark W. *International Conflicts and Collective Security, 1946–1977: The United Nations, Organization of American States, Organization of African Unity, and Arab League.* New York: Praeger, 1979.

Index

velopment, 134, 137, 141; resulting in increments of institutional development, 34–35, 157–59, 175–77, 201, 225; William the Conqueror's, 50–52. See also Political currencies, Transaction theory, Transactions.

Political trust, 38, 234; defined, 40; elite conflict as consequence of, 11–14; examples of political distrust, 65, 75, 131, 134; institutionalized, 33–34

Polk, James K., 93

Popular sovereignty, 175

Populist party, 107

Portes Gil, Emilio, 147–51

Portugal, 164, 186

Pride's Purge, 72, 74

Privy Council, 63, 66–67, 77, 80

Process, and historiography, 4

Progressive party (United States): La-Follette (1924), 107; Roosevelt (1912), 107; Wallace (1948), 107

Pro servicio, 55

Protectorate, Cromwellian, 71, 73, 82

Protestant: clergy, 59; movements, 182

Prussia, 164, 184

Purveyance, 65

Pym, John, 69–70

Radical Civic Union (UCR, Argentina), 166, 168

Radical Republican faction (United States), 101, 104

Reconstruction era, 32, 107

Red Battalions, 137

Red International of Labor Unions, 194

Reelectionists (Mexico), 129

Reform Act of 1832, 32, 82

Regional confederations, 185

Regional institutions, 200, 202

Regional trends, 1

Representation, 56, 82, 132, 148, 216; defined, 26; for Mexican church and caudillos, 122; for revolutionaries, 130; principles of, 188

Representative institutions, British, 47, 56–60, 77–80; comparative, 157–72; development policy for, 174; European, 178–79, 188–92, 199–200; history of, 26–30; Mexican, 113, 120, 122, 130, 141, 147, 152; parliamentary system, 161; relationship to critical transition, 2, 7, 9–10, 19–21; United Nations, 227; United States, 83–84, 87, 92–93, 102, 106, 107–11; world, 215–17, 230–31. See also Cabinet system.

Republican National Committee (U.S.), 233

Republican party (U.S.), 32, 83, 93, 104, 106, 108

Republican People's party (Turkey), 162

Revolution of 1910–17 (Mexico), 112, 117

Reyes, General Bernardo, 129, 132

Richard I (1189–99), the Lion-Hearted, 54

Richard II (1377–99), 54, 56–59

Rodríguez, Abelardo, 149–50

Roman Empire, 23, 179

Romania, 220

Rural police force, 131, 133. See also Militia (Mexico).

Russia, 115, 160, 183–84, 194, 218. See also Soviet Union.

Salinas de Gortari, Carlos, 155

SALT I, 206

SALT II, 206

Sandinistas (Nicaragua), 220

Santa Anna, Antonio López de, 120, 125

Scandinavia, 160

Schuman, Robert, 189

Scotland, 63–68, 73, 75, 78–81

Scott, General Winfield, 97

Scutage, 52–56

Scutum, 52

Seabed Arms Control Treaty, 206

Secession, 98, 100, 103

Second, or Socialist, International, 193, 220

Security Council, United Nations, 209, 211–13, 215, 230–31

Self-Denying Ordinance, 71, 72

Selim III, Sultan (1789–1807), 162

Senate (Mexico), 131, 154

Separation of army and state, 120, 125, 143, 173

Separation of church and state, 125

Separation of powers: U.S. Constitution, 174

Serrano, Francisco, 146

Setlement of 1688–89, 41–43, 54, 70, 77–80, 91, 234. See also Great Britain.

Seven Years' War (1756–63), 81

Shares. See Political currencies.

Sheriffs, 55, 57, 67

Shoguns, 161

Simon de Montfort, 56

Slavery, 94, 103

Soares, Mario, 164

Social currencies, 36; decisional, 37; material, 37; positional, 36

From Warfare to Party Politics was composed in 10.5/14 Sabon on a Merganthaler Linotron 202 by Brevis Press; printed by sheet-fed offset on 60-pound, acid-free Glatfelter Natural, and Smyth-sewn and bound over binder's boards in Holliston Roxite, by Thomson-Shore; with dust jackets printed in 2 colors and laminated by Thomson-Shore; designed by Kachergis Book Design of Pittsboro, North Carolina; and published by Syracuse University Press, Syracuse, New York 13244-5160